ConAgra Who?
$15 Billion and Growing

The Story of
ConAgra's First 70 Years

ConAgra Who?
$15 Billion and Growing

Jane E. Limprecht

Copyright ConAgra, Inc. and
Jane E. Limprecht, 1989.

HD
9009
C66
L567
1990

**ROBERT MANNING
STROZIER LIBRARY**

DEC 5 1990

Tallahassee, Florida

DEDICATION

If there can ever be a proper dedication, let us thank —

- A Board of Directors that played its important role to make the existing system of corporate governance work.
- The *many* members of management that contributed greatly to the first $15 billion of annual sales.
- The thousands of employees who committed their energy to task.
- The many members of the financial community: commercial bankers, investment bankers, insurance company executives and many others whose patience, support and interest were vital to our company's success.

> Charles M. Harper
> Chairman and Chief Executive Officer
> ConAgra, Inc.

ACKNOWLEDGEMENTS

Many thanks to all of the people who generously contributed their time, their knowledge and their memories to help bring the ConAgra story to life. Special thanks go to the Nebraska State Historical Society; the Douglas County Historical Society; the Stuhr Museum of the Prairie Pioneer in Grand Island, Nebraska and its historian, Steve Adams; and the late Fred Glade, Jr., and his brother Henry Dixon "Dick" Glade, both of Grand Island.

Jane E. Limprecht

FOREWORD

The idea of this corporate history first arose out of a growing sense of two urgencies. First, a void of official company historical archives and second, an increasing awareness of the mortality of our key pioneers.

Like many companies caught up in rapid-fire expansions and growth, we simply had not given much thought over the years to preserving historical records or momentos. And most recently, we also had become increasingly concerned about preserving the recollections of those who had played key roles in our early years.

The subject of establishing some kind of permanent record of ConAgra's history kept coming up until finally it was handed to me as a post-retirement project. By that time, we had agreed that we would approach this as a written corporate history, not simply as a file or collection of files of various memorabilia. We set out to convey the sense of pride that ConAgrans everywhere feel for what they and their predecessors have accomplished. Our mission, we felt, was to produce a faithful record of the historical facts and events; but more especially to capture the essence of the quality people who shaped this company through the years — employees at all levels who helped make it into the major enterprise it is today.

At this point I contacted Hollis Limprecht and his daughter, Jane Limprecht. Hollis is the retired magazine editor of *The Omaha World-Herald*. Daughter Jane is an attorney who welcomed the opportunity to write the book while taking a break from her law career to pursue further graduate studies. She now lives in Washington, D.C., where she writes for a legal publishing company.

This formidable combination — daughter creating the entire written narrative and father working with me to gather research from the "key players" whom I identified — proved a marvelously effective partnership from our viewpoint. The result was everything we hoped for: the detached perspective of the Limprechts, daughter and father, led to a more objective, well-rounded picture of the company than we might have produced if we had prepared this internally.

Still, there were concerns that we might be biased in our assessments of the final narrative; and Mike Harper, particularly, was personally concerned that it not be viewed in any way as self-aggrandizing. So we gave the manuscript to several "outsiders" to read, to critique, and to review particularly as to its basic effectiveness in presenting our corporate history. Their comments were very encouraging:

"You don't get the feeling that you are meeting ConAgra from Mike Harper's chair. A lot of people have had a say in this, and the narrative comes at you from a number of viewpoints."

"Reads much better than the usual run of company histories. A complete picture of Mike Harper — not a cardboard cutout."

"Fascinating — remarkably human. Gives a chance for people to view corporate growth in a much more positive way."

"Crisply describes personalities and events."

"Has an honest 'feel'."

These and similar comments led us to decide that we should indeed publish this ConAgra history. Not as a "hyped" event, but simply as the story of the development and growth of an American corporation whose history to date includes some remarkable people, periods, and events.

We understand that its appeal may be necessarily limited to a narrow public or publics, but we hope that those with such an interest in our company will also find this a readable, complete and interesting picture of ConAgra with an honest "feel" for its important milestones and historic past.

Don Amsden
ConAgra Corporate Marketing Associate

TABLE OF CONTENTS

Chapter   Page

1. With Survival at Stake 1
2. The Early Years 17
3. NCM – Building a Reputation 31
4. An Adventure in Consumer Products 49
5. A Trip to Puerto Rico 69
6. Chickens – And More – In the Pot 81
7. The Basics: Econ 101 and Philos 102 103
8. Git Along, Little Dogies: Kasco to Cowboys 121
9. Cold Cash From Frozen Foods 141
10. A Toe in International Waters 159
11. The Center of the Plate..............................179
12. Mike Harper: Hard-Working and High-Flying..........203
13. Toward New Horizons 221
14. Staking a Claim in Cattle Country....................237
15. Nebraska – It's Good for Business 259
16. ConAgra: Building on Basics........................279

Appendix I
ConAgra Leadership from Past–Present

In chronicling the history of ConAgra, it is not possible to give individual recognition to each of the devoted directors who have contributed to ConAgra's success in the recent years particularly. However, a complete list of the board of directors beginning with 1952 can be found on page 285

Appendix II

Chronology of ConAgra acquisitions 287

Appendix III

ConAgra Sales and Earnings history 296

Appendix IV

Index... 299

CHAPTER 1

WITH SURVIVAL AT STAKE

CHARLES "Mike" Harper attended ConAgra's 1974 annual meeting wearing a name tag identifying himself as a corporate officer, although he had yet to receive his first paycheck from the agricultural products company.

"I should have come incognito," recalls the bald-headed, 6-foot 6-inch executive. "ConAgra had announced publicly that it had lost a lot of money and that it had cut out the dividend. Your instinct is to mingle with the crowd so I mingled with the crowd. I tried to make a friend someplace.

"I remember there were two ladies who must have been in their sixties or seventies sitting four to five rows back. I stopped at the row in front of them, leaned over and introduced myself. One of the ladies said, 'I have a question for you. We drove 150 miles from Grand Island to make this meeting.' I didn't know where Grand Island was at that time. Whether it was in Hawaii or what."

Harper later was to learn that Grand Island, in central Nebraska, was involved in the founding of the company. But on this day his concern was an unhappy stockholder. Her question to him was: "When is the dividend going to be reinstated?"

"She had good reason for the question," says Harper. "That dividend was her livelihood.

"I was hardly even an employee of the company yet. I suspect I gave one of those answers where you try to reassure them yet at the same time don't promise anything. But, you know, you think of stockholders as big fat guys in blue suits, sitting on Wall Street, big gold chains thumping their rich old tummies. And here's two elderly ladies who will starve to death unless we get that dividend going."

In its 1973 annual report, ConAgra had declared a record profit of over $6 million from its operations in flour, corn and animal feed milling; poultry raising and processing; and branded and private label grocery products. One year later, the company announced a loss of nearly $12 million. That stunning loss was the reason Mike Harper was at the annual meeting. He had been hired from Pillsbury to help turn ConAgra's fortunes around.

In December of 1973, the ConAgra board of directors suspended dividends on common stock. Preferred dividends were suspended in September 1974. Company secretary Rex Clemons fielded calls from longtime stockholders, some of them former mill employees or their wives or widows, fearful for their savings. Vice president for administration Chris Hansen was accosted at the gas station by an irate investor, who grabbed him by the lapel and demanded to know what was going on. Board

ConAgra's critical situation in 1973—74 leads ConAgra to get acquainted with Mike Harper and vice versa.

members were aware that ConAgra was getting into trouble, but in the beginning none realized how serious the trouble was becoming.

"At first it appeared that ConAgra was a victim of the three-year poultry cycle," board member Bob Daugherty explains. "But that didn't exactly wash because we were doing a hell of a lot worse than some other companies in poultry. We set up an audit committee, and I was elected chairman."

Daugherty, who had been invited to join the board in 1966, headed Valmont Industries of Valley, Nebraska, near Omaha. After World War II, he had purchased a tiny farm machinery business and built it into the major producer of center pivot irrigation systems for agriculture, pipes for gas and oil transmission, street light standards and electric transmission structures. He had grown his company from a one-room shed into an industrial empire.

At about the time ConAgra got into trouble Valmont Industries was going through the process of change, says Bob. "We got acquainted with an industrial psychologist, Dr. Seymour 'Sy' Levy.

"Sy had recently left a position with Pillsbury's human resources department to set up as an independent consultant, and Valmont was his first client. Sy brought to my attention the name of Mike Harper. He gave me a dossier on Harper, a Pillsbury executive who had just sold Pillsbury's poultry operations at a price and in a time period that exceeded all expectations."

Daugherty respected Sy and anyone he would recommend. Thinking Harper might make a good catch as a Valmont employee, Daugherty asked Sy to arrange for Mike to visit. The ConAgra board member met Harper at Omaha's Eppley Airfield and drove him around North Omaha out to Valley.

"After I had met Mike and reviewed his background in depth, it became obvious that he'd be better suited for ConAgra than for a metal manufacturing concern. I appointed myself to give ConAgra's president, J. Allan Mactier, a copy of Mike's dossier and to suggest that he take a serious look at him. If he didn't want him at ConAgra, we'd hire him at Valmont."

Two weeks later Daugherty ran into Mactier, who returned the dossier and said he didn't think ConAgra could use Harper. As a matter of fact, Mactier had already interviewed the disenchanted Pillsbury executive some months earlier.

A native of Lansing, Michigan, Harper had spent most of his boyhood in South Bend, Indiana, and had attended college at Purdue. Midway through his college career, he volunteered for the Army; he spent the period shortly after World War II in occupied Japan. He returned to Purdue to get his degree in mechanical engineering in 1949, and went on to the University of Chicago for a master's degree in business administration.

In 1950, fresh out of Chicago, Harper went to work as an industrial engineer in General Motors' Oldsmobile division in Lansing. Five years later, he answered an advertisement and was interviewed by Harold Schuler, a Pillsbury personnel executive later to become ConAgra's vice president of human resources.

"Pillsbury was setting up an industrial engineering department and I was assigned to go out and find the best guy in the country to head it," says Schuler. "I started a recruiting campaign, found Mike in General Motors, and hired him in the University of Michigan cafeteria, of all places.

"He had the education and the experience, and GM's Oldsmobile division had the reputation of having one of the best industrial engineering departments in the country. And Mike impressed me as the kind of guy — earthy, pragmatic, no B.S. — who would fit very well with our operating management."

Pillsbury initially hired Mike as an industrial engineer, but he soon became director of all industrial, mechanical, plant, chemical and electrical engineering. He was promoted to vice president of research and development, and then to head of the food service supply division. In the late 1960s he was named group vice president of Pillsbury's fresh poultry and food service supply operations.

"He was a student, constantly a student of everything," comments Schuler. "While Mike was in engineering, he was trying to learn more about marketing, or finance, or accounting. He was an insatiable learner."

Harper's ascent was checked in the early 1970s, when Pillsbury's chairman died and a new CEO replaced him. Harper, outspoken and direct, clashed with his new boss on issue after issue, including the decision to jettison Pillsbury's poultry operations. After Harper successfully orchestrated that sale despite his personal opposition to it, he received a run of increasingly uninspiring assignments.

All of which made him ripe for a challenge.

Shortly after Bob Daugherty first hosted Harper in Valley, Nebraska, the extent of ConAgra's financial troubles began to surface. The cyclical troughs of the poultry market were the least of the company's worries. The real culprit was a combination of excessive dependence

ConAgra's Puerto Rico earnings were $6 million in 1973, only $2 million in 1974.

upon offshore operations, enormous debt, peripheral businesses contributing little or nothing to profit, and steady losses in the commodities market.

For 15 years ConAgra had operated flour and feed mills in Puerto Rico. In fact, during fiscal year 1973 the company's island operations generated virtually all of its $6 million in profits. The following year, however, Puerto Rican officials dumped a mill subsidy program while maintaining rigid flour price controls. As a result, ConAgra couldn't recover the cost of the wheat it used to produce flour, and in 1974 its Puerto Rican earnings fell by $4 million.

ConAgra executives had hurried down to Puerto Rico to contest the price controls. They argued that the prices of Minneapolis-milled wheat quoted in the *Wall Street Journal*, and used by Puerto Rican officials to compute the island's controlled price, shouldn't apply to ConAgra's flour. Those prices didn't reflect the high cost of shipping grain from the mainland.

In response to their petition, the company executives received a lecture from the new director of price controls, a Cuban economics professor with very liberal economic theories. David T. "Tom" Peters, now ConAgra's vice president and controller, recalls that after hearing the director's discourse the group was addressed by a tall, gray-haired, stately Puerto Rican who concluded his speech with a broad wink. Some time later the price controls were eased, to accommodate the cost of transporting wheat from Minneapolis to San Juan. In the meantime, however, Puerto Rican profits dipped from the previous year's $6 million down to $2 million.

In addition, the previous seven years had brought a spate of acquisitions and internal expansions. ConAgra had established 12 of its 21 grain mills, 22 of its 32 feed mills, and four of its seven broiler operations during that period. Much of this growth was undercapitalized and the company was saddled with huge financing requirements, in many cases for marginally profitable projects. Skyrocketing interest rates increased ConAgra's interest bill from $3.3 million in 1971 to $16 million three years later. Between 1973 and 1974 the company's interest payments rose by $10 million, a jump of 167%. By 1974, with its stock plummeting to $3 a share, ConAgra had a market value of $10 million and a debt of $156 million.

But the bulk of the company's financial woes resulted from ill-fated commodities transactions which were executed in a wildly fluctuating soybean market — and which culminated in a loss of between $17 million and $18 million.

In a period of skyrocketing interest and wildly volatile commodities, ConAgra sees its balance sheet collapse.

In 1972, El Nino, a warming of the ocean currents off the western coast of South America, jolted world protein markets by forcing the anchovies that were used in fish meal out to sea, away from their normal waters. Fish meal is widely used as an animal feed ingredient, and the shortage greatly increased demand for alternative protein sources, like soybeans and soybean meal.

Another factor was the Soviet Union's entry into the U.S. grain market. For the first time, the Soviets purchased large amounts of American soybeans. They did so with considerable secrecy, and for a while few in the U.S. market knew what was going on. ConAgra officials were among those baffled by this turn of events.

United States export firms were flooded with orders from overseas buyers for soybeans and soybean meal. As demand increased, prices skyrocketed. Soybeans rose to nearly $13 a bushel; soybean meal soared from $270 to $485 a ton. By the spring of 1973, it looked like U.S. traders had sold more soy products to foreign buyers, especially to buyers in Japan and Europe, than could be supplied. A worldwide shortage of soybeans and soy products appeared imminent.

ConAgra needed huge amounts of protein products, like fish meal and soy meal, to feed its hundreds of thousands of broiler chickens. In October of 1972 Allan Mactier had taken control of ConAgra's general hedging policies, replacing Roger "Bud" Morrison, who joined ConAgra as transportation and procurement head with the 1969 acquisition of Montana Flour Mills. By the spring of 1973, ConAgra had reaped several million dollars in paper profits as soybean prices rose.

But these paper profits were in tatters by June. U.S. Department of Agriculture officials, fearful that export sales would leave insufficient stocks of soybeans and soy meal for domestic use, arbitrarily cancelled 50% of all open soybean and soybean meal export contracts.

On the heels of this surprising action, the Chicago Board of Trade issued an unprecedented ruling prohibiting further entry into futures contracts on old crop soybean meal. That meant that while ConAgra had purchased soybean meal at ever-rising levels, it couldn't hedge it by selling

By the spring of 1974, ConAgra starts to sell assets; company's board decides management change must be made.

old crop futures.

A futures contract is an agreement to make or take delivery, during a specific month, of a standardized amount of a commodity at a price established in a commodity exchange trading pit. It's a temporary substitute for the sale or purchase of the actual commodity. When the actual commodity is bought or sold, the buyer or seller liquidates the future position.

Futures contracts are often used to "hedge" against (minimize the risk of) volatile commodity prices. Commodity producers sell futures contracts to protect against price declines; commodity users buy them to protect against price increases.

Explains Morrison: "Those two activities, first by the U.S.D.A. and then by the Chicago Board of Trade, caused the old crop soybean complex markets to collapse. We had released our hedges during the price climb, because every day the meal would go up $10 a ton and we'd get margin calls for $10 a ton times 50,000 tons. We thought, well, we bought this to feed our chickens so why keep paying these margins every day? Then when the Board of Trade said no one could make any new entries on old crop, we couldn't rehedge it.

"ConAgra suffered the entire collapse against its long soybean meal position. We had used part of our supply between March and June, but we still had a four-month supply, or about 50,000 tons. In an attempt to hedge that exposed soybean meal position, we sold new crop soybeans and soybean meal futures contracts. However, rather than moving down with the old crop those also went up, which added to our loss."

ConAgra commodities trader Bill Bates recalls that the soybean market soared to the limit every day, within minutes after the opening bell rang.

"The company was short on soybeans and had futures sold against its cash purchases, so every time those darn things went up 30 cents, we'd get calls for margin," recalls Bates. "I'd have a guy call and say 'Send $2 million.' By 11:00 in the morning he'd be hollering for another million. It was just terrifying."

At first, ConAgra met those calls by borrowing. Before long, however, ConAgra's borrowing power had reached its limit. The company had to swallow the losses. And substantial losses they were — $6.2 million for the fourth quarter alone, and a total of $17 to $18 million for the whole of fiscal year 1974.

Dixie Lily grocery products operations were sold to raise cash.

By the spring of 1974, ConAgra had started to sell assets in order to reduce its debts and interest rates. Cargill, Incorporated bought 13 grain elevators in Montana for over $1 million. A midwestern grain elevator operator bought ConAgra's North Kansas City corn mill. Later in the year Martha White, Inc. bought Dixie Lily branded grocery products for about $5 million.

But the board concluded that only a management change would arrest the company's downward slide.

Bob Daugherty was the key player. As the only outside board member who lived in Omaha, close to the home office, he was the first to conclude that some changes had to be made. He was joined by board member Roy Park of Ithaca, New York, in influencing other board members, and on August 19, 1974, by a vote of 5-3, the board of directors replaced company president Mactier with executive vice president Claude Carter.

Carter, an animal nutrition expert, had joined the company in 1941 to head its new feed division; in 1965 he was named executive vice president and general manager in charge of feed operations. Mactier stepped into the vacant board chairmanship to oversee asset sales and forward planning.

Bob Daugherty and Claude Carter mulled over the possibility of hiring a new man to direct operations under Carter. Daughery suggested Mike Harper.

"We had Tom Brady, executive vice president in charge of finance, whom we had brought in a couple of years earlier," explains Carter. "I told

New President, Claude Carter, hires Mike Harper as Executive Vice President and COO. Cost cutting becomes top priority.

Bob I'd be very interested in talking to Mike about the operations position."

"I came to see Claude and he thought about it," says Harper. "He asked Tom Brady to come to Minneapolis to see me, and Tom and I sat down in the Minneapolis Club and had a pot of coffee. He said, 'Let's talk,' and we did and I was hired. As executive vice president and chief operating officer.

"I did not see the financial statements before I joined the company. I should have. But Bob Daugherty had told me about the situation ConAgra was in, that it was in miserable shape, that it might go bankrupt. I worried a little about coming to a company that was on the brink. But it was sort of fun, too. It had sound businesses. There was no reason to suspect you couldn't make money with them."

Officially Harper started working for ConAgra on October 14, 1974. He had actually begun his new assignment on October 1, but he didn't get paid for the first two weeks. He did, however, get to go to the 1974 shareholders' meeting.

New president Claude Carter assured the quiet audience of investors that the company was not in the control of its bankers, that assets would not be liquidated completely. He emphasized that profitability, rather than size, would be the company's future criterion of success. Bob Daugherty announced that Allan Mactier had resigned as chairman of the board; no successor was named.

"I was prepared to dodge the cabbages and tomatoes," admits Daugherty. "Actually, I thought we got through that meeting very well. There were a lot of tough questions asked and we answered them as best we could.

"The question period had gone on for 20 or 30 minutes and a fellow from Omaha stood up and said, 'We found ourselves in trouble. We're sorry about it, but I think it would serve the best interests of everyone here if we let the current new management and board do their best to solve these problems. We need to work with them.' That just settled everything down. And we ended the meeting."

Carter adopted a participative management style which promoted joint decision-making by top executives. He readily agreed to work with newcomer Harper — to the particular relief of Harper's daughter Carolyn, a flight attendant. After she spilled a Bloody Mary down the shirt-front of first-class passenger Carter, Carolyn had counted her father's days as a ConAgran numbered.

Cost-cutting became the company's top priority. Working together, the general management team of Del Barber, flour milling; Willard Adcox, poultry; Newton Allen and Bob Barnard, animal and poultry feeds, and Ron Hall and Roy Hill, overseas operations, and other top executives slashed administrative expenses by 25% by November 1974. Chris Hansen negotiated the sale of ConAgra's $1 million Lear 25 jet. Cutting back on advertising and sales promotion, dispensing with outside consultants on acquisitions and future planning, and reducing staff as assets were sold all helped to shrink overhead.

"We got going on simple objectives," recounts Harper. "For example, there were 16 flour mills at that time. Every flour mill has a grain elevator that is attached to it. Some have great big elevators, some have little elevators. We were about $160 million in debt. So we said, 'Let's cut back 10% on our grain storage.'

"Now, what the bakery customer wants in a flour is consistent quality. A customer can't run an automatic bakery day after day if the characteristics of the flour change. The flour miller in any particular plant gets consistency only by obtaining large amounts of wheat and blending them. Cut back 10%? Hell, you can't do that.

"Well, we decided to try it. The first 10% cut went great; the flour quality was still good. So we tried for another 10% and some of the mills with a small amount of storage got into trouble. We backed off those mills and tried again with the ones that were left, another 10%, with three or four weeks between cuts. By setting and achieving simple objectives, we got $70 to $80 million out of the balance sheet."

As operations chief, Harper repeatedly stressed the importance of the balance sheet. He encouraged the flour milling management to pursue collection of accounts receivable and to carefully manage inventories.

"Those guys already knew about being very careful about their

(Mill at Chester, Illinois) — *Grain elevator storage helped reduce inventories.*

"Bag of money" concept gives each operating company's general manager the way to think of returns on investment.

costs. We gave them full responsibility for their balance sheets, which they had never had before," he recalls. "We got them a simple balance sheet and asked them to get some objectives on it. That's about as simple as it was."

Frequent meetings of senior staff officers and managers bolstered spirits and cultivated a cooperative atmosphere. The group members met regularly during this period, discussing their new outlook toward the business. Harper and his colleagues introduced the ideas of return on investment, measurement and accountability for results.

They also formulated the "bag of money" concept. Harper told each general manager that he had been given a bag of money and that at the end of the year he'd be expected to return it — plus a little extra.

"I sketched out these things, which is a habit I used to have," explains Harper. "I drew up an 8½ inch by 11 inch transparency showing a bag of money. It gave us a measuring stick. I had to do it in a very simple way, because I'm not a financial guy. We tried to get the general managers to think in terms of return on investment. We worked like hell on our margins and that grubby kind of stuff. And we evolved the phrase that we would try to do a lot of little things very, very well."

"At the same time we changed the relationship between those who had been called 'staff officers' and the general managers," adds Brady. "Raising the stature of the general managers. And calling the staff officers 'resource people' who were to be available to be used by the general managers. Changing the whole philosophy of the company."

Not all of the new chief operating officer's management innovations were enthusiastically received. Shortly after arriving on the job, Harper allocated to each operating division the responsibility for paying its share of corporate costs — financial department expenses, annual report publication costs, top management salaries and so on.

"I went down to Decatur, Alabama, to the headquarters of ConAgra's poultry business," Harper recalls. "I told Willard Adcox, head of the poultry operations, that he was going to have to pay an additional $500,000 a year to support his share of the corporation expenses, meaning me, our marketing v.p. and a few other people.

"Willard is a fine southern gentleman, tall, white-haired, very smooth and soft-spoken. He's got a stainless steel spine right down his back, but it's all covered up. He smoked his pipe, studied on that a little bit.

Finally he answered, 'Well, Mike, I'll pay that. But only if I don't get that much help.'"

With equity of $33 million and debts nearing $160 million, ConAgra naturally became the focus of attention of its 16 nervous bankers. Any one of ConAgra's creditors could have demanded debt repayment, forcing the struggling company into bankruptcy. The task of soothing them fell to L.B. "Red" Thomas, vice president in charge of finance, and Tom Brady, who became chief financial officer in 1974.

Bankers could have closed the company's doors in 1973 and 1974 but ConAgra finance executives worked hard to keep them soothed.

"At one time we were faced with the problem of having to take three or four banks out — pay them off," says Brady. "The remaining banks won't stand for that unless another bank comes in. Northwestern Bank of Minneapolis came into the credit to replace some of the banks that wanted out. I don't recall that it involved more than a couple of million dollars, but it was a matter of each bank not wanting another to get some sort of advantage. They are all together in a credit, but they are fierce competitors otherwise."

"There were times, in 1973, 1974, when the bankers could have closed the door," observes Red Thomas. "They were wise enough to see that was not a smart thing for them to do. History has proven that to be a correct decision."

According to Bob Daugherty, "There's a moral to ConAgra's story. If you're going to get in trouble, get in a hell of a lot of it. Then the banks won't pull the chain."

Thomas and Brady also took on the job of selling company assets that failed to earn their keep. Many of these had been acquired in the late 1960s and early 1970s.

"To pay down our debt we had to liquidate assets," says Bud Morrison. "I remember we had several meetings where there would be eight or nine of us, people responsible for running certain parts of the company, basically trying to decide which things should be disposed of."

Nationwide, poultry industry profits typically followed a three-year boom and bust cycle during which supply first trailed and then exceeded demand. Financial experts, leery of this notorious profit and loss cycle, targeted ConAgra's poultry operations for sale.

Willard Adcox attended one management meeting assuming his business would be next on the auction block. The courtly Southerner bid his fellow ConAgrans farewell. Mike Harper, however, believed that Adcox's poultry operations held enormous potential. He argued in favor

Assets are sold to pay down debt; poultry operations and Puerto Rico businesses close to being sold.

of retaining them.

"The poultry business had cycles, and that concerned some of the financial folks because cycles meant that sometimes you didn't make money and other times you made a lot of money," explains Red Thomas. "But we said that we were a company in cyclical businesses, and that we liked cyclical businesses as long as they earned over the cycle. That was the classic first example. We kept the poultry business, and it was a damn good decision."

ConAgra came even closer to disposing of its Puerto Rican flour, feed and broiler operations, the firm's only moneymaker during the previous fiscal year.

ConAgra has never had a permanent arrangement with an investment banking firm, as its executives have testified before various government agencies over the years. However, Eric Gleacher, later to be head of mergers and acquisitions at Morgan Stanley and Co., had worked with Mike Harper on the sale of Pillsbury's chicken operations, and the two men had become personal friends on the basis of mutual respect for each other's abilities.

In mid-1975 Harper called Gleacher and told him about his new job. Gleacher had never heard of ConAgra.

When Gleacher checked out the company's situation, his first thought was that it was on its way to bankruptcy.

"I said to myself, 'This company is out of business,'" he recalls. "I remember I had just become a partner of Lehman Brothers, and I told my boss that I was going out there. I told him I had met this fellow at Pillsbury and I liked him a lot, but that, boy, this company looked tentative."

So tentative, in fact, that Gleacher's superior wanted him to demand payment up front. Instead, Gleacher took a chance on ConAgra's survival.

After Gleacher met with Harper and Brady, they decided the easiest way to raise the needed cash was to sell the company's Puerto Rican operations.

"I don't recall the number of hours I spend on the company, but I went to Omaha and learned about ConAgra, went to Puerto Rico, saw all the businesses, figured them out, decided who could buy them, went to see the buyers, did the whole thing," continues Gleacher. "I told them how to sell it and who might be some buyers. In other words I produced the buyers and had the deal all set to go, and Mike decided at the last minute that he did not want to sell it."

ConAgra's financial situation had improved to the point where the company could survive without selling its island operations. And those operations produced substantial earnings with a good return on investment.

ConAgra decides not to sell its "crown jewel", Puerto Rico businesses.

"I would have sold it," Gleacher maintains. "But Mike felt in his judgment that over a longer period of time it was a mirror image of the rest of the company. ConAgra understood those businesses, and Mike didn't have a lot else that was going for him at that time. He felt in the long run he could make money in Puerto Rico. And he was right."

"We went so far as to prepare a selling memorandum for Puerto Rico," says Harper. "But that operation was the jewel in our crown; it had earned the money when nothing else had. When it became evident that the company was going to turn around, we decided not to implement our plan to sell."

Instead of carrying out the original ambitious proposal, ConAgra kept all of its Puerto Rican operations except one poorly performing mill on the southern part of the island. That mill had been sold in January of 1975.

Ordinarily, Gleacher would have been left holding an expense check and a hefty file on ConAgra. An investment banker took that risk; no deal, no commission.

"I got Tom Brady and Claude Carter together and suggested that we voluntarily pay him $100,000," explains Harper. "He had worked like hell. That was a lot of money then because it was a big percent of earnings. But that $100,000 has made us a lot; not just friendship but mutual respect."

"Because I had performed my side of the bargain, Mike decided on his own initiative to pay me a fee as though there had been a sale," says Gleacher. "I thought that was very unusual. Most businessmen would have said, 'Well, I'll catch up with you next time.' And here was a fellow whose company was a little bit strapped. That made a big impression on me."

Between the sales of assets — most of them for more than book value, a pleasant surprise under the circumstances — and the general managers' balance sheet belt-tightening, the company raised about $80 to $90 million in a matter of months.

By the end of fiscal year 1975, ConAgra had disposed of nearly $12 million worth of fixed assets for a net gain of almost $4.5 million. And

The "new ConAgra" emerges from fiscal 1975 in strongest financial position in the company's history. Fiscal 1976 earnings set a record.

ConAgra reduced outstanding debt 51%, from its 1974 fiscal year-end $136 million down to $66 million.

Fiscal year 1975 first quarter data showed ConAgra $1.6 million in the red. Second quarter figures revealed net earnings of $2.6 million. By the end of fiscal year 1975, net earnings had climbed to a respectable $4.1 million.

"In March, in the spring, we knew that the thing had turned. The company was not going bankrupt. We were in the black for fiscal 1975, which nobody would have believed," says Harper.

That was just the beginning of the new ConAgra.

The new ConAgra's conservative balance sheet reflected the strongest financial position in the company's history. The new ConAgra's fiscal year 1976 operating earnings were nearly 2½ times higher than ever before. The new ConAgra's increased emphasis on marketing and potential expansion complemented its traditional dedication to low-cost production. Its professional managers developed, committed themselves to, and accepted full responsibility for attaining demanding growth objectives. And its specific, well-documented strategic plans charted the path for achieving both short- and long-range goals.

The new ConAgra: Its roots reached back to the Nebraska frontier, but upon its solid, new foundation it would build a future in the food industry worldwide.

CHAPTER 2

THE EARLY YEARS

THE EARLY YEARS

CONAGRA was relatively new even before Mike Harper arrived. It was christened "ConAgra" on February 25, 1971, and received a listing on the New York Stock Exchange on January 3, 1973. But long before its name was changed from Nebraska Consolidated Mills to ConAgra, the company was well known in the milling industry as a low-cost producer with employees dedicated to superior quality.

Cereal grains have been viewed as symbols of life, as gifts of the gods, since ancient times. At least 60,000 years ago people were pounding grain between two stones to ready it for consumption. The simple pounding stone was replaced by an implement resembling the mortar and pestle; that in turn gave way to the saddlestone, a long stone over which a rounded or elongated stone was pushed or rolled. The millstone — an upper stone revolving over a fixed bed stone — came into existence over 2000 years ago. Scarcely more than a century ago, the millstone remained the most advanced milling tool.

Nebraska's first mill used a set of millstones transported 500 miles from St. Louis, Missouri, and powered by draft animals. In 1819 the first military post west of the Missouri River had been established at Fort Atkinson, far from eastern provisioners; in 1821 the soldiers built the mill to grind wheat and corn for the self-sustaining post. Not until 1847 would the next Nebraska mill be erected, this time by Mormon settlers at their Winter Quarters at Florence, now a part of North Omaha. The settlement was short-lived, and in barely over a year the mill was torn down.

Immigration and settlement burgeoned after the Nebraska Territory was organized in 1854. Pioneers first settled in the southeastern corner of the state along the Missouri River, and later pushed north and west along smaller rivers and streams like the Nemaha, the Blue, the Loup, the Elkhorn and the Niobrara. Adventurous souls bound for the far west followed the wide and shallow Platte. To feed area settlers and to supply westbound travelers, flour was shipped, at considerable expense, from Kansas and Missouri to fledgling river towns in the new Territory.

Settlers soon discovered that Nebraska's soil and climate were well-suited to growing cereal grains. Both corn and wheat produced abundant and profitable crops. A few venturesome settlers built simple grist (ground grain) mills to convert local corn and wheat into flour. Often, the miller ground the farmer's grain into flour for the farmer's use, retaining as his milling toll one-eighth of the amount ground. By 1860, 19 grist mills operated in the state.

In 1867 Nebraska became a state, with flour milling as its leading industry. That same year, Germans Henry Koenig (later to become Nebraska's third state treasurer) and Frederick Wiebe built the first steam-

Back to beginnings; flour milling in early years of Nebraska statehood is a leading industry.

powered grain mill in Grand Island, Nebraska — the State Central Flouring Mill.

In 1862 Koenig and Wiebe opened a general store, the O.K. Store, along the Overland Trail near the Platte River. In 1867, one year after the Union Pacific Railroad arrived at and platted the new town of Grand Island, the two men began processing cornmeal and wheat, rye and graham flour at their new steam-powered mill. They operated the mill until 1883, when they sold it to 39-year-old Henry Glade.

Although Henry Glade died before Nebraska Consolidated Mills was founded, some early-day officials of the company consider him the patron saint of the business, which ultimately blossomed into today's ConAgra. His Grand Island mill was the keystone of the consolidation, and his heirs were active in the business for many years.

Glade, the last of 12 children, was born in Hanover, Germany. When he was 4 or 5, his family emigrated to the United States. Shortly after the Glades arrived in New Orleans, both parents died. Henry and his siblings continued their journey upriver to relatives in Jackson County,

Ravenna, Nebraska mill — one of the four original NCMCo. mills.

Iowa. Henry was raised by his sister Anna Margharetta and the Jackson County man she married, but he struck out on his own as an adolescent. He learned the milling trade in Dubuque, Iowa, and by the age of 14 was managing a mill.

Henry worked in Iowa mills until 1878, when he moved to Columbus, Nebraska, to mill in that town. In 1882 he built a mill at David City, Nebraska, in partnership with his brother-in-law George Etting and William McQuade. The following year he bought Koenig and Wiebe's State Central Flouring Mill. The *Grand Island Independent* reported that the mill's new owner "intends to fix the mill up in first class style, putting all the latest improvements in the line of machinery." Henry Glade lost no time living up to that promise.

After centuries of little change in milling techniques, the 1870s and 1880s had ushered in major improvements. In the 1870s, millers converted to the "new process," or high grinding, technique to increase flour yield. This technique involved raising the fixed bed stone for a second grinding, in order to pulverize the unprocessed wheat particles remaining after the first grinding. After two grindings, the newly invented middlings purifier blew away the middlings — the bran and outer layers of the grain — to be used in animal feed. New process milling produced a finer, purer flour. But the truly revolutionary change in milling technology was the widespread use of the steel roller in the 1880s.

The steel roller mill crushed grain between two cylindrical rollers turning against one another. A series of roller stands contained rollers with successively finer corrugates; the sets of rollers ground and reground grain through a process of "gradual reduction" more sophisticated than that used in high grinding. The ground particles were elevated to the mill's upper floors, where purifiers blew off the middlings and sifters separated the fine flour from coarser particles. The unground grain went through the process again and again, until the maximum amount of fine flour had been extracted.

The roller mill produced flour faster than either the old-fashioned or the new process stone grist mill. Because the miller therefore needed to purchase more grain, he was often able to offer a better price than the miller operating a smaller capacity grist mill.

The 1870s and 1880s usher in major improvements in milling technology. Steel roller mills become a revolutionary development.

Although Nebraska mill power sources included draft animals, windmills and artesian wells, the predominant power sources were watercourses and steam boilers. The winding tributaries of the area's broad rivers offered many excellent locations for water-powered mills, but seasonal floods made dam washout a recurrent problem. (Flooding also caused more unusual maintenance problems; high water carried three live sheep through a window and into a wheat bin in one early water-powered mill.) Steam-powered mills could operate without regard to flood, drought or freeze, but to house the heavy boilers and engines, the mill building needed sturdy construction on a firm foundation. One unfortunate and perhaps unobservant miller lost his expensive capital equipment as it sank into the mill's supporting base — quicksand.

Before the spread of inland rail routes, heavy steel rollers and steam boilers could be transported to riverbank towns, but not beyond. Expanded rail transportation made it possible to ship the machinery into dryland areas, paving the way for millers to establish steam-powered mills on rail lines rather than waterways. Access to rail transportation also allowed millers to buy and sell larger quantities of grain and flour, and to trade with more distant markets. At first, millers dumped excess grain on the ground to store it; the more enterprising and prosperous soon enlarged their mill facilities by adding wooden grain elevators and flour warehouses.

Mill operators often operated sawmills or general stores at their grain mill sites. In the latter part of the 19th century some millers contracted to sell electrical power to their communities, typically using their water turbines to process grain by day and to generate electricity for subscribers at night. And, of course, the dammed "old mill stream" became a popular recreational spot where local folks swam, fished and gossiped.

Henry Glade, an early pioneer miller, and his sons build the new Glade Roller Mill in Grand Island, Nebraska.

With the arrival of the Union Pacific Railroad in 1866, the St. Joseph and Grand Island Railroad in 1879 and the Burlington and Missouri Railroad in 1884, Grand Island was well situated for an ambitious miller. After purchasing the Koenig and Wiebe mill, Henry Glade promptly razed it and replaced it with the newest in technology — a steam-powered steel roller mill. Henry advertised his ownership of the three-story frame building by painting "Glade Roller Mill" in a bold arch across its front. The new mill employed six men and had a daily capacity of 100 barrels (a milling measure equalling 196 pounds) of flour.

In 1886, Henry lost his wife of 20 years, the former Catherine Etting. Henry and Catherine had six children, and by the time of her death the oldest son August had already entered the milling trade. The following year Henry took into partnership Catherine's brother Albert Etting, and changed the name of the business to Henry Glade and Co.

Sons August (Gus) and Arthur went into the family business as soon as their public schooling ended. The Glade boys were hard workers, but they possessed a greater sense of mischief than did their industrious father. Henry married Louisa Brown several years after his first wife died. Her stepsons' antics — dropping a mouse down one co-worker's overalls or igniting a firecracker in another's back pocket — apparently sorely tried her patience.

Sons Filbert (Phil) and Fred Glade Sr. postponed their milling careers to pursue stardom in professional baseball. Phil played for a time in the Western League as a catcher, but it was Fred who made it to the big time. In 1904, pitching for the St. Louis Browns against the Washington Senators, Fred Glade set a new American League record by striking out 15 batters.

The Glade Roller Mill, operated by Henry with his sons and his brother-in-law Albert Etting, prospered in the two decades after its inauguration. Much of the credit for the mill's success is attributed to Henry Glade's unswerving attention to business affairs. Henry was known for his ability to sense trouble in the mill's operations; from blocks away he would detect an alien sound and head back to work to investigate. At times Henry's perfectionism approached the extreme. After contracting to have a new house built, he went to the building site each workday evening — to hammer a second nail in wherever the carpenter had driven the first.

In addition to the Grand Island facility, Henry bought an Abilene, Kansas, mill which his sons operated. Following the practice of the day the Abilene mill distributed free desk blotters adorned with promotional slogans like "It beats the band how our flour sells; it's always in the lead," and "Do not stop to meditate, order our flour now," — not to mention photographs of langourous beauties.

When the family sold the Abilene mill, the *Abilene Reflector* noted the city's sorrow at losing the Glade boys, whose "uniform courtesy . . . strict attention to business and . . . success as millers" had made them "a host of friends." One of those friends was said to be a boy named Dwight Eisenhower, who worked in the ice house down by the mill and played catch with Fred on his breaks.

In December of 1910, Henry Glade died at the age of 66. His obituary stated that few men so active in business were so little known in public life. Henry was portrayed as a hard-working man who belonged to no fraternal orders or societies; in short, "when he was not at work he was at home."

Reorganized and incorporated in 1911, the Henry Glade Milling Company is approached in 1918 by the Omaha Flour Mill owner to merge.

In 1911, shortly after Henry Glade's death, the company was reorganized and incorporated as Henry Glade Milling Co., a closed corporation owned by family members. Lee Etting, Albert Etting's son, was named vice president, with Phil Glade secretary and Gus Glade treasurer. Fred Glade, who retired from baseball in 1908, became president. He had spent his final year in the majors with the New York Highlanders — the forerunners of the Yankees. The third highest-paid man on the team, he pocketed $3,800 for the season. As his son Fred Jr. observed, that's hardly one time at bat anymore.

The Henry Glade Milling Co. was not the only flour mill operating in central Nebraska. However, the smaller mills were growing increasingly scarce. Almost one-third of the more than 300 Nebraska flour mills operating in 1900 were gone 20 years later.

In 1918, Abbott Hartley of the Omaha Flour Mill proposed to Henry Glade's heirs that they strengthen their competitive position by consolidating operations with four other Nebraska mills, including his. During the previous several years Nebraska millers had made at least half a dozen such consolidation attempts. A major stumbling block had been the inability to agree on mill valuations; some millers inflated the values of their mills to obtain more equity in a consolidated company. For example, the Omaha Flour Mill's Mr. Hartley refused to include the mill's brand names and goodwill in his quoted consolidation price, resulting apparently in an inflated asking price. The Glades were interested in consolidation, but the 1918 attempt failed; whether the failure was caused by the Omaha mill's overvaluation or by the promoters' inability to sell the requisite consolidation stock is unclear.

The following year, however, four of the millers reconsidered consolidating their operations. They were fueled by the relentless energy of miller and promoter Alva R. Kinney, the president of Ravenna Mills of Ravenna, Nebraska, who had actively sought consolidation the previous year. The proprietors of the four outstate Nebraska mills — the Ravenna Mill, Hastings Mills in Hastings, the Henry Glade Milling Co. in Grand Island and the Blackburn-Furry Mill in St. Edward — agreed to sell stock to bring about their consolidation.

Thus Nebraska Consolidated Mills was born on September 29, 1919, when articles of incorporation were filed with the secretary of state in Lincoln, Nebraska. Kinney announced the formation of the new company on that day, saying the four properties had agreed to consolidate. In October of 1919, he launched the sale of stock in NCMCo. to the public.

Kinney approached this task with enthusiasm, creativity, and perhaps more imagination than today's Securities and Exchange Commission would endorse. His advertisements declared that the miller makes fortunes without risk; that the security of the milling business is encapsulated in the proverb, "Safe as old wheat in the mill," and the company slogan, "Absolute Safety and Return;" that in Kinney's new company the investor need not consider whether he will make money but only "how much money?" and that consolidating the several mills provides "ABSOLUTE PROTECTION TO THE SHAREHOLDERS AGAINST ANY CALAMITY THAT MAY ARISE."

Nebraska Consolidated Mills Company is born in 1919 merging four out-of-state Nebraska mills, including Glade.

He urged would-be subscribers to act fast, because the offering was certain to attract hordes of eager investors. As it turned out, the $840,000 of stock sold was less than anticipated. Nonetheless, the four millers went ahead with their plan — and on March 15, 1920, Nebraska Consolidated Mills, with a total capacity of 975 barrels a day, replaced the four independent mills.

Grand Island mill — built by Henry Glade in 1883.

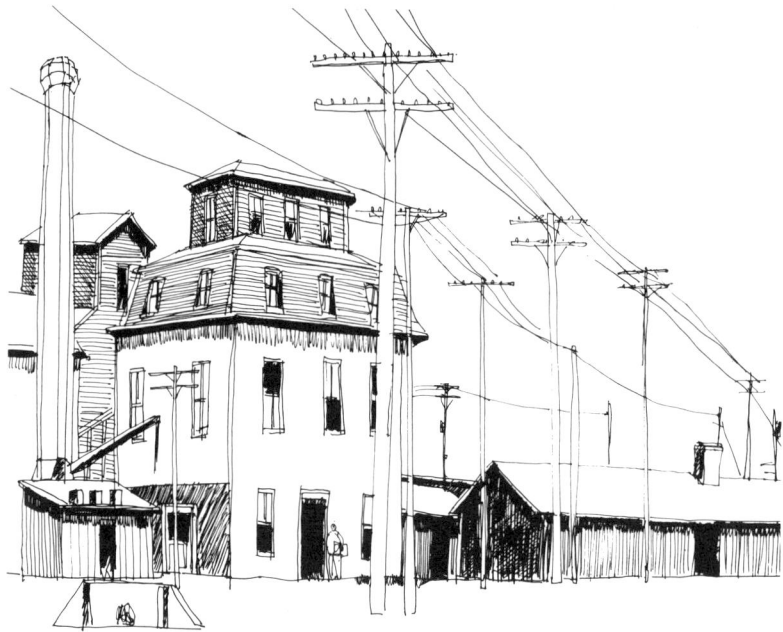

Hastings, Nebraska mill — one of the original NCMCo. mills.

A.R. Kinney is company's first president; his right hand man at the Ravenna Mills, R.S. Dickinson, becomes a V.P.

A. R. Kinney became the president of the new milling enterprise. Kinney grew up in Crete, Nebraska, located about 25 miles southwest of Lincoln, where he attended Doane College and "studied law" as an attorney's office boy. After graduating from Doane in 1897 he went to work for the Crete Mills. Following a brief sabbatical from the milling business — working as a traveling salesman — Kinney, along with several associates, bought the Ravenna Mill in 1904 from A. T. Shellenbarger and C. Davenport.

The Ravenna Mill had experienced almost every misfortune known to Nebraska milling. First constructed in 1891, along Beaver Creek, the mill was washed out three times by spring rains and left nearly high and dry by an intervening drought before it burned to the ground in 1901. Three years after rebuilding the structure, and before further calamaties could strike, the owners gave up and sold to Kinney and his associates.

Kinney's first step was to hire Dan Robinson, a Lincoln man who billed himself as a "damwright". Robinson constructed a wooden crib, filled it with 14 carloads of stone and faced it with concrete. For the first time, the Ravenna Mill could boast of a solid and durable dam — so solid

THE EARLY YEARS

Glade Roller Mill at Grand Island in the early 1900's.

and durable that it took repeated dynamite blasts to raze it 30 years later.

With a reliable energy source, the mill prospered. Over the next decade, Kinney built a new office building, raised the dam to obtain additional power, installed a gas power plant to use during dry weather, installed storage elevators, and increased mill capacity with the new equipment.

With ever-increasing capacity and volume, however, came the need for still more power. Kinney leased electricity from former miller Shellenbarger, who was by then engaged in providing electric power and lights to Ravenna. The service was intermittent and unreliable, and Kinney claimed that between 1910 and 1914 the mill lost up to half of its potential revenue because of inadequate power. In 1918, Kinney strung his own electric line about 10 miles to the power plant near Boelus, allowing the mill to run almost entirely on electric power. In 1919 he prevailed upon his competitors in Grand Island, Hastings and St. Edward to join forces in Nebraska Consolidated Mills.

By all accounts, the mustachioed and impressively built Kinney was a persuasive, forceful and demanding man. Yet he had a soft spot for his family, particularly his ill son, Ray. Alva Kinney and his wife had three children — Louise, Ruth and Raymond. As Louise recounts, her younger brother Ray had contracted polio as a baby, and for years Kinney traveled the country seeking any doctor offering a new cure.

Kinney's resolute search proved fruitless, for little was known about the disease in the early part of the century. Although doctors could not cure his son, they almost universally recommended that Ray swim as much as possible. To permit this, the Kinney family regularly summered in Minnesota.

One weekend when Alva was driving north to join the family, a heavy rainstorm forced him off his regular route and onto the road through Milford, Iowa. There he discovered lovely Lake Okoboji, which was closer to home and offered a longer and warmer swimming season. On Lake Okoboji, Alva Kinney fished and, nearly every evening, relaxed with his wife on a sunset boat ride. The swimming beaches, however, were for Ray to enjoy. Kinney walked in up to his neck, and that was it.

The Kinney family was one of the first in Ravenna to own an automobile — a Buick. Family outings typically consisted of a country drive in the latest Kinney car, punctuated with stops while Kinney disembarked to pick a wheat stalk and grind it between his fingers to test its moisture content. On his drives, Kinney noticed that sweet clover grew abundantly along the sandy roadsides. To determine whether wheat might succeed as well, in his spare time Kinney experimented with raising wheat on a small, sandy farm the family owned.

Before Kinney's only son was born, he started teaching his elder daughter how to use tools and make mechanical repairs. His lessons made an impression; as a Doane College co-ed in 1920 Louise repaired and rewired light fixtures and electrical appliances for her less handy classmates. Kinney also taught her to drive: returning one summer from a Minnesota vacation, the tired miller turned to 15-year-old Louise and asked her to take the wheel.

As Louise grew to adulthood, Kinney took the time also to teach his daughter the milling

Early mill — by the old mill pond.

business. Later married, Louise Kinney Platt became a long-time member of the board of Nebraska Consolidated Mills and ConAgra.

Since 1910, Kinney's right-hand man at the Ravenna Mill had been R. S. Dickinson. In need of a first-rate bookkeeper, Kinney had written to the president of his alma mater, Doane College. The president recommended Dickinson, a promising graduate raised in Columbus, Nebraska. On the strength of that recommendation, Kinney hired R. S. to manage the accounts, sweep up the office and do everything in between. When Ravenna Mills joined Nebraska Consolidated Mills, Dickinson became a vice president of the new company.

Phil Glade was named secretary-treasurer and sales manager of Nebraska Consolidated; his brother Art became operative miller and superintendent of mills. C. E. Dinsmore remained head of the Hastings mill, which he had built in 1895 in association with J. S. Hamilton.

In 1916 fire gutted their mill. With a stiff breeze fanning the flames, the structure burned to the ground in less than an hour. Fortunately the building and its contents were insured, and a newly rebuilt mill opened the following year. This new mill became a part of Nebraska Consolidated Mills just three years later.

The mill at St. Edward, alternately called the Blackburn-Furry Mill, the Blackburn Mill or simply the St. Edward Mill, was the smallest in capacity to enter the consolidation. Earl H. Blackburn, mill secretary, became a Nebraska Consolidated Mills vice president as well as the manager of the St. Edward Mill.

Roughly speaking, Grand Island, Ravenna and Hastings form an equilateral triangle centered around the Platte River. The town of St. Edward is situated 60 miles northeast of the easternmost corner of that triangle, Grand Island.

In 1876 John Gard constructed a four-story, 44- by 32-foot mill housing three millstones to serve the St. Edward farming community. Twenty years later Gard's mill burned down. Joseph Royston rebuilt it, installing steel rollers to replace the old-fashioned grind stones. Shortly after rebuilding the mill, Royston sold it to brothers Samuel and William Crouch, who in turn sold it to Nate Blackburn in 1901. Blackburn renamed it the St. Edward Mill and operated it with various associates including his sons, Glenn and Earl, and Len Furry. Nate and his sons were well-liked by their customers; one

In first 15 months, new company lost $115,000. Stockholders at the first annual meeting are patient. In 1922 NCM reports first profit, $175,000.

81-year-old St. Edward resident fondly recalls the lollipops Nate Blackburn gave her whenever she and her father delivered wheat to the mill.

A. R. Kinney's acknowledged strengths were those of promotion. He well knew that for the Nebraska Consolidated Mills to succeed, he needed the practical milling talents of men like R. S. Dickinson, the Glades and the Blackburns. But even with the benefit of their expertise, it soon became clear that 1920 was not an auspicious year to start a milling venture.

Between March 5, 1920, and June 30, 1921 — a 15-month period — Nebraska Consolidated lost $115,000. Years later R. S. Dickinson remembered the stockholders attended the July 1921 meeting looking for blood. But, as Dickinson recalled, upon reflection they realized their other holdings had suffered just as badly that year. And, a point not to be overlooked, "... they knew that they did not know how to run a mill."

Nebraska Consolidated Mills' officers did. At the 1922 stockholders meeting, Nebraska Consolidated Mills reported a profit of $175,000. The company was paying off for promoter and investor alike.

CHAPTER 3

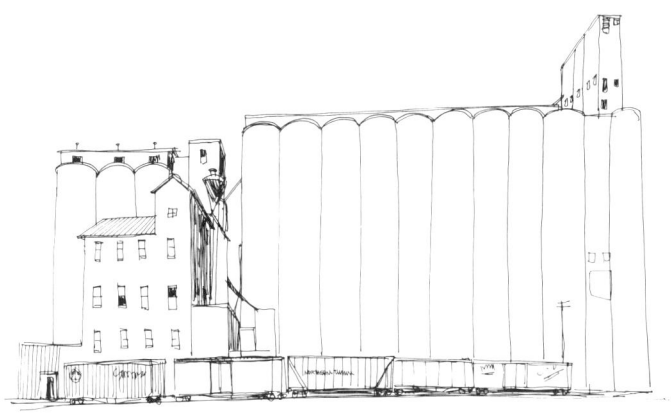

NEBRASKA CONSOLIDATED MILLS — BUILDING A REPUTATION

A LMOST immediately, the new company embarked upon an acquisition program, albeit a small one. In 1922, NCMCo. doubled its milling capacity by purchasing the Updike Mill in Omaha. This meant the company could process enough flour in a week to supply every Nebraskan for a year.

Founded in 1910 by Nelson Updike, the Updike Mill had been closed after World War I when flour exports declined. Acquiring the idle Omaha mill gave NCMCo. officials access to Omaha's grain market and its extensive rail network — advantages they had sought when they originally considered consolidating with the Omaha Flour Mill. With a mill in Omaha, Nebraska Consolidated could obtain a steady wheat supply from a broader area, along with better transportation rates for both inbound and outbound shipments.

In 1922, young Nebraska Consolidated Mills Company buys Updike Mill in Omaha, its first acquisition. Company headquarters moves to Omaha.

When Nebraska Consolidated Mills was created in 1919, company headquarters were established in Grand Island, the largest of the four communities hosting its mills. When the company bought the Updike Mill, headquarters were moved to Omaha. A. R. Kinney and Phil and Art Glade transferred to Omaha. R. S. Dickinson moved from Ravenna to

Updike Mill at Omaha, Nebraska — purchased in 1922.

Now a flour lab, this building was once the company headquarters.

Grand Island to take charge of Nebraska sales.

R. S. Dickinson was known as a hard-nosed businessman, a man of few words, serious and severe about his professional obligations. But he is also remembered as a gentleman, a solid individual who worked alongside his employees, a kind man with a subtle sense of humor. His widow, Mrs. Carrie Dickinson, still treasures a framed tribute to her husband, presented by his co-workers, characterizing him as "a square of that time-honored school who daily lives the golden rule."

In 1914 R. S. eloped with Carrie, a schoolteacher from Norwood, New York. Carrie Clark had rarely ventured outside of her home state when her father received a letter from her great-uncle, the president of the Ravenna school board. He queried whether her father knew of any teachers who might brave the western wilds for a job.

"Without consulting anybody, I thought 'That's my chance to go somewhere,'" Mrs. Dickinson remembers. "And without consulting anybody I came to Ravenna, much to my family's disapproval."

Mrs. Dickinson found life in central Nebraska an agreeable adventure.

"What delighted me most as I rode through Nebraska was my first view of the tumbleweeds rolling across the prairie. I thought that was the most fun thing I ever saw. So on weekends, the other teachers and I would go out and make great piles of tumbleweeds and set them afire. It was a wonderful thing!"

Young Carrie boarded at the home of her great-uncle, the school board president. A young doctor, soon to be married, lived there too. Before relinquishing his bachelor lodgings, he persuaded Carrie's great-aunt to let his room to a friend — an industrious fellow employed at the mill.

"So I lived in the same house with my husband for a year and a half," confides Mrs. Dickinson. "Before we were married."

For the first years of their marriage, R. S. rode the Burlington throughout central Nebraska selling flour to grocery stores; sometimes he was gone from Ravenna for three weeks at a stretch. When they moved to Grand Island in 1922, Mrs. Dickinson found her new home an amiable place, offering a happy and sociable life, though her husband worked six days a week at the mill.

In 1926, the company acquired the Brown Mill in Fremont—markets for its family flour brands spread to many parts of the U.S.

In 1926, four years after the purchase of the Updike Mill in Omaha, the company acquired another facility nearby. Nebraska Consolidated bought the Brown Mill, erected in 1917 in Fremont, just 45 miles northwest of Omaha. The idle mill was refurbished and placed back in service.

Two years later the Blackburn-Furry Mill in St. Edward was shut down. Its location off the beaten trail plus its small capacity — still only 200 sacks a day — kept it from being a money-maker for the firm. And according to St. Edward historian Dean Verhaege, a dispute with an influential local merchant compounded Nate Blackburn's troubles.

Brown flour mill at Fremont, Nebraska purchased in 1926.

The Blackburn Mill, located on Beaver Creek, was at the opposite end of Main Street from the Union Pacific railroad line and had no railroad spur. The only transport between the mill and the railway was by dray down an alley. Nate Blackburn wanted to lay a plank road along this alley to the depot, but the merchant objected because his loading dock lay along the route. So the mill's highest grade flour, Columbian ("Every Sack Guaranteed") was the first Nebraska Consolidated brand to disappear from the stores.

Nebraska Consolidated Mills now owned mills in five Nebraska communities — Omaha, Fremont, Grand Island, Hastings and Ravenna. Its family flour markets dotted the United States: from the Ravenna Mill's clientele in Wyoming, western Nebraska and South Dakota to the Glade Mill's customers in Wisconsin and New York.

Although operative miller Art Glade made sure the various plants turned out flour of uniform quality, each still used its former brand names. Grocers liked to carry exclusive brands, so it wasn't unusual to find each store in town offering a different brand name flour — with the same Nebraska Consolidated Mills product inside each bag. The Glade Mill had long used the names "Mother's Best" and "White Elephant." (German-born Henry Glade apparently thought that a white elephant was something rare and precious; his choice of titles became something of a family joke, according to grandsons Fred Jr. and Henry Dixon "Dick" Glade.) Ravenna's "Peerless" and "Tip Top," Fremont's "Mary Ann," and Hastings "Queen Quality" filled the shelves of their local groceries.

Seventeen-year-old Boise Pannier, fresh from country school, was hired in 1929 to work at Fremont's Brown Mill. The work was tough but it was steady, and jobs were scarce. For 23½ cents an hour Boise worked twelve hours a day, six days a week, closing 800 cotton bags a day of "Mary Ann" flour with hand-tied miller's knots. When Boise finished tying a load, he helped his partner carry the sacks — from "25s" containing twenty-four pounds of flour to "100s" containing ninety-six pounds — to the truck. In the winter, he took breaks from tying and loading flour to stoke the coal-burning furnace that warmed the uninsulated, plaster-walled mill.

The cotton flour sacks Boise hefted had useful lives of their own. Millers customarily packed their products in sacks bearing pretty designs to lure the farmer's wife. After her family consumed the flour, she washed the sacks or soaked them in lye and made them into tea towels, pillowcases and even clothing. One mill offered bordered sacks designed especially for transformation into pillowcases; the more enterprising housewives saved two sacks, slit a seam in each and stitched them together for a bordered skirt. It wasn't unusual for a buyer to choose among several packaging options offered by the same mill. The deciding factor might be the pattern her daughter wanted to wear after the last scoop of flour was kneaded into bread.

Since each of the five consolidated mills produced the same flour, in later years R. S. Dickinson tried to reduce the number of brand names and emphasize "Mother's Best" as the company flour. He didn't reckon with his customers' persistent loyalty to their local mills and their favorite brands. Sack after sack came back to the Brown Mill, toted by irate women swearing that it wasn't the same as their beloved "Mary Ann." To quell their suspicions Dickinson ordered sacks printed with "Mother's Best" on one side and "Mary Ann" on the other, but to no avail. Mill manager Merle Hasson found the solution: he kept a few sacks labeled "Mary Ann" around the place to dole out to the unconvinced.

Retail delivery truck for Mother's Best family flour.

Like Boise Pannier, Merle had considered himself lucky to get his mill job. R. S. Dickinson hired him in August of 1933 to help with the extra business generated by the passage of the wheat processing tax. Farmers could exchange their wheat for flour, based on the prices of wheat and flour minus the processing tax. Every Wednesday and Saturday farmers converged upon Fremont to attend the cattle sales; on their way to the sales barn they stopped at the mill to trade their wheat.

"I don't mind telling you I got a lot of exercise on those days," Hasson reminisces. "The scale was right by the office. I would weigh the truck and run out to dump the wheat. Then the truck came back around and I'd weigh it empty. I'd figure out the amount of flour, go get it and load it in the truck. In other words it was a one-man operation. And it was nothing on Wednesdays and Saturdays to have at least 35 or 40 customers."

Hasson went home bushed, but he appreciated the work. Before he started at the mill he was working part-time running ambulance and funeral calls for the local mortuary. When the funeral director was appointed grand master for the Nebraska Odd Fellows, he paid Merle extra to drive him to evening lodge meetings around the state, so he could cap off the night with a little pinochle. The mortician and his fellow card-

Rebuilding in the 1930's; new mill at Omaha replaces burned-out Updike Mill; Glade Mill is replaced in Grand Island.

players slept in the car as Merle drove them home; wages were $1.50 a close trip and $2.50 a far one.

"My first week at the mill I made $12.50 and I was very happy. And I was awful tired."

On a September afternoon in 1930, fifty-year-old Phil Glade died of a heart attack at his desk. Phil had been vice president and general manager of Nebraska Consolidated Mills and the heir apparent to A. R. Kinney.

That morning Phil's brother Art had married Mrs. Bess Swift in North Platte. They had already embarked upon their honeymoon motor trip to California when brother Fred Sr. overtook them with the news of Phil's death.

Art, as operative miller, was the only remaining family member with an active role in the mill's management or operations. Gus Glade retired nearly ten years earlier, and Fred Glade Sr. left in the mid-'20s. Their cousin Lee Etting had pulled up stakes and gone into real estate in California.

Kinney transferred his protege, R. S. Dickinson, to Omaha to assume the position of executive vice president and general manager. Joe Weaver, a young salesman recently recruited from the Glade Mill's New York agent, was promoted to secretary-treasurer and sales manager.

During the 1930s, Nebraska Consolidated concentrated upon modernizing its mills, maintaining the volume of its family flour sales and production, and nurturing its developing markets for bakery flour. On December 18, 1931, an explosion rocked the Updike Mill in Omaha, destroying that facility. The following year the company built an up-to-date mill. The successful bids for building the new facility were $62,250 for the mill and warehouse and $57,150 for the grain elevators; equipment costs were expected to bring the total price up to $150,000. The increased capacity at the new Omaha mill raised the output of the company to 3500 barrels a day.

In 1936 the company replaced Grand Island's obsolete Glade Mill with a modern facility. Like the Omaha plant, the new mill was built in the expensive "daylight construction" style introduced around 1910. This style emphasized sturdy fire-proof construction, good ventilation, spacious design and natural lighting through large windows. Later "daylight construction" plants often included innovative equipment to collect dust and control humidity.

The new 600-barrel capacity Grand Island mill boasted such

modern amenities as air conditioning for temperature and humidity control, as well as hollow glass block windows that admitted light while diffusing the sun's hot rays. The *Grand Island Independent* bragged about the European millers who convened in Grand Island in 1937 "to inspect the mill as one of the greatly outstanding plants in the world."

Fred Glade's son Fred Jr. was hired to help in the brand new mill before all of the bugs were worked out of its operations. Fred Jr. reported promptly for his first 7:00 a.m. shift; minutes later a "choke" dammed the flow of flour through the machinery. Because during a choke flour can pile up ceiling high, the rollers and other machinery must be shut off immediately. As Fred Jr. stepped off the elevator on the mill's second floor, the head miller bulldozed down the corridor, hit him on the chest with both hands and knocked him to the floor.

"He was going up someplace else to fix that choke. I got up, brushed myself off and I thought, gosh, what kind of a place is this? I no sooner got up and turned around when he came back the other way and gave it to me again."

Mill employees monitored and maintained the expensive machinery, packed and hauled the heavy flour and feed sacks, and experimented

This modern facility replaced the obsolete Glade mill in Grand Island in 1936.

with new ways to improve the company's products. When Boise Pannier married in 1935 he was a flour packer; for the next seven or eight years he worked at the Fremont Mill from 4:00 until midnight six nights a week.

"Even when he got off at midnight I never expected him until 2:00 a.m. because he always put in more than he had to," recalls Boise's wife, Roma. "And in those days you never knew until the day before whether you were going to get Christmas or any other special day off. As I always said, I was pregnant twice and I don't think he ever walked down the street with me because he was always at the mill."

During rest breaks Boise penned his name and address on sacks of "Mary Ann" flour so that far-away customers could correspond with him on the merits of the product.

"I'd get lots of letters from people back East," recalls Boise. "Just to report on the quality of the flour, you know."

Long hours at the mills were sometimes interrupted by hijinks and practical jokes, too. Legend has it that hearty workers grabbed the 96-pound flour sacks in their teeth and raced from the basement of the mill to the top floor and back again. On the other hand, one notoriously indolent employee stretched out for a snooze whenever he stepped outside to weigh sacks of feed. When his co-workers got wise to the scheme they rigged a bucket of water and a string over his favored spot. His next catnap ended abruptly; he awoke to a cascade of icy water splashing down his neck.

Boise and his fellows didn't wear uniforms, but they did change into their oldest, patched togs before starting a shift. Their locker room was a single wooden bench and a post to hang a change of clothes on. One hapless employee arrived for a midnight-to-morning shift to find his well-worn work clothes affixed securely to the post with big, round-headed roofing nails. By the time he ripped his clothing from the post, it was so tattered that he had no choice but to wear his street garb all night long.

More diabolical pranksters placed wire next to the 24-inch belt driving the mill's 150 horsepower steam engine. They ran the wire under the changing bench and stuffed the cracks in the bench with tin — resulting in a shock for any half-dressed colleague unfortunate enough to take a seat.

Most of the Fremont Mill's flour was family flour, often sold to farm women who baked on stoves fueled with wood and corncobs. To serve a sizeable Grand Island bakery, however, the Grand Island mill had started producing baker's flour, with protein content adjusted to provide increased strength and elasticity. Rather than produce a special flour to satisfy Fremont's small bakery trade, the Fremont Mill sold flour milled in Grand Island. Periodically Merle Hasson drove the mill's Dodge truck to

Grand Island and returned with 100 or so 100-pound sacks of baker's flour for the Fremont bakeshops.

In 1936, the same year that Grand Island's clean-lined modern mill was constructed, R. S. Dickinson succeeded A. R. Kinney as president of Nebraska Consolidated Mills. In March of 1936 the manager of the Fremont mill, Kinney's son-in-law Frank Ross, moved to Grand Island to manage the new mill in that city. Not too long afterward, new president R. S. took Merle Hasson down into the Fremont Mill's engine room and asked him if he'd like to be manager.

R.S. Dickinson becomes the new NCM president in 1936; key employees remember his practical, "hands-on" style of management.

"I said I'd sure like to be, but I don't know a damn thing about it. R. S. said 'That's the kind I like.' He said 'If you're willing to learn I'm willing to take a chance on you,'" says Hasson.

Merle remembers R. S. Dickinson as a terrific boss, very opinionated but possessing a quick mind.

"He would go to the last ditch with you, but never cross it. In other words, do it his way and get it done."

One spring in the late 1930s the thawing Elkhorn River rose until it threatened to flood flat Fremont. Local officials had warned the townspeople to head for high ground. The Fremont mill was situated between the raised Union Pacific tracks on the north and the Burlington tracks on the south. The mill ran 24 hours a day to operate at capacity and take advantage of cheaper night-time power rates. It was powered by motors located in the mill basement and the elevator pit; water seepage would ruin the motors. Merle phoned R. S. Dickinson around 9:00 at night to ask whether he should shut down the mill and take the motors out. Hasson vividly recalls Dickinson's reply.

"He said 'Buddy, that's why I've got you there,'" says Hasson. "A cold sweat came out over my face. I thought for a while and decided I'd run the darn thing until I have to shut her down. Well, the water came down and it went south of the Burlington tracks. It was within a block, but we were high and dry."

Dickinson always retained an interest in the practical workings of the company's mills. He and an associate from an Omaha manufacturing company regularly tested new ideas on the Fremont Mill.

"I'd run the thing for three or four days and get all screwed up and then they'd come out and see how it worked," declares Hasson.

One such experiment involved a system to air condition the

Fremont plant. Dickinson directed the mill employees to sink a 50-foot well, install louvers on the second floor, close the windows and doors, moisten the louvers with the well water and pull the cool air through. It didn't work. But Hasson knew that R. S., undaunted, would show up with a new invention before long.

One of Dickinson's major interests was to continually improve the quality of flour produced by Nebraska Consolidated Mills. Employee Arlee Andre, a native of Hendley, Nebraska, graduated from Grand Island's Baptist College in 1928 with a degree in chemistry.

Nebraska Consolidated Mills had advertised for a cereal chemist to perform lab tests for flour quality control. Dickinson figured the company would hire someone and let him go after the harvest rush. Arlee got the job and traveled to Lincoln to take a short course in cereal chemistry at the University of Nebraska.

NCMCo. owned instruments to test the protein content and general condition of its wheat, but lacked baking equipment to test flour performance in the oven. When Arlee returned from Lincoln, he told R. S. about the small ovens and sample loaves they used at the university laboratory. By baking samples, the chemist could determine the exact combination of grind settings, wheat blends and other elements that culminated in the most attractive, mouth-watering loaves of bread. Dickinson was intrigued and told Arlee to buy what he needed.

In 1932 Arlee sent a letter to the company's Omaha office. Nebraska Consolidated produced a pancake flour that Arlee considered

World War II changed emphasis from family flour to commercial bakery flour.

crude. In his letter Arlee discussed ways to improve the mix; he enclosed a sample of his own concoction. A week later R. S. Dickinson journeyed to Grand Island, took Arlee to dinner at the Union Pacific Depot and asked him to replace the company's Omaha chemist. Arlee moved to Omaha to take charge of the bakery lab.

Perhaps because his own route to success had taken him from sweeping the floors of the Ravenna Mill to commanding the operations of Nebraska Consolidated Mills, Dickinson appreciated a diligent employee willing to start at the bottom.

Twenty-one-year-old Del Barber started as an office clerk on April Fool's Day in 1936. After high school Del had moved from his Hetlan, South Dakota, home town at the request of his widower uncle, a United Airlines pilot, who needed help raising two small children. Living with his uncle in Omaha gave Del the chance to go to Creighton University, where he met his future wife, Bernice Stewart. When Del's uncle transferred to Salt Lake City, Del accompanied him and enrolled in the University of Utah. But money was short, and Del quit school to work in a prospect silver mine, with nothing but board, room and stock in the company in return.

"I thought I was going to get rich," Del reminisces. "I made a trip back to Omaha in 1936 to see my girl. She had a friend at Central High School who said a Mr. Weaver had visited the school, looking for a young man to come work for Nebraska Consolidated Mills. Mr. Weaver wanted to interview on Monday."

Del showed up early — on Friday. He got the job. Three months later he married Bernice, and before the year was out he was promoted to city sales. Del drove from grocer to grocer in a panel truck, unloading sacks of flour as he made each sale.

After displaying his salesmanship skills in Omaha, he was transferred to other territories. In their first ten years of marriage the Barbers moved ten times, from Denison, Iowa to Sioux Falls, South Dakota to North Platte, Nebraska to the next town needing an energetic flour salesman.

As a country salesman Del no longer had to haul flour sacks from his truck. Instead, he called on the grocers and the delivery truck followed with their orders. Some country flour routes were worked out of "pool cars." Nebraska Consolidated salesmen criss-crossed the Midwest, selling 10 or 20 100-pound bags at a time to small-town bakers. The pool cars — rail cars loaded with bagged flour — chugged across the landscape, stopping in each town along the sales route to unload the awaited flour.

Rex Clemons graduated with an accounting degree and worked for a Chicago public accounting firm before returning to Omaha in 1938 and walking the streets in search of employment. One day he found himself on North 16th Street, in front of a flour mill.

"I walked in the Nebraska Consolidated Mills Omaha office, saw Mr. R. S. Dickinson, and said 'Do you have a job?' He said, 'What do you do, young man?' and I said 'I'll do anything you want.' So he put me out with the receptionist and whatever loose ends needed tying, that's what I did."

Within two years after Rex was hired, Dickinson transferred him to Grand Island to keep the books for the Grand Island and Hastings mills and the Ravenna elevator. Shortly after Rex started working for Nebraska Consolidated, the Ravenna Mill had burned down, leaving only the country elevator at that location. New on the job, Rex

Millstone relic is preserved at present Montana Flour Mills headquarters.

hadn't even known his employer operated a mill in Ravenna. He was visiting his wife Jane's parents in Lincoln when his mother-in-law remarked that a company mill had just gone up in flames.

The Ravenna mill, the training-ground for both A. R. Kinney and R. S. Dickinson, operated at only partial capacity throughout most of the 1930's. The Depression years were hard on smaller mills throughout the state, especially given the trend toward consolidation of mills in the larger cities. After the mill burned down Dickinson wanted to replace its lost capacity, but he knew that building a new mill in Ravenna didn't make good business sense.

Dickinson proposed that Nebraska Consolidated Mills build its next mill far from its native state: on the Tennessee River at Decatur, Alabama. He felt sure that a vast market awaited the company there; the southeastern states consumed disproportionately high amounts of flour. He also calculated that varying transportation rates permitted raw wheat to be transported, via rail and barge, more economically than finished flour. Why not locate the mill near the customer and transport the wheat there to be processed, rather than locating the mill near the wheat field and shipping the finished product at a higher price?

This would give NCM an advantage for the shipment of hard winter wheat for bread from the Great Plains. It would also locate NCM nearer the soft wheat, grown in Illinois, Indiana, Kentucky and Tennes-

BUILDING A REPUTATION

see, which southern housewives preferred for their biscuits.

The board of directors bought the idea. It was a bold move — and a puzzlement to many industry observers. Twenty years later, the vice president of the Millers National Federation credited Dickinson with being years ahead of other millers in grasping the economies of inland waterway transportation.

The new Decatur mill opened in July 1941, five months before the Japanese bombed Pearl Harbor.

From its inception, the mill fully justified R. S. Dickinson's faith in a profitable southeastern market for family flour. In an era when the door-to-door bread route was already a fact of life for Midwesterners, a great number of families in the southeastern states still baked at home. It was not uncommon for farm workers to bring in their earnings from summer labor and buy a whole winter's supply of flour, to ensure enough food through the coming months.

Dickinson's vision of inland waterway transportation leads him to build the newest NCM mill at Decatur, Alabama — far from the company's native state.

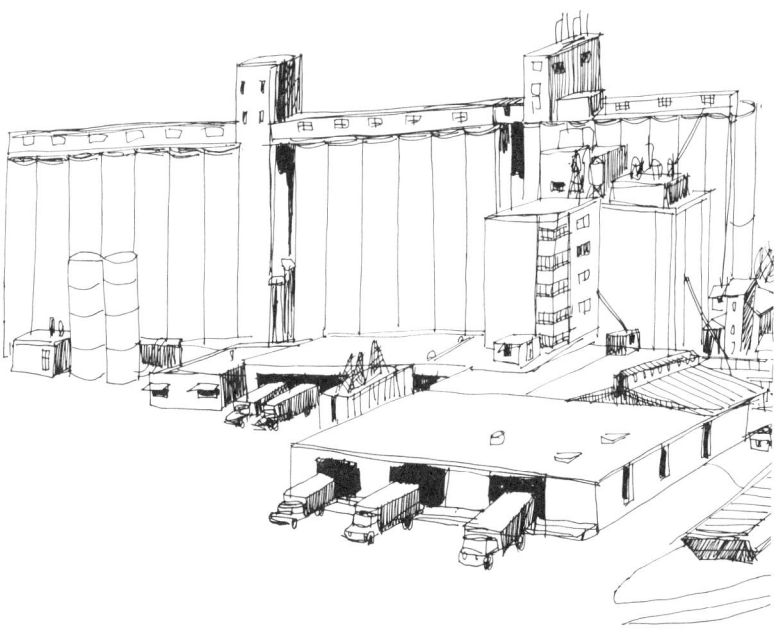

Flour mill complex built on the Decatur river in 1941.

Because of savings from shipping raw wheat, Nebraska Consolidated's family flour profit margins were larger than those of competitors who shipped processed flour from wheat country. The company took full advantage of inland water routes opened by the Tennessee Valley Authority. Wheat harvested in the plains states rode the rails to St. Louis, where it was loaded onto barges to float down the Mississippi River to Cairo, Illinois, up the Ohio River to Paducah, Kentucky, and down the Tennessee River to Decatur.

In later years, as transportation on the Missouri River developed, NCMCo. shipped wheat by barge all the way from Omaha to Decatur from April through October. During the winter, when barge traffic from Omaha came to a halt, the company often purchased wheat from St. Louis mills and grain firms, and occasionally stored grain on barges at Decatur.

Nebraska Consolidated Mills delivered its Decatur corn meal and wheat flour by truck to small grocery stores in the region. Before the advent of the feed distributorship, the neighborhood grocer was also the primary seller of animal feed; the primary buyer was the farmer raising a few chickens or pigs in the back yard.

The by-products of milling – the outer layers of the grain too rough for human consumption – are ideal for use in animal feed. Animal feeds could help make up the tonnage necessary for a milling company to economically deliver flour and corn meal to grocers. To avoid wasting its milling by-products, called the bran and the shorts, or millfeed, Nebraska Consolidated had built a feed mill alongside the flour and corn mills at its Decatur complex. Dickinson set as his goal to sell feed to 90% of the market within the company's "territory" – a fifty-mile radius from Decatur. He firmly refused to seek business beyond the bounds of that circle.

At this time, the feed business was in its infancy. The Decatur mill manager needed an animal nutrition expert to run the company's new feed division. A query at the state ag school yielded the name of Claude Carter, an Alabama native who had recently graduated from Auburn University. Nebraska Consolidated wooed Carter from his job with the Farm Securities Administration; he went to work in March of 1941 developing the formulas for "Mother's Best" hog, cattle and poultry feeds.

"Mother's Best" – it sounded perfect for the kitchen, but not quite right for an Alabama hog lot. So Nebraska Consolidated hired the famous designer Jim Nash, creator of Mobil Oil Company's flying red horse, to think up a more suitable name for the company's latest experiment, animal feeds. Nash suggested "Red Hat Feeds," and Decatur's "Red Hat Feeds" division was in business.

After the United States entered World War II, the challenge of the feed business was not selling the product, but rather allocating it among eager buyers. Shortages of ingredients limited output; salesmen worked hard to maintain the company's good reputation by being fair to all customers.

Claude Carter joins NCM at Decatur to run the infant livestock feed business; "Red Hat" brand is born.

Company operations back in Nebraska felt the wartime pinch too. In August of 1942 salesman Del Barber received a directive from Grand Island. To conserve vehicles and tires R. S. Dickinson advised all drivers to cut the maximum speed on company trucks to 30 miles per hour. As mill manager A. L. Johnson, evidently exasperated with wartime controls, succinctly reminded employees: "We can hire more men I am sure and work them longer hours if necessary, but we cannot get any more tires nor can we buy any new trucks."

Flour sales were also subject to quotas. Merle Hasson, manager of the mill at Fremont, recalls that there was no problem selling the mill's capacity. The problem lay in staffing the mill with able-bodied workers. A defense plant opened fourteen miles south of Fremont, and many area residents preferred the work offered there to heavy mill labor.

Decatur mill developed the Red Hat brand for feed products.

"It was nothing to run through fifteen or twenty guys a day," calculates Hasson. "We were handling 25- and 50-pound bags of flour, and 100-pound bags of bran. The new workers would go in there, work an hour and decide that wasn't for them. They'd just get up and leave, they wouldn't even come in and get a check for their hour.

"I did put on three or four women. Two of them weighed at least 200 pounds. I mean they were big ladies. They couldn't handle the 100-pound sacks but they could handle the 50s pretty well. And they liked to work."

As more and more women entered the workforce during the war, they turned increasingly to the commercial bakery to provide convenient and inexpensive baked goods. Fewer women had an abundance of either the time or the ingredients necessary to make home-baked bread. They suffered the same trials that Carrie Dickinson recalls experiencing during World War I rationing. Mrs. Dickinson's Ravenna neighbors assumed, to her great indignation, that having a miller husband ensured her all the flour she needed. On the contrary, lacking white flour she once tried to make a cake out of rye flour. As she describes it, "Very unsuccessfully."

During World War II, Nebraska Consolidated produced about 40% of its products for military and government buyers. Despite wartime wage and price controls, Nebraska Consolidated Mills' new Decatur complex proved profitable. Through it the company established a foothold from which to later expand its southeastern operations, and demonstrated itself eager to compete beyond the Midwest.

CHAPTER 4

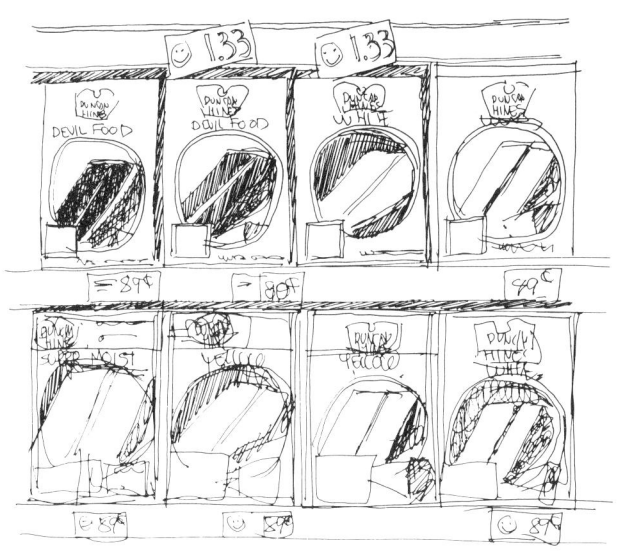

AN ADVENTURE IN CONSUMER PRODUCTS — DUNCAN HINES CAKE MIXES

WHEN J. Allan Mactier went to work selling flour for Nebraska Consolidated Mills in the spring of 1946, he was quickly introduced to the recovering postwar agricultural economy. His first assignment was to search southeastern Nebraska to find wheat for sale.

The Omaha native was fresh from duty as a Navy submarine officer when he started at Nebraska Consolidated. On an eventful day two years earlier, February 26, 1944, Mactier had graduated from the University of Michigan with a bachelor's degree in economics, received his commission in the Navy and married R.S. Dickinson's daughter Ann.

During his first years with Nebraska Consolidated Mills, Mactier sold flour in Nebraska and Iowa. At that time the company's family flour sales techniques were changing. Rather than delivering directly to grocery stores, NCMCo. salesmen began doing "resale work," calling on grocers to sell flour to be delivered by a certain wholesaler. By 1948 Mactier had been transferred to the company's Omaha headquarters at 1521 North 16th Street to work in sales and advertising.

The end of the decade marked the end of operations at the Hastings mill, the last of the four original facilities consolidated in 1919. The Hastings elevator horn, which sounded automatically to signal a scale full of wheat, had long been a city institution. Unofficially, the horn may have been used for other purposes; the story goes that night-shift workers blew it to warn coal scavengers at the nearby railyards that the coal company watchmen were approaching.

While long-established milling operations were drawing to a close in Hastings, Arlee Andre, by now chief chemist for Nebraska Consolidated Mills, was experimenting with something new in the Omaha laboratory. Nationwide, a number of companies were marketing packaged cake mixes to give housewives and working women the satisfaction of home baking with less of the time-consuming fuss. The trouble was, the cakes didn't taste like much. Convinced that he could improve upon the available product, Arlee began spending evenings in the bake lab experimenting with flour, shortening and flavoring formulations.

The right combination was elusive. Rationed during the war, shortening was still scarce; Arlee had trouble locating a steady supply of the kind having the best baking qualities. Using dried eggs in a mix produced a cake too reminiscent of C-rations for a war-weary market to welcome. And choreographing the precise blending sequence tested even Andre's extensive knowledge of the science — and art — of baking.

Andre recalls that one West Coast cake mix producer, Cinch, had access to a ready supply of shortening. Cinch shipped carloads of mix across the nation, selling it for 15 or 20 cents a box, with minimal compe-

Allan Mactier joins NCM as a family flour salesman; teams up with chief chemist Arlee Andre on plan to produce cake mixes.

tition because other producers lacked a shortening source. In Andre's estimation, however, Cinch's mix made a pitiful sort of cake.

The demise of post-war rationing made Andre's task a little easier. Night after night, he concocted new recipes, financing his experiments with bake sales to his fellow employees — 15 cents a cake. Their reaction to his handiwork guided his research; he eliminated anything anybody said "I don't like."

"I had a system," Arlee divulged. "I would make up a mix which was about 90%, then I would use a little more flour, a little more sugar, a little more of whatever I wanted to make my balance. After I completed that I would take my calculator and work out the actual percentages for the mix."

By 1950 Andre was satisfied with his creation. He presented Allan Mactier and R.S. Dickinson with slices of Pillsbury cake and slices of Andre cake. The two sipped their coffee between bites. The Andre cake disappeared to the last crumb.

Mactier enthusiastically began developing a plan to produce and market Andre's formulation. Dickinson had his reservations about the venture. The memory of a mid-1930s retreat from the biscuit mix business still smarted. Nebraska Consolidated Mills had tried to sell "1-2-3" biscuit mix but "Bisquick" carried the day. For the first time since its first year of operation, the company lost money. Dickinson was left with cases of unsold "1-2-3" to remind him of the folly of entering the consumer goods market.

Nonetheless, he grudgingly promised to back Mactier's and Andre's radical enterprise — with a grand total of $25,000 capital.

"I remember he said 'You can lose $25,000 doing this, but when that's gone that's all there is, young man,'" Mactier jokes. "Dick always set out to 'stop this fooling around in the lab,' as he called it. Dick liked Andre, and he'd visit him over in the lab nearly every day. But then he'd say to me, 'I see that lab is going again on what I stopped them from doing.'"

Once Dickinson had committed the company's $25,000, it was up to Mactier to figure out how to sell the new product — including what to name it. Neither of the two consumer brand names NCMCo. already used — "Dixianna" and "Mother's Best" — had quite the right ring. "Dixianna" might not go over well outside of Dixie and "Mother's Best" was too close to "Mother's Oats" for the comfort of the Quaker company.

In the midst of this dilemma Mactier picked up an issue of the

ADVENTURE IN CONSUMER PRODUCTS 53

advertising trade magazine *Tide*. Inside, he found an article describing how New York public relations man Roy Park and noted restaurant critic Duncan Hines were licensing Hines' name to appear on first-rate food products.

Intrigued, Allan called Roy. Roy agreed to meet him and Allan traveled to Ithaca, New York, along with fellow employee Joe Weaver, Jr., whose father was then secretary-treasurer of the company.

"They came over and wanted the franchise," says former North Carolinian Roy Park. "They were very bright, very frank, and had a nice open western approach. It seemed to me that maybe they would be people that we could work with better than we could some of the other folks from the big city. I'm kind of a country boy, and I like country people, and we got together."

Roy's partner Duncan Hines was a native of Bowling Green, Kentucky, who had worked for a Chicago printing company in the early 1930s. Hines and his wife enjoyed dining out, and he started keeping note of his favorite restaurants and distributing the list to friends and neighbors. When the list grew popular, he sold it for a dollar. The demand became so great that in 1936 he published the first edition of his book *Adventures In Good Eating,* which made him famous.

Hines quit his sales job and concentrated on touring the U.S., Canada and Mexico to seek out the best dining for the traveler. The next twenty years brought forty-seven printings of his book, each adding new eating establishments. Because of his books and his many food reviews, people associated Duncan Hines' name with "good food."

To help the tourist, who was otherwise faced with choosing between one "greasy spoon" and another, Duncan Hines developed rigid standards by which he judged restaurants. His top priorities in any dining establishment, whether humble or swank, were cleanliness and good food tastefully prepared. A restaurant rating his approval could display a plaque, unless he removed the establishment from his book for later transgressions.

Many readers wrote Hines to express their appreciation for his writings or to detail their own dining experiences. The courteous critic insisted that each fan letter he received be answered — on the day it arrived, if possible. But fame and a reputation for integrity brought him less welcome correspondence, too. From real estate developers to purveyors of exotic kitchen implements, they sought Duncan Hines' endorsement on their products. He firmly and repeatedly refused to oblige.

In 1948, when a friend told Duncan that a New York P.R. man wanted to talk with him, Duncan could have dismissed the idea as one

Looking for a brand name, Mactier reads about a New York PR man (Roy Park) who is licensing the Duncan Hines name.

more attempt to capitalize on his good standing.

Roy Park operated an advertising, research and public relations firm based in Ithaca, New York. In 1948 his agency was retained to handle Tom Dewey's "Rural America" presidential campaign. After Dewey's defeat, since Park's agency was publicly allied with the gentlemen not residing in the White House, a number of principal clients chose to switch public relations firms. Of Park's remaining projects, one of the most promising was the development of a brand or franchise name for a group of farm co-operatives which marketed various food products.

After initial research, Park informed his farm co-op clients that launching a new brand name would cost at least $2 million. That move didn't enhance his popularity. Then he told them that the only existing franchise name available was "Donald Duck." That almost got him thrown out of the room.

Park tried a new tack. He held a contest among his employees to come up with a catchy new brand name that would be appealing for food products. Of the five hundred or so entries he received, the name "Duncan Hines" stood out. But how to contact and work out a deal with the noted critic?

The photocopy machine not yet being an office fixture, Roy sent an employee to the library to photograph articles about Hines. Roy poured over the reading material. It was clear that Duncan had never endorsed a product and wasn't going to start now. But, through mutual friends, Roy wangled himself a telephone introduction to Hines. He told Duncan he had an idea he wanted to share with him and asked to pay him a call.

"I told him I was from North Carolina and I told him a few things about himself so he would know that I was not just giving him a line of baloney," says Roy. "He said that he got to New York from time to time and maybe we could get together there. I think by not telling him what I wanted to talk about I kind of piqued his imagination. I guess he wanted to know what it was."

Hines called Park some time later from New York City and the two arranged to meet. When Park entered Hines' room at the Waldorf Hotel, he found Duncan on the phone heatedly refusing to endorse a particular make of car.

"I don't know whether he was putting on a show or not," says Roy. "But he told the fellow from the automobile company that he would not endorse any car, and certainly not that make because it shook his life and his liver too much."

Undaunted, Park launched into his presentation. Roy informed Hines that the capacity of the human stomach is 40 fluid ounces, and that all too frequently that stomach is stuffed with the wrong kind of food. Roy believed that people would pay a little more for premium-quality food. He wanted to license food producers and packers to sell high-quality foods — approved and carefully monitored by Hines, Park and professional nutritionists — under the brand name "Duncan Hines."

In 1951, NCM launches Duncan Hines Cake Mixes.

"When Duncan told me his policy was never to endorse anything I said, 'Yes, Mr. Hines, I know that, because I've studied about you a great deal. I'm not asking you to endorse something. What I want to do is to name a quality product for you.' Then I had sense enough to shut up," recalls Park.

After they parted, Roy didn't hear anything about the food writer for the next couple of weeks. Then the friends whose names he had given as references began to call and ask what he was doing with Duncan Hines. Hines had been carefully checking those references. At length, captivated by Park's idea and satisfied of his integrity, Hines agreed to a six-month contract; Park created the new Hines-Park Foods, Inc., based in Ithaca.

Six months went by and Park had nothing to show for the endeavor except for his out-of-pocket expenses. He asked Hines to extend the contract for six more.

"Duncan said to me, 'You've invested quite a lot in this, haven't you?'" Park recalls. "I said 'For me, I have.' Then he asked me why I hadn't asked him to help. I told him I didn't think I could afford him. He said 'I think you can. I like what you're doing. All you need to do is pay my expenses.' So from there on, I had the world's greatest trademark."

Shortly afterward, the Hines-Park enterprise came to Allan Mactier's attention. He lost no time in getting Duncan Hines and Roy Park to taste a forkful of Arlee Andre's cake.

Hines liked Andre's cakes. He and Park had blind taste tests run on other dessert lovers. They liked Andre's cakes, too.

In June of 1951, Nebraska Consolidated Mills launched its new Duncan Hines Cake Mix. The single flavor was the Three-Star Special, which made a white cake with the addition of water and egg white, a yellow cake with water and a whole egg, or a chocolate devil's food cake with water, an egg and cocoa. The Three-Star Special was produced under

Mactier gambles his entire $25,000 capital on his hometown market, Omaha, introduction is a huge success.

contract by Omaha's Omar bakery; the audacious new Duncan Hines Cake Mix Division had no production facilities.

Allan Mactier was vice president and general manager of the fledgling division, with Del Barber in charge of direct sales and Joe Weaver, Jr. heading broker sales.

The Duncan Hines Division's competition included General Foods, Betty Crocker and Pillsbury, along with half a dozen other regional and local brands. Mactier still had his $25,000 to spend.

At the urging of NCMCo.'s St. Louis-based advertising agency, Gardner Advertising Co., Mactier decided to shoot the works in the hometown market, Omaha. First came the radio commercials, bolstered next by TV and newspaper.

Del Barber staked out his territory in front of the Omaha Potato Mart; he greeted incoming shoppers and offered an orchid to each one who tried a package of Duncan Hines cake mix. The store owner admonished him to quit fooling around with orchids and start couponing his product. Nebraska Consolidated direct-mailed a 10-cent coupon to every household in Omaha. Too late, the company realized that area grocers

First Duncan Hines Cake Mix product was this Three-Star Special.

hadn't stocked enough of the new mix to satisfy the resulting demand.

"Our salesmen took trucks and we just peddled that cake mix all over town, to every grocer," recalls Del. "And they were waiting for us to come because people were clamoring for our cake mix. It was an overnight success."

The company had gambled everything on its first try, and had been wildly successful.

After the mix went on the market, Arlee Andre conducted his own informal marketing surveys.

"I was walking through Elmwood Park. I went down to the picnic area and I'd hear the women say 'Have you tried this Duncan Hines mix? The texture is so good.' Then I'd walk a bit farther and hear more ladies talking about it. And I'd question them a little bit, ask what's different about it. They had no idea I had anything to do with the mix. I'd get kind of a pleasure out of listening to them talk, of course."

Nebraska Consolidated set an initial yearly sales quota of 100,000 cases of mix. In the first six months, sales were six times that amount. NCMCo. hired 60 new employees to staff the Cake Mix Division, and purchased a four-story fire-wrecked building at 802 Jackson Street where the company began producing its own mixes in 1952.

NCMCo. began producing cake mixes at this Omaha plant in 1952.

That year production reached 36,000 boxes a day and Duncan Hines Cake Mixes were available in twelve states, including most of Iowa, Nebraska, Wyoming, Colorado, Utah and Idaho. The mix quickly became the best seller in the majority of the larger cities where it was introduced, like Omaha, Des Moines, Kansas City, St. Louis, Birmingham and Denver.

In 1952 Mactier hired as advertising manager Gould Flagg, formerly the assistant sales manager of *Nebraska Farmer* magazine, an agricultural publication read by many NCMCo. customers. Mactier was well-acquainted with the magazine. Shortly after Allan had obtained the Duncan Hines franchise, he had asked the employees of *Nebraska Farmer* to pick out a mailing list from their subscribers. Nebraska Consolidated sent a questionnaire to the selected subscribers asking them if they had heard of Duncan Hines. The great majority had said yes — fortunately.

Gould worked extensively with Gardner Advertising Co. to create the Duncan Hines Division's unique advertising and sales campaigns. Although perhaps homespun when compared with today's precise and sophisticated market testing and segmentation tools, the marketing techniques used by the Duncan Hines Division were innovative and even daring for their day.

Nebraska Consolidated used "grass roots" merchandising — primarily promotions and local newspaper advertising — to reach housewives and, in particular, the country's estimated 19 million working women. With the help of a media blitz, the company tried to quickly dominate each market it entered.

Mrs. Mary Prince, widow of long-time NCMCo. attorney Harold Prince and a former member of the Nebraska State Board of Control, which supervised state penal and mental health institutions, remembers a trip to Chicago for promotional festivities with food editors and brokers.

"I was working in Lincoln and I rearranged my schedule because Allan had specifically asked me to go. I'd never been a part of a promotion and it was an eye-opener for me. I could move around the room, chat with people and expatiate about the cake mixes. I could tell people how when my mother, a marvelous cook, came to visit I'd bake a Duncan Hines cake and convince her that I was as good as she."

NCMCo. was the first packaged mix company to present a cake, bigger than life, on a full page newspaper ad — and in color, no less.

Newspapers were experimenting with improved methods of printing color. An out-of-register piece of cake could look very unappetizing, and do more harm than good for the advertiser. So the Gardner agency worked with the newspaper industry to set uniform standards for run-of-paper four-color printing, to ensure that a Duncan Hines yellow cake looked as appealing in the *Minneapolis Star* as in the *Omaha World-Herald.*

"I'm not too sure that the first color ad didn't appear in Omaha," says Roy Park. "Nebraska Consolidated always asked for page three if they could get it. They wanted the right hand page, and they wanted to be the first ad in. When the person got there and saw that full-page color ad, why, it really did generate excitement. By today's standards it was crude, but it was unique then and it certainly got the attention."

The Duncan Hines Division innovates with full page, 4-color newspaper ads and product close-ups on TV.

On television NCMCo. worked with close-up photography. Rather than showing a happy family around a table, presumably feasting on the barely visible product, the Duncan Hines spots zoomed in on the sliced cake, which was frosted with India-inked shaving cream and topped with a dollop of grease-cutting hand soap.

"Since TV was all in black and white, we varied the shades of gray in the shaving cream to make it look like a yellow or chocolate frosting," ad man Flagg explains. "For ice cream, we used that kind of soap that comes in a big can; it had the same kind of texture and it didn't melt. In those early days the 'cake a la mode' looked pretty bad in real life but fine on the screen. Of course it's a lot more fun to film in color, because you can eat the product."

NCMCo's television ads lingered over a bite of cake, showing luscious frosting stretching between cake and mouth, much as today's ads depict ribbons of gooey cheese linking pizza to person.

"It's kind of sloppy but it has appetite appeal," says Flagg. "Because that's the way it is when you eat it at home."

NCMCo. also introduced an innovative packaging design. Instead of the typical indistinct reproduction of a wedge or square of cake, each box of Duncan Hines mix displayed a vivid close-up of the entire cake with a wedge cut out. The enticing picture, printed using the expensive rotogravure process, covered the box front and continued around the side.

At the end of its first year in Minneapolis, the home of giant competitors Pillsbury and General Mills, NCMCo. staged an anniversary parade. Over 30 trucks loaded with cake mix sported banners showing their store destinations. Sound trucks at the parade's head and tail played the popular tune "If I Knew You Were Coming I'd 'A Baked a Cake." A motorcycle escort guided the whole caravan.

There was just one detail Nebraska Consolidated hadn't taken into account. It was January in Minneapolis. It was 15, maybe 20, degrees below zero. There was nobody on the streets. The parade could be heard from blocks away, but the only on-lookers were those watching through ice-glazed office windows.

When the Duncan Hines Division invaded the West Coast markets, the company held another parade. Although the Minneapolis extravaganza had failed to attract cheering throngs, it had clearly succeeded in boosting sales. And Los Angeles winters were a lot warmer.

But Nebraska Consolidated didn't ship mix to the west coast by truck. The company used trains. So NCMCo. worked with Union Pacific to put together an entire trainload — some 30 or 40 cars — of Duncan Hines mix. Each boxcar wore a banner announcing its destination. Photographers took pictures in Omaha as the train rounded a curve. They took more pictures as the obliging engineer backed the train up and rolled her forward again and again.

Well before the trainload parade arrived, Gould Flagg and an advertising agency colleague had lined up the promotions and advertising in each western city. At the heart of their marketing program was Duncan Hines himself, whom Roy Park described as the country's only walking, talking trademark.

Each time the company entered a new city with its product, Mactier and Park cajoled the mayor into proclaiming a "Duncan Hines Day." Restaurants approved by Hines donned signs welcoming the well-known food critic. Often, the mayor presented him with the key to the city. Hines spoke at cocktail parties and supermarkets, over the radio and on the new rage — black-and-white TV. As Park recalls, "Television was hunting for a lot of ways to get somebody on."

Because of Hines' major role in improving quality, sanitation and inspection in the restaurant and hotel industry, he enjoyed a nationwide reputation as a consumer champion. To preserve this popular appeal, NCMCo. carefully kept Duncan Hine's identity separate from that of the company. But Duncan Hines Cake Mix shone in his reflected light nonetheless. Gould Flagg estimated that during NCMCo's first month of sales in its West Coast markets, the company received around $2 million in free advertising — the equivalent of $15 million or $20 million today — from publicity surrounding Duncan Hines.

Furthermore, Hines' presence at a Nebraska Consolidated reception ensured a good crowd; since chefs outdid themselves to please the gourmet critic, invitees knew they could count on a lavish spread. NCMCo. hosted a gala reception at Salt Lake City's Utah Hotel, owned by the Mormon Church.

Knowing that Mormons avoid alcohol, Gould Flagg asked a local food broker whether the company should alter its usual practice of offering cocktails. The broker advised Flagg that although the Mormons would not try to influence his decision, it might be best to dispense with the cocktail hour — especially since NCMCo. had invited not only the governor and the mayor, but all the elders of the Mormon Church.

Duncan Hines took a personal role in many market introductions; NCM associates remember his collection of watches.

"Well, Duncan loved Kentucky bourbon before dinner," Gould remembers. "He'd say, 'A little bourbon and a little branch water.' I told him before the reception that there would be no drinking and he thought that was fine. Right after dinner, he motioned me to come over. He said he had to go to his room, and asked me to go with him. I thought he was ill, so I said we could go right away. I got him to his room — we just kind of disappeared from the reception — and I was ready to help him into his bed. Then he said, 'Let's have a drink.' He was a charming, thoughtful guy."

Despite his high standards regarding food preparation and service, Duncan once confessed to a newspaper reporter that his own culinary proficiencies were limited to fried eggs, steak, toast and coffee. Not that he regularly indulged in steak and egg breakfasts, however; his favorite morning repast was oatmeal and ice cream.

According to Mactier, Hines was not a naturally gregarious conversationalist. Because his role as food critic and franchise spokesman frequently put him in the limelight, he developed something of a performance revolving around his numerous timepieces. He carried eight or ten or twelve watches all the time — in his cufflink, in his pen, in his eyeglasses, in his belt buckle. His standard explanation during interviews was that winding and setting all his clocks kept him so busy at night that he hadn't the time to spend chasing young ladies.

Hines' watches made a particularly striking impression upon Rex Clemons' wife, Jane. When NCMCo. had begun producing its mixes in 1952, Rex was recruited from the accounting department to become the Duncan Hines Cake Mix Division purchasing agent. As he recalls, he learned by the seat of his pants how to scout out the best buys in cocoa, burnt sugar, lard and sundry other ingredients.

Rex was named assistant secretary of Nebraska Consolidated Mills in 1952 and secretary-treasurer in 1954. Whenever Hines and his wife visited Omaha, Rex, Jane and other top executives entertained them at the

By 1954, Duncan Hines mixes were in all or part of 35 states; new flavors and continually improved products meet with great success.

elegant Blackstone Hotel, now an attractive office building. The hotel staff put out their very best five-course meal for Duncan, but he barely tasted his portions.

"They flew in a brace of pheasants from Illinois," says Jane Clemons. "He would take one little pinch from each — they were probably prepared in different fashions — and then he'd write something down in his book. He ate very little because every place he went he was served a rich thing. And then he wore watches all over himself. He had watches on his fingers, in every pocket, two or three on a wrist. He collected most unusual watches so all evening the conversation would be about watches. And all the time we were eating they would be chiming and setting off alarms. I sat next to him once. Maybe that's why I remember it so well — all those watches dinging around me."

By 1953 Duncan Hines Cake Mix was sold nearly everywhere west of and including Ohio, Kentucky, Tennessee and Georgia. The new Omaha plant was already too small to handle demand.

The yearly sales goal announced in January 1954 was 121 million boxes of mix. This announcement accompanied another of even more far-reaching effect: J. Allan Mactier would replace R.S. Dickinson as president of Nebraska Consolidated Mills on February 1, 1954. Mactier was thirty-one years old. Characteristically enthusiastic, the young president-elect predicted that, with mix production slated to increase by 60% that spring, the Cake Mix Division would surpass its 121-million-box goal.

The company now distributed its mixes in all or part of 35 states. In September of 1954 NCMCo.'s general offices were moved from North 16th into three floors of leased space at 314 South 19th Street. Early in 1955, Del Barber was promoted, at the age of forty, to vice president in charge of sales and advertising for the Duncan Hines Cake Mix Division. Gould Flagg and Joe Weaver, Jr., became marketing manager and advertising manager, respectively.

As Duncan Hines carried the Cake Mix Division's promotional message from state to state, Arlee Andre, whom Dickinson had named vice president and director of research, continued to develop and improve the product. Elaborating upon the Three-Star Special, Andre refined and expanded the company's repertoire of flavors, relying upon his unrivaled ability to distinguish subtle nuances of taste and smell.

"Mr. Dickinson used to say 'Nobody in the world has a taste factor like Arlee's,'" recalled Andre. "It was just some sort of a God-given talent that I had. As a young man I never smoked, and somehow I could examine or classify tastes and blend them together."

Andre worked with a Chicago flavor manufacturing company to obtain his precisely developed flavor combinations. He insisted upon a hint of maple in his chocolate flavoring and a dash of lemon in his vanilla. His superior flavor formulations were so coveted that competitors weren't above trying to pirate them.

One young former co-worker sent the Chicago flavor manufacturer an order for a flavoring agent created especially for Nebraska Consolidated. A vigilant employee called the Duncan Hines Cake Mix Division. Did the fellow have the right to order the flavor? Andre responded that the young man, by then working for a new employer, most definitely did not have the go-ahead to purloin his ingredients.

Andre not only had a special talent for formulating flavors, but he also had a knack for putting together the whole mix in just the right way. As a child, he learned to bake by watching his mother. At home, he had tinkered with his wife's angel food cake recipe until it consistently yielded perfect cakes — breaking down spousal resistance to his kitchen invasions.

Andre knew that, in addition to a sense of flavor, moistness was essential for an excellent cake. The secret to a cake mix that resulted in moist cakes lay in properly combining the flour, sugar and shortening, and in leaving the eggs for the consumer to add fresh at baking time. Andre commissioned a finer grind of flour to better absorb his flavorings. He also found a new shortening that blended more thoroughly and provided the superior "keeping" qualities needed to ensure a high, moist cake, even if the mix spent months in the consumer's cupboard.

"It was just a matter of saying if you add this, you get this result," said Andre. "That's what formulating is. If you do certain things, you get certain results."

In addition, if mix ingredients were blended in the right sequence — first combine the sugar and shortening, then add and completely blend the flour and flavoring — the resulting product was easier to handle. And because the most carefully-balanced formulation was worthless if misused, Arlee composed the package instructions.

"I stood over that mixer and watched it day after day after day. I watched the formation of the batter and I watched how it worked out. Pretty soon other manufacturers began changing the mixing directions printed on their cake mix boxes. They used to say, 'We don't know why these instructions turn out a better cake — but that's the way Andre does it and it works!'"

Andre sent his fellow employees home with cake mixes, unmarked except for instructions, to test on their families.

"Did we bake cakes!" says Jane Clemons. "Our family got fat on the cakes we tested."

Mrs. Clemons wrote critiques for Andre: the pound cake was too eggy-tasting and her kids wouldn't touch the burnt sugar cake. She had no problems getting the cakes to rise, however; they outdid the pan more than once.

Unlike Jane Clemons' brood, Mary Prince favored the burnt sugar cake. Her suggestions for Arlee involved improving his white cake, which she found too dry. Arlee and his chemists took her advice.

Frances Schuster, who worked as Rex Clemons' secretary at the time, enjoyed gossiping with the cake mix salesmen when they reported in at the end of the week. As one Friday afternoon drew to a close, the salesmen gave Mrs. Schuster and the other secretaries packages containing the company's new chiffon cake mix. A few freshly baked chiffon cakes would go over well at the sales meetings scheduled for the following Monday.

"Well, when I made mine, it was a flop," Mrs. Schuster admits. "I was embarrassed to bring it into the office Monday morning — but when I got to work I saw that mine was one of the better ones."

It was back to the lab for the chiffon cake mix.

Arlee considered his wife, Thelma, his best counselor. To test his recipe changes, he regularly toted cakes home for her opinion. Angel food was her preference.

"I never saw anything like it," Andre declared. "I used to take home angel food cake halves and quarters. I'd ask where she put the cake. 'Well, I ate it,' she'd respond."

On the other hand, R.S. Dickinson and Allan Mactier didn't rank high on Arlee's list of discriminating tasters. In Arlee's opinion, his bosses lacked a well-developed sense of flavor analysis. They just knew what they liked.

As the popularity of Arlee's cake mixes soared, quality control became a more complex operation. In 1948 Arlee had hired Joe Nigro, a brand new graduate of Omaha's Creighton University, to run flour analyses in the mill laboratory. Joe received his diploma — with a double major in chemistry and mathematics — on Monday, June 14, 1948; got the job with Nebraska Consolidated on Friday, June 18; and started working Monday, June 21.

Joe worked with Arlee as he perfected the Duncan Hines cake

ADVENTURE IN CONSUMER PRODUCTS

mixes. When Joe returned from military service in Korea from 1953 to 1955, he was offered the position of Duncan Hines quality control chief.

In Joe's absence, the laboratory had been expanded from a single room in the mill building to a spacious four-kitchen spread in the company's former headquarters at 1521 North 16th Street. Over 500 dealers and company friends had toured the facility, which Arlee Andre helped design, during its three-day open house in June of 1954.

To test the mixes Nigro and his staff took a sample of each batch, performed a chemical analysis to verify that it met formula specifications and ran a bake test to ensure that it resulted in an excellent cake. A sample of every batch was stored until the lab approved packaging. Each batch that passed its exams was packaged, coded and approved for shipping.

In 1955, sales of 180 million packages constituted 2/3 of NCM's total dollar sales. But annual advertising costs approach the company's total net worth.

Early in NCMCo.'s cake mix production career, the cake mix plant produced 16 batches per shift, three shifts per day. That meant 48 cakes a day from Nigro's diligent bakers. After the new lab opened, Duncan Hines staffers baked as many as 400 cakes daily. To deal with this abundance of cakes, the lab doled them out to employees who dropped by.

"I got a little tired of eating cake," says Joe. "But we never had to throw any away."

Sales remained vigorous. In 1955 NCMCo. sold 180 million packages of mix; the company's mix operations constituted two-thirds of its entire dollar volume. The Cake Mix Division's fifteen or so products — including yellow, white, chocolate, devil's food, lemon, burnt sugar, angel food and chiffon cakes, plus brownie and muffin mixes — captured as high as 75% market share in some areas of distribution. At its peak sales volume, NCMCo. sold more packaged mix in the Midwest than all of its competitors combined. The company worked with food brokers located over the western two-thirds of the country: in Cleveland, Minneapolis, Sioux Falls, St. Louis, Kansas City, Denver, Salt Lake City, Los Angeles and San Francisco.

But there was a dark side to the story. Freight costs squeezed profits from western markets. Even more crucial, annual advertising figures began to approach the company's current net worth.

"When we tackled Los Angeles and San Francisco, we finally realized that we had stretched so far on our freight that to go national we needed a West Coast plant," says Del Barber. "We also learned that while

Mactier decides to sell his cake mix division to Procter and Gamble in 1956; NCM pockets an after-tax profit of about one million dollars. you can advertise in one newspaper in Omaha or Des Moines or Sioux Falls and get the whole job done, when you get into an area like L.A. or San Francisco it becomes more expensive to try to reach the consumer. The national brands were using national magazines and national TV and radio networks. And because of their volume, they could buy TV and radio time at about 40% less than we could."

NCMCo. found itself less able to successfully open new markets. Other companies were discovering the secrets to moist and flavorful cakes, and new and more unusual flavors introduced under the Duncan Hines label were less enthusiastically received.

"In the early days we had a distinctly unique product," explains Mactier. "As others caught up with us, it became less so. We began opening new markets at a loss. It seemed to me that a one-product company, with high advertising and sales expenditures, was going to be at a big disadvantage against the multiple-line companies who got quantity discounts on advertising. Our company's net worth was less than $4 million and our advertising and promotion budget was approaching that figure. You don't just spend it all like a table stakes game and hope it comes back."

Confronted with the problems ironically stemming from the success of his company's product, Mactier decided to sell the Duncan Hines Cake Mix Division while it could still bring top dollar.

In August of 1956, D. H. Food Co., a subsidiary of Cincinnati-based Procter & Gamble Co., snapped up the inviting bait. Procter & Gamble Co. was the nation's largest producer of soap and detergents. Although P & G's Crisco shortening was popular with housewives who baked from scratch, the purchase of the Duncan Hines Cake Mix Division marked the company's entry into the prepared cake mix business. Nebraska Consolidated's after-tax profit on the deal — around $1 million.

Nebraska Consolidated pared its clerical staff from 60 to 13 and squeezed back into its former headquarters on North 16th Street. The company disbanded its grocery products sales organization and began re-emphasizing flour and feed production and sales.

Arlee Andre and Gould Flagg headed to Cincinnati to work as consultant and marketing manager, respectively, for Procter & Gamble. Flagg left Procter & Gamble in 1961; Andre stayed until his retirement in 1965. Andre still baked regularly until shortly before his death in 1989 at the age of 89.

"My specialties — when I bake for the church or for special occasions — are angel food cake and brownies," said Arlee. "And I never bake from scratch. I always use Duncan Hines cake mix."

Duncan Hines died in 1959 at the age of 78, but Procter & Gamble still produces successful baking mixes bearing his name. D.H. Food Co. operated the original Omaha plant until mid-1987, when its packaged mix operations were closed and consolidated with those of two plants in other locales.

Though short-lived, Nebraska Consolidated Mill's Duncan Hines venture was the key to the company's subsequent diversification. Del Barber credits NCMCo's packaged mix experience with changing the whole complex of the company, impelling its growth into a large corporation.

"It's only once in a blue moon that a small company like ours establishes a new national brand in the food business," observes Del. "And we did it."

CHAPTER 5

A TRIP TO PUERTO RICO

A TRIP TO PUERTO RICO

IN 1956, Nebraska Consolidated Mills retreated from its aggressive competition with the food industry giants. It was back to basics, back to the milling operations the company grew up with. But soon the "back to basics" road took a turn that company executives didn't anticipate when they closed the deal with Procter & Gamble.

Cake mix profits finance a new NCM milling venture in a unique location—Puerto Rico.

After the Duncan Hines Cake Mix Division was sold, company operations had been scaled down; the office pace had slowed. Allan Mactier and his wife, Ann, were building a new home in the wooded Ponca Hills area northeast of Omaha. Ann's sister Jean suggested they take the opportunity for a needed vacation. A relaxing visit to some sunny retreat would help dispel the strain of the last five years.

Allan and Ann took Jean's advice and flew to the Virgin Islands. On their return trip they stopped in Puerto Rico to visit family friends. Mactier headed to the local bank to chat with an acquaintance of NCMCo.'s New York City banker. The island financier led Mactier to Flamento, the Puerto Rican Economic Development Administration, where he was informed about investment opportunities in Puerto Rico.

"Our interest in Puerto Rico really developed from that trip," recalls Mactier. "It turned over something to look at. After the trip we spent a year or two investigating it."

Investigation showed that Puerto Rico had no flour mill; the flour consumed on the island was imported already packaged. Like the southeastern United States, Puerto Rico had a high level of flour and corn meal consumption. Combined with the fact that the small island had twice the population of Nebraska, that meant a sizeable market for NCMCo.'s product. There were also transportation benefits similar to those R.S. Dickinson took advantage of in the company's Decatur expansion. NCMCo. could ship bulk grain by rail and barge to ports on the Gulf of Mexico and from there transport it to Puerto Rico. By processing the grain on the island, NCMCo. could sell it more cheaply than the imported, packaged flour and still garner a profit.

Furthermore, to attract desirable investment the Puerto Rican government operated an industrial development program called Operation Bootstrap. As a qualifying business, NCMCo.'s island operation would be exempt from all Puerto Rican income taxes for 10 years and from most property taxes and municipal levies for eight years. After the period of complete tax exemption, NCMCo.'s Puerto Rican plants and equipment

A $3,900,000 milling complex is completed on San Juan Harbor by spring of 1956. Includes flour mill, corn mill, feed mill and grain elevators.

would be eligible for flexible depreciation.

After they reviewed the situation, Dickinson, Mactier, Claude Carter and Owen Cotton (who was hired as chief industrial engineer in 1954) concluded that Puerto Rico provided a unique location where NCMCo. could apply its special talents and resources. They decided the company should build a milling facility on the island commonwealth. Profits from the Cake Mix Division sale, along with cash released from inventory and receivables, would initially finance the venture.

Industry skeptics declared it impossible for NCMCo. to run a successful milling business in Puerto Rico. They claimed that the market was too small and that shipping bulk grain across the Gulf would prove expensive and impractical. In addition, they questioned how the company would dispose of the huge amounts of millfeed generated by the facility.

But NCMCo. officials trusted in their proven abilities to gauge market potential and transportation economies. They also believed that if the company helped develop Puerto Rico's small dairy and poultry industries, a steadily growing feed market would result. They commissioned plans for a facility roughly the size of the Decatur plant, consisting of a flour mill, a corn mill, a feed mill and a grain elevator.

Late in 1957 construction crews broke ground for the new facility on a 4½ acre waterfront site in Cataño, Puerto Rico, on the west side of San Juan Harbor. The Puerto Rican public relations service excitedly reported the new venture, Caribe Mills, Inc., characterizing it as "a figurative sun in an expanding industrial solar system."

In 1958 Nebraska Consolidated Mills changed the name of its subsidiary to Molinos de Puerto Rico, Spanish for "Mills of Puerto Rico." By the spring of 1959, the new Molinos plant was finished, complete with facilities to dock ocean vessels drawing up to 32 feet. The $3,900,000 complex had annual milling capacities of 1,400,000 hundredweight of flour, 400,000 hundredweight of corn meal and 3,200,000 hundredweight of feed. Its 225-foot-high elevator held half a million bushels of grain.

Nebraska Consolidated Mills employees had monitored and directed the plant's development. Allan Mactier moved his family from their brand-new home to spend several months in Puerto Rico. Joe Nigro traveled to the gleaming new plant to install baking laboratory equipment needed for flour analysis and bake tests. Owen Cotton moved to Puerto Rico to serve as vice president and general manager of the new operation.

The gala grand opening of Molinos de Puerto Rico took place in April of 1959. On hand were a host of island and mainland dignitaries. As the bishop of Puerto Rico blessed the mill, Nebraska Senator Roman Hruska and the Puerto Rican secretary of state raised the flags of their respective homelands.

The governor of the commonwealth stood before his official residence across the San Juan Harbor and pushed a button, causing floodlights to bathe the complex. To cap off the festivities Mactier presented the governor with a set of 15th-century documents signed by Spanish King Ferdinand and Queen Isabella, instructing the royal storehouse to provide biscuits for Christopher Columbus' second voyage.

Behind the hoopla of a gala opening were lots of hard work and frustration. The language barrier and unskilled work force provided real challenges.

Behind all the hoopla, however, were hard work and frustration. Most of the plant's Puerto Rican employees had never seen a flour mill, let alone worked in one. Few of NCMCo's American employees spoke Spanish so they taught the basics of mill operation to bilingual Puerto Rican supervisors, who transmitted the instructions to their subordinates.

Frank Mathias, former general manager of Molinos de Puerto Rico, explains that producing flour in the quantities that NCMCo. anticipated was at first quite foreign to the company's new employees.

"When you expect to start making 4,000 sacks of flour a day and your employees have never made one sack, it's pretty hard for them to understand," says Mathias. "It's sort of like a 40-year-old man deciding he's going to drive when he's never even ridden in a car before. It took us awhile to learn that if an employee made a mistake, we shouldn't become too excited about it. We just needed to show him again. There's an old saying, 'If you're going to teach somebody, tell him, show him and check back.' We might have told them but we didn't always show them, and when we checked back, if they weren't doing it right, we got upset. It took us a little bit more time, a little bit more patience, and a little bit more understanding to get things to come together."

The language barrier and the inexperienced workforce aggravated the usual problems of opening a mill. Rex Clemons and his family spent the summer of 1959 in Tersi, Puerto Rico, managing Molinos de Puerto Rico while Owen Cotton and his family returned to the states for a vacation.

The mill was brand new and there were plenty of bugs in its operation.

"First thing after I got there, there was a frantic call in the middle of the morning," says Clemons. "A machine sold by somebody from England who was supposed to know all about milling machines jiggled itself out of the cement. So there was no operating until that got fixed. And when something like that happened you couldn't just stick your head out the window and yell at somebody to get it fixed."

Nebraska Consolidated employees taught more than milling techniques. Joe Nigro visited bakery customers, to help them and to learn about the flours they needed to make baked goods for the Puerto Rican consumer. NCMCo. agricultural personnel worked with local dairy and poultry farmers, teaching more productive agricultural methods to build up the market for animal feed.

"At one time practically all of our effort was going to Puerto Rico," remembers grain expert Bill Bates. "We had mill production guys and we had guys helping the farmers. It seemed like we didn't have anybody working up here anymore; everybody was in Puerto Rico working to get it going."

From the Omaha office Bates lent a hand in the effort. Bates had been hired in 1957 to manage the NCMCo. mill in North Omaha; in the spring of 1958, Mactier placed him in charge of procuring and shipping grain for Molinos.

Bulk grain transport ship unloads at Molinos de Puerto Rico.

"When we first started we were pretty green," admits Bates. "Coming from Nebraska, we didn't know anything about ocean shipping."

Mactier and Cotton contacted several ship brokers. They arranged to have NCMCo.'s midwestern grain, which was transported by barge from the Omaha area, transferred to ocean-going vessels at New Orleans, Louisiana. Unfortunately, in the late 1950s, port and elevator facilities on the Gulf of Mexico weren't as well-developed as they are today. New Orleans' few grain elevators were publicly held and storage space was available only on a first-come, first-served basis. To compound matters, NCMCo. quickly discovered that with its capacity of 500,000 bushels — a little over one boat-load of grain — Molino's elevator wasn't nearly large enough.

"We had to keep pushing the grain over to Puerto Rico so we didn't run out, yet we didn't have enough room to unload it when we got there," says Bates. "With our limited space in Puerto Rico, we couldn't afford to be on a first-come, first-served basis in New Orleans. Having to stand in line in New Orleans meant we'd be running out of grain all the time over at Cataño. So we decided New Orleans had too much business, and we routed our shipments through Mobile, Alabama, instead."

That still didn't solve the problem created by insufficient elevator

The Molinos milling complex dedicated at San Juan harbor in April, 1959.

space at Molinos. NCMCo.'s ship broker hatched the idea of using an old war-time coal carrier for supplemental storage. The collier, minus its engines, was towed to Puerto Rico and tied alongside the Molinos wharf. When a boatload of grain arrived, a tugboat shoved the collier from the wharf while grain was unloaded directly into the Molinos elevator. Then the collier was tied outside the grain boat to take on the excess grain; Bates recalls that it held about 150,000 bushels. When the collier was full, the tug moved it away from the grain boat so the latter could leave the harbor. Finally, the tug pushed the collier back into position alongside the wharf.

"It was a real operation," says Bates. "But that barge was our lifesaver until we got some money to build more storage. Then we hauled it off to the scrap pile."

Life in Puerto Rico brought other eye-opening experiences for Nebraska Consolidated's midwestern employees and their families. In 1958, Puerto Rico was an eight-hour prop plane flight from Miami, Florida. Even Nebraskans accustomed to plains heat waves were unprepared for tropical living.

"We stayed in the Cottons' home while they vacationed back in the states," explains Mrs. Clemons. "The upstairs was air-conditioned so we could sleep at night but downstairs there were just louvers to keep the house cool. So everything went in and out of the house — lizards, insects and so on.

"Once we entertained some of the American men who were living there without their families. I thought I'd fix a chicken dinner, to give them a piece of home. I was stirring the gravy when a swarm of termites decided to come in one side of our house and fly through to the other side, in the meantime diving into the gravy. I didn't know it, but Harry Thomas, the milling superintendent, was standing behind me watching me spoon them out. Well, when we got to the dining room table, every time I looked up, Harry was saying, 'More gravy, please.'"

Every morning at 6:00 Rex Clemons used the radio-phone to call Claude Carter about developments regarding a poultry operation the company was assisting. Because the radio-phone's reception was unreliable and service was often interrupted, the Clemons household awoke early to shouts of "HELLO, CLAUDE! CLAUDE?"

After his daybreak phone calls, Clemons drove to the mill where he often worked until the early evening, skipping the islanders' midday siesta. His wife recalls that San Juan traffic was so heavy that anyone who didn't get home by 3:00 in the afternoon gave up trying until 7:30 or so.

"Drivers crowded five cars in three lanes," says Mrs. Clemons. "And there was always one that broke down. So we'd sit there and visit with somebody next to us until traffic started to move again. One time we found some very close friends of ours in the next car and arranged to go out to dinner with them."

Puerto Rican businessmen involved with the mill entertained frequently during the Clemonses' stay. As is typical in many Spanish-speaking lands, dinner was served right around the average Midwesterner's bedtime. NCMCo.'s American employees, largely an early-to-bed and early-to-rise bunch, were perplexed by the Puerto Ricans' late hours.

Life in Puerto Rico offers eye-opening experiences for key employees brought in from the Midwest; late dinner hours, siestas require adjustments.

"When we were invited out, we felt we were doing fine if we sat down to dinner by 10:00," comments Rex. "Once we made the mistake of going at the time we were invited for. It was 7:30, and nobody was ready for us. We went home and came back at 10:00."

"If we were in the states we couldn't have stayed out one night after another until midnight and still worked like that," adds his wife. "I don't know what it is about Puerto Rico, but we could do it."

Frank Mathias found the Puerto Rican lifestyle extremely slow

New feed mill at Las Piedras gave Puerto Rico farmers Red Hat products.

In first two years of operation, Molinos de Puerto Rico lost money but by 1961 transportation, market and tax advantages began to produce profits.

when he first arrived in San Juan. Recently widowed, he had gotten accustomed to running his personal errands over the lunch hour.

"When I first came to Puerto Rico, everyone took siestas," recalls Frank. "I'd leave my office to go shopping for a shirt or some socks, and there wouldn't be a store open anywhere. But eventually I learned not only how to do things, but also how to ask questions. At first I assumed it was just like the states. Well, it's not. And it never will be."

Unlike some of his fellows, Mathias ultimately adjusted quite comfortably to the Puerto Rican lifestyle. In 1963 he married a Puerto Rican dairy farm owner and the two raised a family on the island.

"They used to say I'd do anything to sell feed," jokes Mathias. "I even married my customer."

By the time Mathias met his future wife, that joke was funny. But in 1959 and 1960, the thought of taking drastic action to succeed was no laughing matter around the Molinos plant. The first two years it operated, Molinos de Puerto Rico lost money for NCMCo.

Rex Clemons recalls the day Molinos' first grain shipment pulled into the harbor. Skeptical about the financial stability of the new venture, the ship's operator demanded that Rex pay him as the cargo was unloaded.

"He thought we'd go broke," explains Clemons. "And that he'd end up standing in line for his money."

L.B. "Red" Thomas, now secretary and vice president of finance for ConAgra, started in NCMCo's Omaha headquarters in 1960. He'd been on the job for a week when Mactier took him to Chicago to talk to the company's bankers. In its first year Molinos had lost $1.4 million: 20% of Nebraska Consolidated Mills' entire equity capital.

"We were going to explain to the bankers why that happened," says Thomas. "I didn't even know how to spell 'Puerto Rico,' let alone what happened, because I really was brand new."

The concentrated training that NCMCo. gave its employees as well as its customers, combined with the transportation, market and tax advantages that led the company to Puerto Rico, started paying off after Molinos' first two financially precarious years. By 1961, Molinos had begun to show a profit.

That year, the island plant exported 15% of its volume to the

Caribbean Islands and Latin America. Funds were budgeted for the desperately needed grain elevator addition. Construction was underway on a poultry pathological laboratory to provide free services to local poultry growers; just 25% of the poultry consumed in Puerto Rico was raised on the island and NCMCo. hoped to boost that figure.

Molinos had expanded its workforce to 225 people, only six of whom were from the mainland. Puerto Rican officials estimated that company and trucking payrolls, as well as the added value of Molinos' manufactured products, annually injected an additional $4 million into the island's economy.

Between 1962 and 1966, half of NCM Company's profits came from Molinos and tax-exempt status reduces company's federal and state tax ratios.

Between 1962 and 1966, half of NCMCo.'s profits came from the operations of Molinos de Puerto Rico. And because of Molinos' tax-exempt status, as this proportion increased NCMCo. reduced its federal and state income tax bills; for example, between 1961 and 1962 the company's income taxes decreased by 54% — from $822,199 to $377,106.

Like NCMCo.'s Decatur milling operations and its Duncan Hines Cake Mix Division, Molinos de Puerto Rico expanded the company's research and experience. NCMCo. employees gained experience in launching a foreign operation and in working with people from a different culture. The lessons from NCMCo.'s expansion into the Caribbean proved invaluable when the company reached across the Atlantic Ocean later in the 1960s.

But for the immediate future, Nebraska Consolidated Mills executives had other plans. It was back to the mainland to strengthen the company's U.S. milling base and to take on yet another challenge — the chicken.

CHAPTER 6

CHICKENS – AND MORE – IN THE POT

ONAGRA'S fortunes have been strongly linked to the poultry industry, which has undergone many changes in recent years.

At the turn of the century nearly every American farmer, large or small, raised a henhouse full of chickens for the family table. But it wasn't until after World War II that raising chickens and selling them to the public became a major part of U.S. agriculture.

The broiler business started in the locale known as Delmarva, made up of Delaware, eastern Maryland and northeastern Virginia. Mrs. Wilmer Steele of Ocean View, Delaware, is credited with tending the nation's original broiler flock — 10,000 chickens — in 1923.

In Mrs. Steele's day the average chicken yard was home to around 75 birds. The egg-layers were usually the valued creatures, while the unlucky roosters and non-laying hens ended up in the stew pot. Farmers who raised broilers shipped them live to market by overnight rail, and handlers plopped wet mash into their cages at the charges' customary dinnertime. The birds sold for a tidy sum: 50 to 60 cents a pound on average and a dollar a pound at Easter.

During the 1920s and 1930s, new discoveries from poultry disease research allowed safe large-scale confinement raising, and lowered the cost of poultry production. Feed researchers developed heat-processed feeds to replace messy and cumbersome mixes of grains, dried milk and animal scraps. The growing poultry industry spread into Alabama, Georgia, and Arkansas for a number of reasons — the southern states' mild climate, rural small-farm economy, marginally productive farmland, abundant labor and need for a cash crop.

World War II created a new need for expanded poultry production. Because food supplies were limited, feed efficiency became vitally important. While beef cattle typically consume seven to eight pounds of feed for every one pound of meat produced, a chicken can convert about two pounds of feed into one of flesh. In 1944, Howard Pierce, the national poultry director of A&P Food Stores, sponsored a contest to spur the development of a meaty, broad-breasted chicken that most efficiently converted the least amount of feed. Largely because of Pierce's futuristically named "Chicken-of-Tomorrow" contest, broiler production jumped 18% in the next six years.

During this period of expansion, many new broiler growers financed their operations with credit from a feed supplier. As Allan Mactier recalls, "As time went along, broiler growers began growing increasing numbers of broilers. The feed mills started to finance those growers. But when a grower overproduced in response to demand, he'd find himself in a credit crunch and leave the mill with a big account receivable. The mills

Nebraska Consolidated decides to make a full scale move into the poultry business to protect the company's feed operations.

were really in a spot. If the broiler grower went broke, a mill was left with bad credit, but if the grower made money he built a mill and started producing his own feed."

In 1956 Nebraska Consolidated Mills built a feed mill at Tunnel Hill, Georgia, primarily to supply a local broiler operator. The grower sold his operation, leaving NCMCo. with a feed mill and no customer. To safeguard its feed operations, NCMCo. reacted quickly.

"We bought somebody else in the same boat," explains Mactier. "And the integration of the business began for us."

The poultry industry requires a grower, a hatchery, a feed mill, a processing plant and a distribution system to handle the finished product. Originally all of those operations were separate businesses. The industry's cyclical nature, however, ultimately caused those businesses to consolidate into huge broiler production companies.

NCMCo's. relatively small broiler operations experienced only modest success through the early 1960s. Board chairman R.S. Dickinson decided that a full-scale move into the poultry business was essential to protect the company's feed operations.

Typical broiler growing facility houses large numbers of birds in semi-confinement.

"As an offensive move, we began looking for a poultry grower and processor who did not have a feed mill and who was located in the area that we could service," recalls Claude Carter. "Our idea was not to sell feed but to get into the poultry segment of the business. One of our primary prerequisites was that we buy a good business that had the best management possible. We found that company in Dalton, Georgia."

Nebraska Consolidated Mills purchased the Dalton Poultry Co. in April, 1963. Dalton Poultry Co. consisted of a feed mill, hatchery and broiler grow-out operation along with a processing plant which employed 170 people and produced 6,000 ice-packed broilers an hour. Sales for 1962 exceeded $6 million. The "best management" NCMCo. had looked for was Dalton's general manager, Willard Adcox.

With purchase of Dalton (GA) Poultry Company in 1963, NCM Co. gets top management skills of Willard Adcox; joins ranks of fully integrated major poultry producers.

Dalton began in the 1920s as an ice and coal plant and expanded into the meat locker business during World War II. In 1951 the company constructed a poultry processing facility; in 1954 it built a hatchery and feed mill.

Adcox joined the Dalton Ice and Coal Co. in 1941. A native Alabamian, after graduating from high school he attended business school in Chattanooga, Tennessee, for six months.

"I ran out of money and took a job at $15 a week in the circulation

Commercial table eggs are graded by this plant worker.

department of the Chattanooga newspaper," says Adcox. "After a few months I went to work for Dalton. When we started the poultry business we only had two employees who had ever been inside a poultry plant. One lady had worked in a processing plant, and we hired a plant superintendent with some experience. Then we hired 125 new people. We didn't have any more sense, I guess.

"We started out processing about 8,000 birds a day and increased that over time. The poultry business had changed between 1945 and 1950; it had become an operation of large producers. Chicken houses in those days were 3,000 to 6,000 square feet. When we started our program we tried to get people to build 6,000-square foot houses. Now I suppose the average size is 25,000 to 30,000 square feet."

With the purchase of Dalton, NCMCo. officially joined the ranks of integrated poultry producers. Nebraska Consolidated Mills contracted with breeder farms to produce eggs from 75,000 breeder hens, hatched 200,000 chicks a week from the eggs at its hatchery, contracted with 250 growers to raise the chicks for a specified number of weeks on NCMCo.'s Red Hat feed, contracted with catchers to conduct night-time chicken round-ups and processed 250,000 ice-pack broilers a week in its own processing plant.

Banks of incubators hatch baby chicks for growing.

"The key to raising a chicken is management," explains Adcox. "There are close to 100 items you can monitor in the cost of producing chickens. You don't think in terms of pennies per pound, you think in terms of hundredths of cents per pound. You keep feed in front of them all the time and encourage them to eat all they want. The formulas you use and the ingredients that go into your feed can make a tremendous difference. You formulate feeds to where it will take the least number of pennies' worth of feed to produce a pound of chicken. This gives you a great advantage over pork and beef producers because it takes far fewer pounds of feed to produce a pound of chicken."

In August of 1963 NCMCo. doubled the poultry processing operations of its Red Hat Poultry Division by purchasing Sweet Sue Poultry Co. in Athens, Alabama. Six months later NCMCo. completed a new hatchery in Moulton, Alabama, with a 320,000 chick-per-week capacity.

Poultry processing line at ConAgra's Athens, Alabama plant.

To supply the company's two processing plants, the number of broilers grown had increased to 560,000 a week.

These 30 million hungry birds chowed down some 110,000 tons of Red Hat Feed per year. But by 1965, NCMCo's. southeastern feed business was primarily a segment of the company's integrated poultry operations. As explained in NCMCo's 1965 Annual Report, "Our Southeastern feed business has moved with the changes in agriculture in this area... The primary product which we now sell is no longer feed, but chickens and eggs." In June of 1966, Dalton's Willard Adcox was elected NCMCo. vice president and general manager of the Poultry Products Division.

An adventurous NCMCo. didn't limit its poultry operations to Alabama and Georgia or, for that matter, to chickens. In December of 1965 NCMCo. bought Maplecrest Turkeys, an Iowa firm with a turkey hatchery, two growing farms and a processing plant. Several years later the company started a broiler program in Puerto Rico, shipping hatching eggs by air freight to the island every week.

As it developed a booming poultry business out of its southeastern feed operations, NCMCo. also expanded feed sales into the West and Midwest. On September 28, 1963, Nebraska Consolidated Mills acquired

As it develops poultry operations in Southeast, NCM Co. also expands feed production and sales in the West and Midwest.

Sheridan Flouring Mills. Located south of Sheridan, Wyoming, the mill was Wyoming's leading producer of flour, feed and pancake mixes. NCMCo. reformulated the Sheridan Mills' Tomahawk feed, and produced and marketed it in Wyoming and Montana under the Red Hat brand name.

In March of 1964, NCMCo. acquired Nixon Feed Company. Nixon Feeds ran two feed mills in Nebraska, at Omaha and Albion, and three in Iowa, at Des Moines, Sioux City and Washington. Nixon produced a complete line of feed for animals big and small — including Maplecrest's nearby turkeys — but its midwestern clientele bought mostly cattle and hog feed.

Urging the customer to "Buy Direct and Save," Nixon cut costs by selling directly to the farmer, feedlot operator or rancher. Nixon located its plants next to the stockyards and its novel "Drive-In" feed distributorships next to meatpackers and livestock sales barns. A cattle feeder who came to town with a truck full of livestock could pick up a load of feed at the "Drive-In" on his way back to the farm. With no feed salesmen, dealers or deliverymen on the payroll, Nixon offered low prices to entice midwestern livestock growers.

Owen Cotton became general manager of Nixon Feeds. Claude Carter, who had joined the NCMCo. board of directors in 1964, was named executive vice president and general manager in charge of domestic

Decatur complex is expanded in '60s as feed mill and flour operations grow.

and international feed the following year. NCMCo. moved its Feed Division headquarters to Omaha and set up a modern quality control lab at the Omaha flour mill.

One of NCMCo.'s most successful — and adventurous — moves of the decade in the feed business was its 1965 agreement to share ownership of a Spanish feed mill with Bioter S.A., a Madrid-based firm founded in 1953. Located in La Coruna, Spain, the new feed mill was christened Saprogal. A new Red Hat hatchery built near the mill supplied high quality chicks for Spanish poultrymen, and a hog breeding operation furnished local farmers with breeding hogs, feed, veterinary products, farm building plans and marketing expertise.

A most successful move in the feed business takes NCM Co. to Spain; also two less auspicious ventures in Australia and the Dominican Republic.

Early in 1966 NCMCo. hired Ron Hall, a native of England who studied at Oxford and Stanford Universities, as general manager of its European operations. Hall had flown in from London to Omaha to interview for the job.

"I decided that my chances of getting the job would be better if I arrived bearing presents," said Hall. "I therefore bought a gross of daffodils from Covent Garden, the famous London flower market, only to be told in London that it was forbidden to carry fresh flowers into the U.S.A. However, on my arrival at the Chicago airport I told the customs officials that the flowers came from the market where the first scene of 'My Fair Lady' was filmed and, surprisingly, they let me bring them in.

"Imagine landing in a blinding snowstorm in Omaha carrying 144 daffodils! These were distributed to Mrs. Mactier, Mrs. Carter and Mrs.

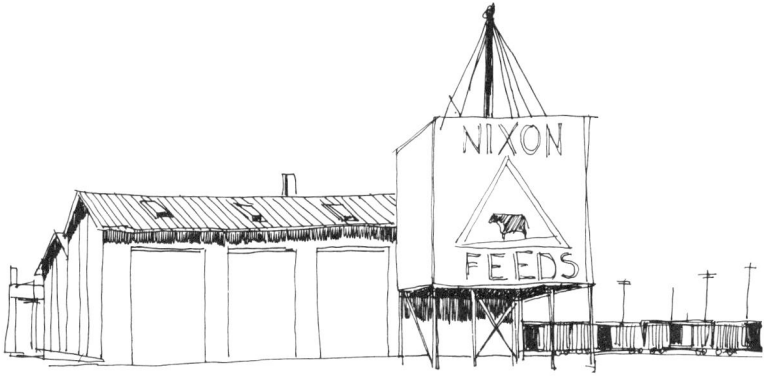

One of several Nixon Feed Drive Ins built to serve Midwestern livestock producers.

Modern Saprogal feed mill at La Coruna, Spain.

Cotton and after a brief interview with Allan Mactier I was hired. I should just have sent the daffodils."

NCMCo. enjoyed an amicable relationship with its partner Bioter from day one. La Coruna's feed volume grew 27% between 1967 and 1968 and 40% between 1968 and 1969, and the Spanish enterprise continued to prosper in the following years.

Not all of NCMCo.'s early forays into the international business scene were so triumphant.

In 1966 Nebraska Consolidated Mills obtained a small feed mill located in northern France at Pierrepont-Sur-Avre, on a World War I battlefield. The mill had a capacity of 6 tons an hour, and its machinery was housed in a structure surviving from the 19th century.

Soon after NCMCo. concluded its negotiations with the owner of the French mill, the fellow was heard bemoaning his decision to sell. According to the company grapevine, when the miller visited the local watering hole his friends chided him so mercilessly about selling to the Americans — France being in an anti-Yankee humor — that he wanted to scrap the deal and start over.

Stateside sentiments were much the same. In 1967 Nebraska Consolidated Mills decided to sell the business and withdraw from France, at a loss of around $695,000.

"France probably just didn't have the growth opportunities for us that Spain had," explains Allan Mactier. "In Spain, we had a good concept, a good partner, and good management. To start with, we knew a whole lot about animal agriculture. We had some knowledge of the Spanish language. We knew that Spain was somewhat backward within Europe but was rapidly going to catch up.

"I had a driver who spoke excellent English. I would talk about business with him and tell him that Spain could do this or that. And he'd reply, 'No, we can't do anything since we lost our money. Things have never been any good since Spain lost her money.' I asked him when Spain had lost her money. He said, 'When the Armada went down.'"

That was in 1588.

"We believed that transferring our knowledge in the form of selling feed and selling our services would be profitable," concludes Mactier. "And we found a very good partner and had very good management."

Yet another far-flung undertaking — an attempt to operate a former United Fruit Company plantation in the Dominican Republic — cost NCMCo. $1,140,000 after taxes in 1967. NCMCo's plan was to cultivate the fertile 30,000 acres to grow grain, and then sell plots to interested local farmers. Unfortunately, NCMCo. executives didn't take into account the 8,000 banana workers left behind when their employer departed, or the limits of tropical agriculture.

Nebraska Consolidated cleared the land and built housing to complement an existing commissary and school for the plantation residents. To provide work, NCMCo. decided to plant labor-intensive crops like strawberries, cantaloupes and peanuts. Tennessee strawberry plants were shipped to the lush island country. The strawberries, great big ones, tasted fine when picked but quickly turned mushy. Air shipping to the mainland was too expensive; by the time the fruit arrived in the states by boat it was inedible. Accountant Jack McGill recalls the ill-fated operation, and jokes about the "$100,000 bowl of strawberries" he breakfasted upon one morning.

Reflects Mactier, "One observer said that I don't even keep the water-grass out of my front yard, so what made me think I could run a 30,000-acre plantation in the Dominican Republic? We were going to grow milo and corn, things that probably wouldn't grow there, and we should have known that to start with. The land was good for tropical agriculture. It had been bananas, but the world banana market was no good. After we sold it, it went back into sugar."

Topping off NCMCo's inauspicious year abroad, in 1967 company officials wrote off expenses for an Australian land-development venture. NCMCo. had joined a group of investors, including entertainer Art Linkletter, to develop 1 million acres of arid rangeland in northwest Australia.

Gladiola flour mill at Sherman, Texas, acquired with Fant Milling Company.

Like central Nebraska, the plains of northwest Australia contain vast amounts of underground water. NCMCo. thought it could tap those subterranean reserves and use the water for irrigation like Nebraska farmers do. The Annaplains Land and Cattle Co. planned to grow milo, or grain sorghum, and soybeans.

NCMCo. shipped irrigation equipment and a combine to the remote Australian site. The company hired a ranch manager and set him up with a station house, as well as a commissary and school to serve the anticipated sizable community.

Then Annaplains established a 200-acre test plot. It failed. There was not enough power available to extract the water. Without irrigation, the arid land couldn't bring forth a stalk of milo.

On top of this disappointment, the station's location — 3,000 miles from Perth, the nearest big city — meant sky-high grain transportation costs. The whole arrangement was too much for NCMCo.'s dwindling financial resources, and the company pulled out at an after-tax loss of around $210,000.

Linkletter, who had access to more capital, stuck it out with the investment. In the mid-1980's the success story of the venture, which he renamed the Australian Cattle and Land Co., appeared on the pages of *National Geographic*.

As Nebraska Consolidated Mills experimented — successfully or not — with new poultry, feed and land development endeavors, it continued to expand its original and largest business segment, flour milling. In 1957 NCMCo. had purchased Garland Mills, Inc. of Greensburg, Indiana, and the flour mill and elevator of Lillie Mills of Franklin, Tennessee. Unlike most midwestern plants, these mills produced and distributed the soft winter wheat flour that commercial bakers used to make cakes, cookies and crackers.

Several stateside acquisitions, including winning a bidding war for Montana Flour Mills Company, help NCM's flour milling operations to span the U.S.

In 1963 Nebraska Consolidated Mills ranged to the Rockies to acquire Sheridan Flouring Mills. Between 1965 and 1968 NCMCo. spread its flour milling territory still further. NCMCo. acquired Fant Milling Co. with its flour mills at Sherman and Gainesville, Texas; Harris Milling Co. with flour mills in Michigan and North Carolina and a feed mill in Michigan; Mauser Mill at Treichlers, Pennsylvania; Birdsey Flour Mills in Macon, Georgia; and Red Lion Milling Co. of Red Lion, Pennsylvania. Several of these mills, particularly those located in Pennsylvania, increased NCMCo's access to lucrative metropolitan commercial bakery markets located on the eastern seaboard.

With the acquisition of Montana Flour Mills in 1969, NCMCo's flour milling operations spanned the United States. Montana Flour Mills operated a mill in Great Falls, Montana, and in Fergus Falls, Minnesota, but the company's most coveted plant was located on the San Francisco Bay in Oakland, California.

The Montana Elevator Company was founded in 1904 by Charles R. McClave, Austin Warr, and Norman Holter, three Montana businessmen banking on the fortunes of the approaching railroad. To handle the grain merchandising trade they counted upon the new rail traffic to bring, the three built a grain elevator in Moore, Montana, on the rail-line's intended site.

The elevator business thrived as new rail branches transported increasing supplies of grain; homesteaders needed not only wheat for their families but also locally scarce oats for their horses and mules. By 1910 the Montana Elevator Company owned four elevators, and that year, after shipping the first carload of improved "Turkey Red" winter wheat seed into the state, the company acquired its first mill, the Grafton Roller Mills in Harlowton, Montana.

Two years later the newly incorporated Montana Flour Mills

acquired the Judith Basin Flour Mill in Lewistown from a group of gold mine owners, and in 1915 the company built a mill and elevators in Great Falls. More acquisitions followed, as did the advent of a South American export business. In the wake of a 1919 crop failure, a rail strike prevented delivery to South American customers. Mountains of flour spoiled on the wharves before the landlocked product was dumped into the ocean.

Dry years continued through the early 1920's. In 1923 all of Lewiston's banks closed, over-extended by loan demands. Montana Flour Mills took over the banks' functions. The company sold local merchants bank drafts for use in cities where it maintained accounts; it also brought in $5,000 a day from the Helena Federal Reserve Bank to cash checks.

In the ensuing years Montana Flour Mills kept expanding and experimenting. The company bought mills in the eastern and central states to obtain a reliable supply of spring wheat. In 1930 the firm became a national leader in cubed animal feeds by installing an innovative "Sizer" cuber imported from England. During World War II, Montana Flour Mills produced a fermentable alco-meal for chemical plants and developed an 80%-extraction bread flour to use more of the wheat kernel. In 1947, the Montana Elevator Company entered the agricultural chemical business; it shipped in the state's first carload of ammonium nitrate fertilizer, which took a year to sell.

By the early 1960s the western milling firm owned 47 elevators, three flour mills, three feed plants and two seed plants. When Nebraska

Montana Flour Mills acquisition included this Oakland, California mill.

Consolidated Mills bought Montana Flour Mills in 1969, Montana had recently sold a Cleveland mill, bought the Fergus Falls mill and opened its modern mill in the populous San Francisco Bay area.

Roger "Bud" Morrison was first vice president and general manager of Montana Flour Mills. Bud Morrison was born in 1925 in Marshalltown, Iowa, and grew up in Minneapolis. He entered the grain and milling business in high school, working as a country elevator operator helper in North Dakota during summer vacations. After serving 2½ years as an Army second lieutenant, he studied for another two at Macalester College in St. Paul, Minnesota.

In 1948, Morrison took a job with the Minneapolis-based McCabe Co., starting out as second man in its Glendive, Montana, elevator. He rose within the company until McCabe properties were sold 10 years later. For the next three years Morrison worked for Cargill as assistant manager of country elevators in the company's northwest region. In 1961, Morrison joined Montana Flour Mills to head its country elevator division; in less than a year he was first vice president and assistant general manager.

"When Nebraska Consolidated Mills bought us, we were a flour milling company headquartered in Montana," recalls Morrison. "We had built a new flour mill in Oakland, and still operated mills in Great Falls and Fergus Falls. We also operated a formula feed business and a fertilizer chemical merchandising business out of Great Falls.

"After we started the Oakland mill, there was a lot of consolidation of milling companies going on. Some of the directors felt that if Montana Flour Mills could join with a larger company, it would increase the value of Montana Flour Mills stock. The company was publicly owned, although the McClave family owned about 18% of the stock."

For two or three years negotiations proceeded sporadically between Montana Flour Mills and several milling companies. Then in 1968 Fisher Flouring Mills of Seattle made an exchange-of-stock offer which sparked action by other mills. Centennial Mills, owned by Seattle-based Univar Corporation, bid next.

"Between the Fisher family and the Centennial group, they had run our stock up from around $22 a share to $30," recounts Morrison. "One day in early December I got a call from Allan Mactier, whom I knew through the Millers' Federation. Allan knew these other companies had been bidding and he wanted to get in too. So pretty soon we had three companies involved. And Nebraska Consolidated topped the rest of them at about $34, $34.50, for cash. Not stock, but cash."

In January of 1969, Montana Flour Mills stockholders tendered

The company's 50th birthday in 1969. Flour is still king, providing 40% of total sales, but feed and poultry account for 24% and 21% respectively. Dickinson retires and Mactier takes over.

their stock to Nebraska Consolidated Mills, increasing NCMCo.'s milling capacity by nearly 20%. Bud Morrison, Montana Flour Mills vice president and general manager, signed on with NCMCo. as vice president of procurement and transportation.

That year was NCMCo.'s 50th birthday, and the steadily growing firm proudly proclaimed its accomplishments. During NCMCo.'s anniversary year, return on average common equity was 21%, and over the past six out of seven years it had averaged 19%. From 1959 to 1969 earnings per share showed a compound growth rate of over 20%, as net earnings increased from $342,875 to $5,096,090. In the same period, feed production grew 360%, and poultry sales increased elevenfold. Providing 40% of total sales, flour still represented the company's largest business segment, but feed and poultry accounted for 24% and 21% of total sales, respectively.

After 18 years as company president and 16 years as board chairman, R.S. Dickinson retired from active service in 1970. Just a year later, on July 12, 1971, he died at the age of 82. Noting that several of Dickinson's business decisions became turning points in American milling history, the *Southwestern Miller* paid tribute to him as a pioneer in American milling. As the industry magazine observed, Dickinson was dedicated not only to his company but to the progress of his community and industry as well. He served for many years as a director of the Millers' National Federation, founded the Nebraska Chamber of Commerce and set the Nebraska Grain Improvement Association on a course of wheat variety and quality improvement that became a model for other states and regions.

Throughout the 1960s, outside acquisitions had generated 55% of NCMCo.'s sales growth; both acquisitions and new construction continued apace in the early 1970s.

In 1970 NCMCo. acquired McGehee Poultry Co. in Louisiana. With its processing plant in Arcadia, feed mill in Choudrant and hatchery in Downsville, McGehee Poultry increased NCMCo.'s broiler volume by 25% and annual sales by $6 million. Capacity at the Athens and Dalton poultry processing plants was expanded by 25%. In 1971 the company purchased Harrell Poultry in Enterprise, Alabama. Meanwhile, NCMCo.'s branded "To-Ricos" broilers proved popular with Puerto Rican consumers. By the time it acquired a broiler complex in Birmingham, Alabama, in 1973, the company was the nation's seventh largest broiler producer.

Flour sales reached a landmark $100 million in 1970; by 1973, with its 18 flour mills, the company was the nation's second largest commercial bakery flour miller. NCMCo. built new mills in Tampa, Florida; Martins Creek, Pennsylvania; and Guanica, Puerto Rico; and bought one in Omaha. It acquired H.C. Cole Milling Co. in Chester, Illinois; Fruen Milling Co., a Minneapolis oat mill specializing in oat products and formula feeds for high performance horses; and a Kansas City corn mill that produced grits, brewers' grits, and corn flours and meals.

A family fiesta for 5,000 launched operations at NCMCo.'s second Puerto Rican feed mill, located near Las Piedras. NCMCo. opened a new feed mill at Vigo, Spain, and helped organize Sapropor, a Portuguese sister to Saprogal, to sell feed and swine breeding stock. It acquired Feedright Milling Co. in Augusta, Georgia, and Security Mills, Inc. in Knoxville, Tennessee. As the firm moved up to sixth place among U.S. feed manufacturers, it consolidated six regional feed brands under the new name "Formax."

In 1970 NCMCo., expert in the care of furred and feathered beast, entered the element of the finned with the purchase of Stral Catfish, an Alabama company that raised and marketed farm-fed catfish. And in 1973, for owners of hounds and hamsters, NCMCo. acquired Geisler, an Omaha pet food and accessories concern, and Kasco, a dog food manufacturer selling primarily to professional breeders and trainers.

This flurry of acquisitions and internal expansion vastly extended the reach of the hard-working midwestern milling firm. By the early 1970s NCMCo.'s business operations, once concentrated in a small triangle in central Nebraska, stretched from coast to coast in the continental United States, dipped south into Puerto Rico and crossed the Atlantic into Europe.

The growing company took pride in its heritage — a consolidation of flour mills in Nebraska. But the name "Nebraska Consolidated Mills" no longer described the company's varied operations, and its distinctly regional tone even hampered business relations in some areas. In the late 1960s Allan Mactier had set in motion the search for a new name. Mactier felt that the firm had outgrown its original name back in 1941, when NCMCo. first set up operations beyond Nebraska's borders. By 1971, the business was a diversified food company with 53 plants in 13 states, Puerto Rico and Spain. In fiscal 1971, annual sales had grown to over $272 million and the company had 4,105 employees.

"'Nebraska Consolidated Mills' no longer fit where we were or what we were doing," says Mactier. "We tried developing names and couldn't get anywhere, so we hired a consultant specializing in corporate communications to change the name, the image, the whole job."

On February 25, 1971, Nebraska Consolidated Mills shareholders officially approved the adoption of a new company name — ConAgra, Inc. A corporate design firm from New York, Sandgren and Murtha, Inc., developed the name. "ConAgra" was derived from Latin roots for "with" and "land", and signified the company's past and future "partnership with the land". As company literature explained, "ConAgra" is pronounced "con" as in consolidated and "agra" as in agriculture, with the emphasis on the Ag.

Along the route to the shareholders' vote for "ConAgra" lay discarded contenders like Agrifoods, Cerecon, Consol, Heartland, Homestead, Nebco and Nebcon. The name change cost ConAgra about $200,000 — half spent to find the new title and half spent to advertise and promote it to investors, industry customers and the general public. No mere random combination of syllables would have sufficed. For each nominee the consulting firm had to ascertain whether any other company claimed the same or a similar name; whether the name accurately depicted a growing NCMCo's present and future operations; and whether the name bore unfortunate meanings or connotations in any foreign language.

"I didn't like 'ConAgra' at first," admits Mactier. "I don't know why. It's a great name, but I didn't like it."

Before long Mactier reversed his stance, and he enthusiastically promoted the firm's new identity. ConAgrans celebrated the new name with a daytime party at the company's Kiewit Plaza offices and an elegant dinner for executives and their wives at the Radisson-Blackstone Hotel. Coincidentally, that dinner marked the 27th wedding anniversaries of two of the prime movers behind the change — Allan Mactier and Maurice Malin, coordinator of the name change project.

Employees accepted the new name with a minimum of fuss.

"The company was changing a lot, and it had gotten so much bigger," recalls Bill Bates. "A lot of our companies were still going by their own names. We were Mauser Mill Company in Treichlers, Pennsylvania. Down in Decatur we were the Alabama Flour Mills. And at Sherman, Texas, we were Fant Milling Company. The idea was to get all those names under one. I think all the employees were a little amused at the name change, but other than that, it didn't cause too much consternation."

CHICKENS AND MORE

As Jane Clemons concludes, "It was a little hard for us old Nebraska Consolidated people to accept that 'ConAgra' for awhile. But we all wore our buttons and we all 'ConAgra'd' each other until we got used to it."

On a wintry day less than two years after Nebraska Consolidated Mills was rechristened ConAgra, the company first saw that name on the Big Board in New York City. Trading of ConAgra common stock on the New York Stock Exchange began promptly at 10:00 a.m. on January 9, 1973. ConAgra was the exchange's first new listing of 1973; the firm's official symbol was CAG.

As company grows far beyond its original state and businesses, a new name, "ConAgra" is adopted in 1971. Less than two years later the company's stock is listed on the NYSE.

ConAgra was in select company. Only five other Nebraska entities were listed on the New York Stock Exchange: Fairmont Foods, Union Pacific, Northern Natural Gas Co., and Pamida, Inc. for their corporate stock, and Mutual of Omaha for its "Mutual Interest Shares" closed-end fund. In fact, as of January 9, 1973, ConAgra became only the 1,507th business — out of 1,700,000 U.S. businesses — to hold a spot on the NYSE.

New name ConAgra goes up at entrance to Decatur complex.

Unloading caged broilers at Enterprise, Alabama processing plant.

ConAgra management had applied for the listing during the previous year. Historically the company had been traded over the counter, but Mactier and other executives believed that the New York Stock Exchange — with its average daily trading volume of $545 million in 1973 — offered a better trading market for buyers and sellers, a larger pool of potential stockholders, greater national and international recognition and easier access to capital.

ConAgra met the criteria for inclusion in effect at that time: three consecutive years of at least $2 million pre-tax and $1,200,000 after-tax earnings; at least 1 million shares of common stock outstanding, with certain requirements regarding distribution of ownership; net tangible assets exceeding $10 million; and an aggregate market value of publicly held shares of at least $12 million.

"Going on the New York Stock Exchange seemed to be a natural progression, a way to enhance the price/earnings ratio, the value of the company," comments Mactier. "It seemed like an important step."

ConAgra's stock ownership base was already spreading nationwide. Between 1967 and 1972 the number of stockholders increased by 60% to nearly 4800. Whereas in 1967 only 38% of company stockholders lived outside of Nebraska, by the time ConAgra applied for its NYSE listing that percentage had risen dramatically, to 65%.

The firm's debut on the Big Board was filled with fanfare. As the day's trading commenced, Allan Mactier purchased the first 100 shares of stock at $16.50 per share. An enthusiastic horseman, Mactier later donated the stock to the United States Olympic Equestrian Team. Del Barber gave 500 loaves of bread to the New York Salvation Army. During a reception at the Wall Street Club, Mactier met with over 100 security analysts and news media representatives to brief them on this relatively unknown Midwestern conglomerate.

Boise Pannier will never forget that reception. Pannier, who started work at NCMCo.'s Fremont mill two days after the stock market crash of 1929, was the company's longest-tenured employee. Gould Flagg suggested that Boise appear in New York on behalf of the company's 4300 workers.

"ConAgra had a private plane and pilot and I rode back there to New York," recalls Pannier. "Allan Mactier gave a talk and they introduced me to the crowd. I told them about the Fremont mill, when they bought it and how old it was. Then we came back on the plane that night. It was just for the day.

"But I didn't get any dinner. I was out sightseeing and they had dinner at noon. When I came back, why, it was all over with!"

They don't eat that fast in Fremont.

CHAPTER 7

THE BASICS: ECON 101 AND PHILOS 102

ECON 101 AND PHILOS 102

C ONAGRA had a new name. It had a listing on the New York Stock Exchange. It had business operations extending across the Continental United States, firmly established in Puerto Rico and comfortably developing in Spain.

But by mid-1974 ConAgra's board of directors recognized that the company also had nearly fatal losses.

Much of its recent growth had been undercapitalized. Assets had been consumed for various intriguing — but marginally profitable — ventures. The company relied too heavily upon Puerto Rican mill profits cramped by price controls. And disastrous events in the soybean markets had almost toppled the whole shaky structure to the ground.

Company president Allan Mactier stepped down in August of 1974. Claude Carter became the new president. In October he hired Pillsbury executive Mike Harper as ConAgra's first "chief operating officer."

Harper focused on simple goals: Reduce assets, trim inventories, track down unpaid bills, and give managers responsibility for their balance sheets.

The company parted with its most salable asset in late 1974, when it sold Dixie Lily, a packaged baking mix business with control of several popular brand names, to Martha White, Inc. Although top management regretted losing Dixie Lily, that sale was important. It proved to ConAgra's creditors that the company was resolved to sacrifice in order to recover its financial footing.

In January of 1975 ConAgra sold the J.F. Imbs Milling Company, a packaging concern at Martel, Ohio, to Pillsbury. Red Thomas recalls the firm's state-of-the-art computerized warehouse system, in operation when ConAgra purchased the plant. One ConAgra representative watched the progressive new system at work: a computerized mechanism traveled along a track to a designated pallet, picked it up, traveled back to the loading area, ran into the wall and dropped the load all over the floor.

That same month ConAgra sold its mill at Guanica, on the south coast of Puerto Rico. This sale enhanced Thomas' and Tom Brady's reputation for adroit bargaining. By introducing milling competition on the island, the transaction quieted local officials' concerns about an incipient milling monopoly. Coincidentally, it rid the company of a lackluster performer — at a good price.

Recalls Red Thomas, "They used to call Tom Brady and me the junk salesmen."

At the end of fiscal year 1975, ConAgrans breathed a collective sigh of relief. In that year ConAgra had pulled earnings of $4.1 million out of the previous year's $11.8 million loss. By concentrating on basic objectives, the company had turned the corner.

Asset sales continued as the new, and brighter, fiscal year advanced. In September of 1975 the Peavey Company paid $600,000 for ConAgra's Grand Island plant. The attractive brick mill, a model of "daylight construction" when Nebraska Consolidated Mills built it in 1936, was already closed. Peavey wanted the elevator for grain storage space.

A few months later ConAgra sold several Nixon Feed properties. Nixon's "Drive-In" feed sales had dried up in the late 1960s, when Omaha meatpackers started journeying to the farmer to buy livestock. That meant that cattle farmers no longer trucked their livestock into town, or stopped at the Nixon store for a load of feed before heading home.

Fortunately, ConAgra's poultry operations had eluded the clearance sale sweep of 1975. Harper's faith in the chicken business appeared ready to pay off in excellent — not merely respectable — fiscal 1976 profits for ConAgra.

As ConAgra improved its financial position, it also struggled to boost its reputation among stockholders, investors, and securities analysts. The recommendations of these experts could decide a firm's standing on the financial pages. After ConAgra's dismal showing in 1974, brokers' reactions to the suggestion that they recommend ConAgra stock ranged from the polite to the profane.

"If we were ever going to be able to use the company's stock as currency in our deals, we had to improve its value in the public market," explains Tom Brady. "I'll never forget sitting down with some local brokers at the Omaha Club. One broker told us, in a gentle way, that until he saw something he could live with he wasn't going to do much about ConAgra stock. Then another announced that ConAgra had disappointed him so many times he wouldn't deal in our stock if his life depended on it."

ConAgra found the right man to regain the financial community's confidence — Warren McCoy. Shortly after Harper came to Omaha, McCoy, 59, had left his job as Pillsbury's director of financial relations. He had worked for Harper's former employer for over 30 years.

"When we heard about that, we arranged for him to come visit Omaha, and Claude Carter hired him," says Harper. "This guy has made more money for our shareholders than any other guy I know. A quiet man, not flashy, but boy, is he good."

In January of 1976 McCoy signed on as ConAgra's director of public relations. His task was to reclaim a modicum of credibility for ConAgra among the security analysts. While at Pillsbury, McCoy had developed a reputation for honesty and dependability. Industry experts knew he would tell the bad news as quickly as the good.

"When Warren left Pillsbury, a group of the top food analysts in New York flew to Minneapolis to give him a going away party," remarks Harper. "Well, Warren got us in to see those guys."

Shortly after his arrival at ConAgra, McCoy mentioned to Mike Harper that the objective of a financial relations program was to earn a fair market value for stock.

"Mike's response was 'If fair equates with $50, then I agree,'" McCoy recalls. "That's $50 a share at a time when the stock was selling for maybe $13 or $15.

"About this time ConAgra's personnel department asked me to describe my objectives. I saved myself a hell of a lot of time. I put down '$50 a share'."

Establishing a financial relations program. Objective: To earn fair market value for stock.

With missionary zeal, McCoy and Harper spread their message to analysts, brokers and potential investors. Improving investor relations meant riding a turbulent grasshopper flight to Sioux Falls, South Dakota, for a breakfast meeting with stockbrokers; taking a mid-morning hop down to Sioux City, Iowa, for a brown-bag lunch discussion; then reboarding for the weary last leg home — in time for a 4:00 p.m. chat with brokers at the Omaha Club. Along the way, Harper learned a few painful lessons about financial P.R.

"One time Warren got us a meeting with a top analyst from a New York bank," he recalls. "We made our pitch. At the end of it this guy said he'd watch ConAgra for three years and then decide whether to do a paper on us. Warren was delighted, because now the analyst knew about ConAgra. But I was crushed. I expected the stock to go up five minutes after we left the man's office."

In addition to catching the attention of the financial analysts, McCoy tried to garner some publicity for ConAgra's management. He contacted an internationally known public relations firm for help.

"I remember Warren and I went to lunch in New York with those people," says Harper. "They really had a full court press on us. They told us what they could do for me, including becoming president of the United States. They appeal to the ego of the top management. That's the way they sell.

"Warren and I decided not to do that. We would use advertising firms to sell products, but not a public relations firm to sell the corporation. I'm rather proud of that, because I think our own staff has done a great job getting us publicity."

In May of 1977, ConAgra got its first visible support from Wall Street when an analyst issued a strong buy recommendation for the company. It took over three years for the business press to follow suit. Then, within the same week in December of 1980, both *Business Week* and *Forbes* featured ConAgra. In January of 1981 ConAgra's name graced the front page of the *New York Times* business section; three months later *Barron's* profiled the company.

According to McCoy, there's a herd instinct at work among the financial community. If one analyst or publication comments favorably upon a company, others follow. The hard part is to break in, to communicate why a given firm merits attention.

"If I taught Mike how to talk with the analysts, it's because I emphasized honesty, integrity, and openness with them," explains McCoy. "Some executives try to talk and say nothing. Mike always tried to get his objectives for the company across to his audience. As the analysts heard him more and more, they couldn't help but sense how strongly he believes in the objectives he was putting forth for ConAgra.

"The analysts are very heavy on performance. 'Let us see what you are going to do.' Then if you do it, and they recall you said you were going to do it, that helps."

"I remember the one thing Warren used to tell me to do when I spoke to the analysts," comments Harper. "He said 'Make your answers shorter'."

Maybe Harper had needed some lessons in investor relations. But his overall savvy in the food business didn't go unnoticed at ConAgra.

Claude Carter explains, "When I became president of ConAgra in August of 1974, my big job was to save the company. And to save the employees. When rumors start going around that you are bankrupt or that the banks are going to take you over, your competitors don't just sit by and twiddle their thumbs. They go after your jugular vein — your business and, more importantly, your key employees.

"Having gone through that traumatic episode, I could see two things. One, Mike Harper wasn't going to stick around and wait for me to get to be 70 years old to run the place. And, two, his abilities really were terrific. It was evident that he was a leader. I felt that for the good of the stockholders it was a good move for Mike to move into the presidency."

In August of 1975 Harper had been appointed to the board of directors to fill the unexpired term of Louise Kinney Platt, daughter of the firm's first president, A.R. Kinney. On March 15, 1976, the board of directors voted Harper president and chief executive officer of ConAgra. Bob

Daugherty, who had been elected chairman of the board in February, 1975, retained that position. Claude Carter became board vice chairman.

As CEO, Harper was free to plot the future course of the company.

"When a fellow is made CEO he gets a couple of phone calls and some nice letters and a few pats on the back and then that's all over," says Harper. "But he has a clean slate to work with.

"ConAgra had just survived near-bankruptcy. We'd darn near gone under. That really gave us an opportunity to open a window and look at ourselves pretty objectively about what we wanted to become. I believe it is very hard for most companies to do that. They go through the motions, but to get that window open, that fresh breeze, is very hard."

So Harper wrote a white paper. A stack of 8½-inch by 11-inch paper, typed, with all the normal misspelled words.

"The paper attempted to deal with the kind of company we wanted to build, from a management standpoint," says Harper. "It dealt with things like environment, culture, quality of people, quality of the product, and objectives of the company."

Harper circulated the draft among his top corporate executives and operating officers for their comments and contributions. They weren't shy with their opinions.

"You would think we were trying to write the Old Testament," recalls Jim Kennedy. "We wrote it and rewrote it, wrote it and rewrote it. Every word and the context in which it was stated took hours, after Mike had labored hours on it."

Senior managers took the "white paper" and shared it with middle managers, both to improve the language and to ensure that it was understood.

"Maybe we built a communication bridge between people so they knew what the words meant to each other," suggests Harper. "Because all of a sudden the process accelerated and everything fell into place."

Midway through 1977 Harper presented the rewritten manuscript for the board of directors' perusal.

"By then we had wired everybody from top to bottom on the language," he explains. "That language — and the concepts underlying it — developed into what we finally called the 'ConAgra Philosophy.'"

Harper had taken inspiration for his "white paper" from co-workers who influenced him throughout his career. Industrial psychologist Sy Levy, a Pillsbury alumnus, promoted openness and conflict and stressed the significance of a company's environment and culture. Bob Keith, a former Pillsbury CEO, emphasized the importance of having the best employees in the business. Another former Pillsbury chief, Terry Hanold, showed Harper the value of periodically looking beyond the day-to-day details to play with broader concepts.

Terry Hanold describes a company culture as the sum of all employees' shared experiences, and the total values drawn from those experiences. The values form a system of guides for decision, conduct, evaluation and judgment of past conduct. This value system creates the set of attitudes that all employees in an employment community share.

To emphasize the importance of a company culture and the personal commitments required by top managers and board members to achieve it, Harper published the final version of the "white paper." Even though the 16-page, brown-covered booklet was only intended for use within ConAgra, fixing the company's objectives and aspirations in tangible form was risky. What if those goals weren't met?

Recalls Jim Kennedy, now vice president and corporate director of marketing, "We resolved the issue by deciding that the booklet described what we were striving to be. Not with respect to our objectives; those were clear. But for the more esoteric things — the environment, who we are, what we're trying to do. We may never get there but if we're striving to get there that is worthwhile."

At first ConAgrans used the booklet for its stated purpose — as a primer on basic goals for the company's management style and internal culture, against which to regularly measure individual and company performance. Gradually, though, Harper made an interesting discovery.

The overriding management objective: maximize stockholders wealth. From the ConAgra Philosophy.

The philosophy set forth in the slim pamphlet intrigued desirable employment applicants and acquisition candidates. The booklet helped Warren McCoy explain the new ConAgra to dubious investment analysts. Red Thomas started to show it to ConAgra's bankers. The original internal purpose of the "white paper" remained paramount. But the published "ConAgra Philosophy" helped convince outsiders of ConAgra's whole-hearted commitment to a new, cooperative yet individualistic management style.

The ConAgra Philosophy sets forth one over-riding management objective: to maximize stockholders' wealth. The cornerstone of the ConAgra Philosophy is the prescription for meeting that objective. "The company's success will depend on entrepreneurial leadership coupled with professional management operating in an atmosphere of openness that encourages top-quality, innovative, profit-motivated people to achieve results."

According to the ConAgra Philosophy, creating the proper work environment is probably management's most important task. The ideal work environment encourages the pursuit of high goals and standards; the development of people and ideas; participation and involvement between managers and employees; and collaboration and close professional association among peers, with energies put into unifying objectives rather than rivalries.

To achieve all of this a work environment must have certain key characteristics.

First, employees need to feel free to act vigorously, without inhibitions caused by the fear of being wrong. They should expect their fellows to judge their work, but in an atmosphere of helpfulness rather than of second-guessing.

Harper believes that a working environment should foster good decision-making and reduce mistakes. A dictatorial atmosphere invites the fear of failure. A fair and supportive environment frees employees from the anxiety and irresolution that often results in error. Ultimately, mistakes occur less frequently in an open atmosphere in which an error is a learning experience, rather than an invitation out the door.

"When I hear people — especially young people — talking about the 'politics' in a corporation, I think of what that corporation is losing," says Harper. "Imagine the loss, for instance, if somebody really thinks something is wrong but can't or won't speak up because of 'politics.'

"I know of some corporations that have built an atmosphere of fear among their people. Some of these are enormous, powerful companies. The management styles in these companies may not mean the companies won't succeed. But it's my belief that the degree of success — and security — is dependent on the management style. Besides, would you really want to work in a company where people are constantly afraid of making a mistake?"

In Harper's opinion, errors can be fruitful if they encourage learning. As board member and business owner Bob Daugherty notes, that viewpoint is essential for managing a large company in an entrepreneurial fashion.

"You've got to be willing to let people try things," Daugherty notes. "Some things work and some things don't work. If you learn from the things that don't work you're going to be well ahead."

Under the ConAgra Philosophy, employees are free to act, but they are also responsible for getting results. While a perfect batting average isn't expected, employees should expect to be measured on the basis of end results. Performance evaluation serves the employees, by allowing them to demonstrate their worth to the company and to learn how to improve.

"Giving a person responsibility is the greatest training device in the world," says Harper. "It's fundamental. People love responsibility — particularly good people."

Subordinates aren't the only ones who get evaluated on their performance. In addition, managers are accountable for developing their subordinates' talents.

The ConAgra Philosophy recognizes that strong employees won't stay with a company unless they feel, perhaps selfishly, that they are growing personally. Each key executive must provide his or her employees that opportunity to grow.

The brochure states it well: "We will not, and cannot, force people to grow; but the nature of most people in a business is that they want opportunities. Particularly those who would be our future leaders will leave unless they have these opportunities. We cannot maintain the type of working environment that we want in the future without personal growth founded on opportunity, encouragement and feedback."

Fundamental to the ConAgra Philosophy is the belief that the workplace must be an open environment, founded on trust and confidence, in which people can be open with one another.

Employees must take the risk of trusting in their subordinates, peers and superiors. They can show that trust through actions like admitting uncertainty; inviting critique and feedback; asking for and giving support; offering ideas and suggestions or challenging traditional methods; and openly and directly confronting issues and people.

The ConAgra Philosophy encourages the freedom to disagree. Harper subscribes to the theory that "you can't really mean yes unless you can say no." Subordinates who are consistently coerced into agreement become compliant rather than creative and challenging.

In Harper's opinion, an employee should feel free to tell his boss to go to hell. And Harper doesn't just prescribe behavior for other people; one of his own top executives threw a punch at him during a heated exchange.

However, positive conflict resolution isn't simply a license to curse the boss. It serves a vital purpose. Well-directed, it permits a manager to determine the roots of a problem, to ferret out the causal factors so the problem doesn't resurface next week, or next year. Open disagreement between employees can lead to these discoveries; the key is to keep the dispute centered on issues rather than personalities.

According to industrial psychologist Sy Levy, "A business is a difficult, problematic environment. The critical issue is to try to get as much data and feelings out in the open as possible, on the assumption that the

ECON 101 AND PHILOS 102

more data we have the greater the chance of coming up with some resolution useful to the parties, the task and the problem."

Levy feels that a top executive who allows himself to be challenged by subordinates demonstrates his freedom from the stereotyped behavior of his role. Far from reducing the top manager to the level of his employees, it raises him. But Sy doesn't preach this to non-believing CEOs. If they're ripe to convert, they convert themselves.

ConAgra's CEO not only swears by open conflict, he also celebrates individuality.

Harper feels that many corporations mistakenly try to fit their employees into a mold. Instead of seeking the "organization man", Harper wants the unique individual.

Observes Harper, "Only by being ourselves can we bring energy and uniqueness to our work. New ideas come from individuals, not clones.

"We were and still are trying to build a culture of responsibility, commitment, and openness, and an entrepreneurial environment. With freedom to act, freedom to fail, a lack of fear. Freedom to disagree and freedom to challenge. We are trying to create a culture that releases the power of the individual."

In Harper's view, sharing a common goal shapes individual behavior and enhances, rather than restricts, the power of the individual. Under the ConAgra Philosophy, each individual works to achieve company goals in his or her own way.

"Commitment to a shared vision will move an organization toward that vision," declares Harper. "Commitment is a voluntary act. Commitment can only be made by individuals who feel a sense of power."

ConAgra pays a premium for top quality people— seeking the best individual in the industry for key positions.

To get these powerful and committed individuals, the ConAgra Philosophy calls for top management to fill each key position with the best individual in the industry. The company aims to have fewer but better people than the competition. Because the best people expect reward for their competence, ConAgra pays a premium for top quality — rewarding both the high achiever and the manager who gives growth opportunities to subordinates.

In general, the ConAgra Philosophy holds that most people want to be involved meaningfully in their work. The greater their involvement, the greater the intensity of effort and thought they apply to their tasks. People want a sense of belonging. They want to achieve significantly and be rewarded appropriately. They want to set goals and use their energies to attain those goals.

Roger "Bud" Morrison, who as transportation and procurement head helped refine the "white paper", wholly endorses that philosophy. He believes that employees who push themselves and take on more responsibility experience greater job satisfaction.

"A good employee is a happy one," Morrison asserts. "Employees should enjoy what they're doing, understand the job and set goals for the job and themselves."

For nearly a year, Harper's draft "white paper" filtered through the ranks of ConAgra managers, each eager to leave a mark on the new company philosophy and culture. Meanwhile Harper determined that the firm needed a new set of financial, as well as cultural, objectives. ConAgra was functioning again, but that didn't satisfy Harper. He wanted it to excel.

Former board member Terry Hanold contends that the barrier to excellence is moderate success.

"This is expressed in the fine old phrase 'If it ain't broke, don't fix it,'" he explains. "'It's not the greatest in the world, but it works and we're getting along.'

"A lot of operations are going nowhere but are pretty comfortable. To a great extent that had been the old ConAgra's position. It had average growth, it had average return on capital, it had a decent position in its industry. Its prospects were average good. When catastrophe freed us from the company's past, it freed us to opt for a new ConAgra. And the cost of saving ConAgra deserved a lot better reward than simply restoring the average conditions that had prevailed."

Vail 1976 Conference— to forge a new set of financial objectives for the company.

So Harper hustled a select group of top managers and directors out of Omaha to forge a new set of financial objectives. For two and a half days in October of 1976, the seven men rented three private houses in the mountains of Vail, Colorado.

Earlier in the year, ConAgra had flown several of the country's top securities analysts into Chicago to meet at the O'Hare Inn. ConAgra executives asked the analysts what they thought the company should do to earn a reputation as a good investment.

"They talked about 'quality of earnings,'" Harper recalls. "We had to get stair-step earnings. We had to get into the kinds of businesses where we'd have earnings increases year to year or quarter to quarter. That was their advice.

"We told them that we didn't know just what we were going to do, but we were going to set our own strategy. Wall Street could evaluate us, but we were not going to let Wall Street set our strategies. We laughed as we said it, but we were serious."

The time had come to set that strategy.

Jim Kennedy came to the Vail meeting as ConAgra's new marketing expert. Harper wanted him to inject some marketing thinking into the company's commodity-oriented outlook. Kennedy started at ConAgra in April of 1976, after seven years with Armour Food Company, which had wooed him from a job as Pillsbury's new products chief. In 1952, Kennedy had joined Pillsbury as one of its first marketing managers — helping to lead the campaign against competitor Nebraska Consolidated Mills in the fledgling cake mix business.

Bob White came to Vail as a top-notch strategic planner. After Harper helped develop ConAgra's first three-year plan in the fall of 1975, he suggested hiring a management recruiter to track down a planning expert. The recruiter found White at General Mills, managing venture development in the corporate growth department. Before joining the Minneapolis-based food company in 1966, White had worked in Chicago as a management consultant for Booz, Allen and Hamilton. In March, 1976, ConAgra hired him to help company management build a strategic planning process.

"Back then when we were assembling our team, we called ourselves the Washington Redskins," notes Harper. "At that time they were a bunch of has-beens and retreads, yet they were in contention for the championship."

Tom Brady attended the meeting as the company's authority on money. Two board members joined the entourage: entrepreneur Bob Daugherty and creative thinker Terry Hanold. Harper got to go along because he called the meeting. Sy Levy refereed.

The crew split up among the three houses for sleeping, and picked the roomiest for their daily huddles. Breakfast arrived at the meeting house at 7:30; over bacon and eggs the seven dove into the topic at hand.

Their wrangling continued over luncheon sandwiches. A break for an afternoon walk among the aspen trees, blazing with autumn color, cleared cobwebs out of the brain. Snacks and cocktails at the house preceded dinner in a local restaurant; all the while, conversation steered a steady course — ConAgra.

"It was such an intense and complex subject that your mind got working and you couldn't really turn it off," explains Kennedy. "People came into a session with ideas that they favored. But the cross-stimulation would spark another idea, would either take someone to a different place than he was coming from or add to the point of view he held before. And that just kept going, over lunch or dinner or whatever."

The first question was so simple it was profound. What was ConAgra's business? After selling off various peripheral assets, the company had two primary segments left – flour and chickens. Industry analysts looked askance at flour milling; fierce competition in the 1960s had crippled many U.S. millers. And food experts shunned the broiler business, fearful of diminished returns during the down periods of the three-year poultry cycle.

But Harper had come to Vail armed with studies of several other major food companies specializing in basic foods, notably the highly successful Cargill Incorporated. Because Cargill was privately held, its record was not widely known or easy to find out. Several years earlier, however, former Pillsbury president Terry Hanold had prepared a report comparing Pillsbury and Cargill.

The comparison clearly showed Cargill's superlative growth records with respect to profits, size and capital. It lent credence to the viewpoint that ConAgra, too, could prosper in the basic food business.

Unlike many industries in which a few huge companies controlled major market shares, basic foods – which Harper defines as anything remotely connected to food – was a fragmented industry offering ConAgra ample room to flex its muscle. Contrary to popular wisdom, commodity foods companies frequently enjoyed much higher rates of return than the narrowly focused, consumer packaged foods enterprises that investors favored. And the world's swelling populations and improved living standards meant ever-increasing food consumption, making basic foods good business.

Terry Hanold pointed out that ConAgra lacked the production, sales, marketing, research and development resources needed to compete on a national level in the grocery products arena. But the basic field presented the company with opportunities suited to its resources and talents. ConAgra could cope with the competition.

First decision: A basic foods company that would focus on return on equity.

"We decided to become a basic food company which included, but didn't limit itself to, packaged goods," says Harper. "To work the entire food chain. We sell inputs to farmers, we buy their production, we convert that into food ingredients along with other food companies, we buy those ingredients and we process them into fine consumer and food service products."

ECON 101 AND PHILOS 102

If ConAgra pursued basic foods operations, however, the company's management team had to be prepared to cope with the swings in commodities markets. Managers would have to stay on course through the tough years in the commodity cycles, when returns were scant. On the other hand, peak years in the cycle could bring exceptional rewards. If executives managed for the long term — instead of playing for quarter-to-quarter or even year-to-year gains — basic foods offered the potential for excellent profits.

So the Vail team agreed that ConAgrans would plan for the duration, riding the ups and downs of the commodities cycles instead of proceeding in strict quarterly and yearly formation. But if ConAgra followed this unorthodox route, how could management measure the company's financial progress?

Clearly, the nation's top securities analysts were partial to measurement of stairstep earnings gains. Terry Hanold recommended throwing out these standard notions.

"My point of view was that if we were going to follow the basic foods course there was no point in hampering ourselves with a stairstep obligation," he recalls. "It wouldn't make sense. If we attempted to follow it, in tough times we'd make decisions that we would regret."

Hanold suggested that for a company operating in cyclical businesses a focus on return on equity, calculated by dividing net income by common stockholder's equity, best served the stockholder. On average — over the fat and the lean years — the earnings returned would ultimately build up the company's value.

"Sure it looks funny, and the earnings go up and down," Harper acknowledges. "But on average — on average — if you earn more than somebody else on your investment, for which we used equity, then you'll do a better job for your shareholder.

"That is not what we were counseled to do by these fellows out of the East, these security analysts. But we finally settled on that. We seized it. We said 'We will be a return on equity company.'"

Bearing in mind the earnings of similar food businesses, the seven executives fixed their standard of financial success. ConAgra would consistently earn in excess of a 15% return on common stockholders' equity, and would strive to increase that average return to 20%.

For this return on equity standard to be meaningful, however, the company needed standards governing the proportion of debt to equity on the balance sheet. After all, as Red Thomas explains, a dollar's worth of earnings represents 20% return on equity if the company is leveraged to the point where it has five dollars in equity. Harper and fellows agreed that a 40% long-term debt-to-total capitalization ratio would keep the balance sheet healthy.

Furthermore, they strictly limited the use of short-term debt. In previous years the company had dangerously increased its short-term debt, in some cases using that debt to finance long-term assets. The Vail participants decided that the company would pay off or pay down all short-term debt at the end of each year.

As with several of the other financial objectives, company managers were already working toward this goal. Beginning with fiscal year 1976, ConAgra's fiscal year had closed at the end of May rather than June. By coinciding with the food company's natural low point in inventory investment, this adjustment — which meant a 48-week fiscal year 1976 — helped whittle year-end short-term debt.

The firm's dividend policy remained a sensitive subject. At that time, many companies distributed between 40% and 60% of their earnings as dividends. ConAgra had paid no dividends for over a year. It had resumed distribution of preferred stock dividends in November, 1975, and of common stock dividends in January, 1976. What kind of dividends should the new ConAgra pay?

Again, Harper and his colleagues had come prepared. Before the meeting they had researched various theories of dividend payment, including the theory that shareholders gained the most when they did without. According to this line of thought, a company that reinvested earnings instead of distributing them benefited its shareholders by providing them with capital gains, which were then taxable at a lower rate than the ordinary income of a dividend.

Statistics on ConAgra's stockholders decided the issue. The vast majority of investors were individuals, most of them with relatively small holdings and a significant number — like the elderly ladies Harper met at the 1974 annual meeting — at least partially dependent on the company's cash dividend for a living.

When ConAgra suspended dividends, top managers had fielded calls from frightened widows and furious workmen. That experience fresh in mind, the Vail group decided to reinstate the dividend, but at a ratio lower than the prevailing industry one. They pledged to distribute from 30% to 35% of earnings in the form of dividends.

The last piece of the financial puzzle — how fast to increase earnings — then fit into place. If the company paid out 30% of its return on equity in dividends, then it retained 70%.

ECON 101 AND PHILOS 102

Say that the company's return on equity equalled 20%. Seventy percent of a 20% return on equity is 14%. That meant that if ConAgra earned a 20% return on equity and paid out 30% of its earning in dividends, earnings should grow by 14% each year.

Harper notes the advantage of this proposal: "It's a very simple, Midwestern kind of formula."

This underlying earning power would be measured over the long haul, not quarter-to-quarter or year-to-year. The Vail troop dubbed it "trend line" earnings.

30-35% dividend payment, conservative debt policy and 14% average earnings growth completed the financial standards.

Plugging a slightly lower, 15% return on equity into their Midwestern kind of formula, the group resolved to increase ConAgra's trend line earnings per share on an average of more than 10% per year, starting from the company's 1973 fiscal base. They chose 1973 as the base year because it was the record year before the company restructured. They planned to reach 20% ROE by fiscal 1977; then, according to their handy formula, trendline earnings would rise to 14%.

ConAgra had created its financial strategy. Now to tell New York about it.

The ConAgra executives agreed to publish their new financial objectives on pages four and five of the 1977 and subsequent annual reports. That would openly establish their commitment to the standards of performance.

"Some said this was risky," comments Harper. "But our company had no credibility, so we couldn't lose any. People laughed a little bit when this company that had just come up to the brink started saying 'We're going to be the best earning food company in the United States.'"

One observer, later to join ConAgra's board, bluntly offered his assessment of the decision: printing its financial aspirations made ConAgra either the smartest or the dumbest company he'd ever seen.

The Vail group gathered at their meeting house on Saturday morning with one pressing strategic issue unresolved. That issue was size. Should the company carve out a niche to occupy, or should it strive to operate on a larger scale? Terry Hanold cautioned against bigness for the sake of bigness. After all, inadequately monitored acquisitions and internal expansions had contributed to ConAgra's near-collapse in 1974.

His advice was well taken. But others in the group maintained that size offered certain fundamental advantages. Size enabled a firm to generate the kind of profitability and return that ConAgra wanted. It helped a company become a low cost provider, vital in an industry of 1% margins. It made a company a more important supplier to its customers. Above all, it helped attract the best employees.

In 1969, on ConAgra's 50th anniversary, former company president and board chairman R.S. Dickinson had succinctly observed: "Growth is the mark of all successful U.S. business — it's grow or fall behind." In any number of ways, size helped a business withstand competitive forces in the battle for survival in the marketplace.

Before leaving for Colorado, Hanold had shown Harper and Kennedy a cartoon depicting two vultures sitting on a branch. The caption read "Patience, my ass. I'm gonna go kill somebody."

Harper thought that described ConAgra's situation in a nutshell. He asked Kennedy to order a set of personalized plaques made, each sporting the hunkering vultures. If an agreement came out of Vail, Kennedy would distribute the plaques before the group dispersed; if nothing jelled, he'd have a heavy suitcase on the trip back to Omaha.

"Mike felt we were going to do something as a result of our meeting," recalls Kennedy. "We were not just going to have a nice discussion and then walk away and go back to business as it was before the meeting. That explains the 'Let's kill somebody.' It points out that, in his mind, the importance of growing the company in a hurry was foremost. I guess that if he had a pre-set agenda, it may have been that. And if we didn't get agreement, those plaques were still in my suitcase."

Late Saturday morning Harper gave Kennedy the thumbs-up to unveil the vultures.

The ConAgra executives had agreed to seek well-planned company growth, to diversify within the broad classification of basic foods. They had set a new expansion goal: to increase sales from $500 million to $1 billion. It was time to go on the hunt.

CHAPTER 8

GIT ALONG, LITTLE DOGIES: FROM KASCO TO COWBOYS

THOSE avid hunters returned from their first wilderness expedition with tails dragging.

Mike Harper and marketing director Jim Kennedy had determined that expanding into the consumer food market would help counterbalance the cycles of ConAgra's commodity businesses. It would also entice analysts and investors attracted to industries more seductive than flour and chickens.

"My mission was to try to bring some marketing thinking into this totally commodity-oriented business," explains Kennedy.

ConAgra had few consumer products to work with. Kennedy first tried to resuscitate the company's grocery store family flour sales. After the asset sales of 1974 and 1975, the company barely maintained a position in this market. The revival attempt failed.

Not to worry. If humanity remained unmoved by ConAgra's marketing overtures, maybe the animal world would respond.

For several years, ConAgra had sold Formax dog food through its feed distributors. But in 1973, with the purchases of the Kasco and Geisler companies, the company had also entered the consumer side of the pet products business.

ConAgra enters pet products business with purchase of Kasco and Geisler.

Kasco, originally an acronym for Keiser and Son Company, was founded in 1884 in Haverstraw, New York. In 1954, the Keiser family sold its interest, and Kasco operations were moved to National City, Illinois. After ConAgra purchased the company it had increased production of Kasco's high-performance dog foods — painstakingly formulated, right down to the delectable beef tallow coating — to keep up with demand from breeders, kennels, trainers and handlers. Kasco also produced tons of feed for other animals, from catfish to zoo exotics. Satisfied customers included the Omaha Henry Doorly Zoo, which informed ConAgra that its charges performed best on Kasco products.

Like Kasco, Geisler enjoyed a long-standing reputation in the pet industry. And Geisler was a home-town firm for ConAgra. In 1888, German-born Max Geisler crossed the Atlantic to sell some inherited land in Omaha, Nebraska. Instead of returning to his native Bremen, he settled in Omaha and established the "Max Geisler Bird Co.," importing canaries from Germany's Harz Mountains and selling his own brown-paper-bagged canary food. Geisler pioneered in the use of mail-order catalogs, mail-order pet sales and consumer promotions. His company shipped live birds nation-wide to *Ladies Home Journal* and *Good Housekeeping* readers, and conducted demonstrations of trained birds to promote department store canary sales.

In the 1920s Geisler's sons opened branches in New York City and Hanover, Germany, to handle the growing demand for canaries as well as more exotic animals. By 1925 many zoos relied upon the Max Geisler Bird Co. for their supplies of tigers, leopards, elephants, bears and chimpanzees. When the Depression curtailed zoo expansion, the Geisler company stopped importing wild animals, although it continued to ship canaries and parakeets until 1952. For the next two decades Geisler concentrated on developing small animal and fish foods, litters, treats and remedies. When ConAgra acquired Geisler in 1973, the company handled over 500 pet products and accessories.

That same year Americans spent an estimated $3.3 billion on their pets; by 1975 that figure had grown to $4.25 billion. And while the growth in the nation's cat and dog population slowed in the mid-'70s, dry dog food — rather than the more expensive canned and semimoist varieties — claimed an increasing proportion of the pet food market.

Because of ConAgra's successful experience with Kasco and Geisler, it seemed natural to expand in the growing consumer pet market.

"Kennedy came up with a number of approaches for marketing dog food," recalls Mike Harper. "This was going to make us rich and important in the consumer food business. We came up with the damnedest concept; we thought we could make a fortune."

Early in 1976, ConAgra had acquired Norso Distributors, Inc., a California-based pet accessories business. ConAgra executives had contacted Norso president Robert Holmes through a California investment banker. Tom Brady and legal counsel John "Jack" North flew to California and booked a suite in a local hotel to impress Holmes. As Brady recalls, after they talked business for nearly an hour, Holmes suddenly said, "Hey, wait a minute, are you guys here to buy my company? I thought I came here to buy your pet accessory company."

Acquisition of Norso pet supply distributors, leads to birth of Snoopy dog food.

Norso distributed pet supplies and accessories from over 40 different manufacturers to discount stores, supermarkets, variety stores and drugstores in California, Virginia and Texas. Combined with ConAgra's Geisler and Kasco sales, Norso increased the company's pet business sales to around $18 million in 1976. Norso's major attraction to ConAgra, however, was that it owned the rights to use the "Peanuts" comic strip characters in consumer advertising.

The pet business had long been dominated by two names: Hartz Mountain in pet accessories and Ralston Purina in pet foods. With the acquisition of the "Peanuts" rights, Kennedy and Harper foresaw the creation of a new giant in the pet industry — ConAgra.

In fiscal year 1977 ConAgra started test marketing dry dog food under the "Snoopy" name, using different formulas and packages for the "Puppy Dog," "City Dog," "Suburb Dog" and "Working Dog" canine lifestyles. "Snoopy" marketing also pushed Geisler pet accessories — dog treats, dog collars, little green mice for cats, and so on.

In January of 1977 ConAgra purchased Pet Dealers Supply Company, a pet product distributor serving retail pet stores and tropical fish stores in five western states, Alaska and Hawaii. Later that year, ConAgra bought Bow Wow Co., Inc., the Missouri-based manufacturer and distributor of "the dog food dogs ask for by name." ConAgra also acquired the Victoria Feed Company of Davenport, Iowa, to produce wild bird feed for sale under the aegis of "Woodstock," Snoopy's spike-feathered friend.

Market research showed that 65 million people a day read "Peanuts," and that 95% of Americans not only recognized Snoopy, but also strongly identified with his qualities and characteristics. When queried, consumers said they would choose a Snoopy-endorsed product knowing the lovable beagle would not support an inferior product.

To protect the integrity of the "Peanuts" cast, the United Feature Syndicate, Inc., closely scrutinized both the products and the management of potential licensees. Cartoonist Charles Schulz retained artistic control over his creations, reserving the right to approve the artist chosen to draw the ad poses. To preserve Schulz's characterizations, each picture of a "Peanuts" family member had to either duplicate a pose drawn by Shulz or receive Schulz's specific approval.

Furthermore, Snoopy's and Woodstock's performance contracts prevented them from directly endorsing their namesake products. Licensing restrictions prohibited "commercial" quotes from filling those balloons floating above the characters. Instead, Woodstock toted picket signs sporting slogans like "I'm For the Birds" and "Take a Bird to Lunch," while Snoopy leaned forward, eyes closed and lips pursed, next to a resoundingly non-commercial "SMAK."

The "Peanuts" characters definitely had crowd appeal. Geisler sales representatives completed their presentations to chain store buyers before revealing the "Peanuts" promotional giveaways they brought along. Once the adult audience members got their hands on the complimentary stuffed toys, they ended up playing with them and ignoring the sales pitch.

Unfortunately, that crowd appeal didn't translate into skyrocketing market shares in the pet business.

Popularity of Snoopy doesn't necessarily translate into market share and sales.

"We were going to put Ralston Purina out of business," Harper recalls ruefully. "We thought we'd build up our dog food sales and get in the grocery store business, flying in the face of Ralston. But we just couldn't budge Ralston. We couldn't spend the money; the risks were too high.

"It was funny, though. 'Bow Wow' had the largest share of the market in St. Louis, the home of Ralston Purina. Ralston couldn't change that, and we couldn't change the rest of the country.

"We're still using old shipping cases of 'Snoopy' dog food. And we have an adequate supply of 'Suburb Dog,' 'City Dog' and 'Working Dog' shipping cases as well. We see them from time to time and they remind us of how smart we are."

According to marketing chief Jim Kennedy, ConAgra's dog and bird food ventures failed for several reasons. One was transportation. The "Bow Wow" plant was located in Rolla, Missouri, about 120 miles west of St. Louis. As long as the company could use local corn and soybeans, transportation costs were reasonable. When volume increased to the point where grain had to be shipped in, the high freight rates prevented "Bow Wow" from being a low cost producer.

"So 'Bow Wow' was doomed in the beginning by having a poorly located plant," says Kennedy. "That was one reason. Second reason: we relied very heavily on the 'Snoopy' awareness. We felt all we needed to do was get the product in distribution and it would walk off the shelves because of the comic strip's popularity. That turned out not to be the case.

"At the same time, we tried to replace St. Francis as the patron saint of the wild bird by introducing a line of 'Woodstock' wild bird food. I found out nobody had ever done any marketing in that business. I'd go to a big buyer and give him the whole package, including advertising and promotion, and our price. He'd book the order. Almost 100% of the time, within a week I'd get a phone call. The buyer had just talked to another guy willing to sell bird seed for less. No one kept his word. If he'd get a better price — boom. We had two options in that situation: reduce the price or get out of business. To this day there's no marketing in the wild bird food business."

While it lasted, however, "Snoopy" pet food served at least one purpose.

"Before we knew that the dog food business was a failure, it filled a little hole," concludes Harper. "We had nothing to talk about in this company. You can't talk too long about a feed business when you're talking to the analysts. It's hard to bash the cymbals and beat the drums when you're talking about a chicken. Go to New York to talk about hogs and it takes a while to get them excited. So when we went to the analysts we talked about 'Snoopy' dog food and they all loved it. It gave us some pizazz with the investor."

But, Snoopy dog food gives ConAgra something to interest financial analysts and investors.

While "Snoopy" dog food grew stale on grocery shelves in city and suburb, ConAgra embarked on a radically different consumer venture. In the latter part of 1977, ConAgra acquired the operations of Texas-based Mr. Beef, Inc. — a total of 24 Taco Patio Mexican fast-food restaurants in Texas, seven Mr. Beef sandwich shops and 18 Mr. Chuc Wagun units.

ConAgra executives had their eyes on the Taco Patio outlets. Market studies showed that "away-from-home" food sales were on the rise while grocery sales stayed flat, and market researchers predicted that the Mexican fast-food market would grow by 20% a year into the 1980s. Plus, Mike likes tacos.

Harper faced an immediate problem — a budding trademark conflict with RJR/Nabisco, the owners of "Patio" frozen foods. Taco Patio needed a new name.

"The biggest problem was to avoid defacing the signs on the restaurants, to change names as quickly and as economically as possible," explains Jim Kennedy. "So I was given the job of coming up with a name that had 'Taco' in it and that had a second word that began with 'P' and had five letters. I spent a lot of time going through the dictionary before coming up with 'Taco Plaza'."

Unfortunately, changing the restaurant marquees didn't address the Mexican chain's deeper problems. What Ralston Purina was to pet food, competitor Taco Bell was to Mexican fast food. And Taco Plaza was too weak to oust the leader. Like ConAgra's consumer pet food venture, Taco Plaza struggled in vain. Later, in a bit of irony, ConAgra bought the Patio brand from RJR/Nabisco.

"Norso, Pet Dealers Supply, Bow Wow dog food, Taco Patio — those were mistakes," admits Harper. "These mistakes, however, helped materially in founding the new ConAgra. We instituted a practice of critiquing our failures. We learned why Taco Plaza didn't win. The restaurant business was an area unfamiliar to our operating management. And the Taco Patio acquisition was too small to attract and retain the best

Taco Plaza restaurant — one of Mexican food chain in Southwest.

management in the industry.

"If we are going to go outside our normal operating areas, then the business has to be big enough to attract the best management in the industry. That was a lesson we learned directly from Taco Patio's failure."

"What Bow Wow dog food and Taco Plaza also taught us was that buying a small piece in a large market ordinarily is not going to get you anywhere," says former board member Terry Hanold. "But if you can buy a large piece of a large market, you can add small pieces to it very effectively."

"We bought small-scale with the idea that we would grow the business," adds Harold Schuler, former senior vice president of human resources and administration. "But we didn't have the know-how for these specialty retail businesses in our own management. The management that we acquired with the businesses hadn't been able to grow their firms without us, and they weren't going to grow them with us."

Harper quickly learned something else from critiquing those experiences. He learned to hire an outside consultant to perform an extensive "due diligence" study from time to time on potential acquisitions.

Harper builds acquisition know-how by lessons learned from pet food experiences.

After Harper reaches an "agreement in principle" with a prospective seller, a due diligence study is launched. The due diligence team spends several weeks reviewing the target company's strengths and weaknesses. The consultants evaluate the firm's expected earnings and cash flows, and the amount of capital required up front. They determine whether the firm meets ConAgra's standards for return on equity and earnings growth. They call customers and suppliers. Meanwhile, ConAgra's lawyers do a legal due diligence study, researching insurance, tax, legal title, labor, patent, trademark and similar issues.

"The outside consultants have a certain amount of objectivity, because we don't ask them for the answer we want," says Harper. "We ask them for the 'right' information. Based on their study, we make our decision. And we hope we're right, because there is nothing infallible about any forward projection."

"Before we close a deal the consultant hands out copies of the report and gives a briefing," describes corporate controller and vice president Tom Peters. "Everyone gives his views. At the end, we may ask the consultant to get more information. Or we may make the decision to buy or not to buy. We may decide to restructure the deal. The deal may fall through. The price may prove to be too high. Or it may be apparent that the opportunity we thought was there actually wasn't."

"At first the outside consultants balked at doing the study, afraid that if we acted on their advice and got burned we'd sue them," explains Harper. "But it has worked out, and the objective due diligence study has at times been a successful part of our acquisition process."

Even though it sometimes pays to ignore the consultant's advice.

New York investment broker Eric Gleacher kept ConAgra in mind after the company rejected his advice to sell its Puerto Rican holdings in 1976. He watched for good business opportunities for the Omaha-based agribusiness concern. In 1978 Gleacher's co-worker, Dennis Kelly, suggested that an agricultural chemical company he'd heard about might interest ConAgra. Gleacher doubted ConAgra would want to enter the chemical business, but he and Kelly called Harper nonetheless.

Enter agricultural chemicals and a business new to ConAgra.

The enterprise was called the Balcom Group. It was a casually organized collection of 20 or so formulators and distributors of agricultural chemicals — herbicides to eradicate weeds, insecticides to kill bugs, and fungicides to control fungi growth. Formulators combine basic chemicals into herbicides, insecticides or fungicides, and package them in usable form. Each company was independently run, with the whole assemblage loosely supervised by a fellow named George Doering.

Doering grew up on a farm in Georgetown, Texas. He entered Texas A & M University to study veterinary medicine. He also played professional baseball.

The vet school had a strict policy: either straight through the program or out the door. When the dean told Doering he could either be a veterinarian or play baseball but he couldn't do both, Doering's choice was clear. He played ball, and studied agriculture and entomology — the science of insects.

In 1959 George graduated with his B. S. in agriculture. In 1961 he earned an M. S. in entomology; in later years he picked up 30 credits toward a Ph.D. For fun he helped his wife, Gayle, raise, race and sell quarter horses.

Doering served as an ag entomology consultant for two years before landing a job with Monsanto in 1963. Five years later he left the corporation. He and a financial partner purchased Balcom Chemicals, an agricultural chemical distribution business based in Greeley, Colorado.

Before too long, Doering's partner wanted out. Doering wondered whether he too had made the wrong move. A former Monsanto colleague, Phil James, heard of George's troubles. James was managing Midwest Ag Warehouse in Fremont, Nebraska, for a wealthy fertilizer and feed dealer named John Anderson. Confident in Doering's abilities, James floated the idea that Anderson help him out. Anderson bought out Doering's original partner and told George to run the company as he liked.

Doering set about expanding the business. His first new units were located in Dumas, Texas, and Kearney, Nebraska. Driving from Greeley to Dumas, Doering's truckers crossed the sales territory of Willis J. "Tuffy" Holland's Pueblo Chemical Company, headquartered in Garden City, Kansas.

"Balcom decided to fill that territory in with their own customers," explains Holland. "That put them on a collision course with me. They spent a whole year and took one of my customers away. And took two years to get paid.

"That year George Doering called me and we met in a bar in Colorado Springs. I didn't know him and he didn't know me. He said we ought to look at putting our companies together. He sat and talked about it and philosophised for about four hours and finally I said, 'Hell, we think the same. Let's shake hands on it. We'll do it on the basis of the net worth book value of the two companies right now. We'll do it for a year without signing any papers, and if we like each other we'll sign papers. I think we got around to signing papers four years later."

The Balcom Group continued to add new distributors and formulators — in Texas, Montana, Idaho, Washington, Oregon, Alabama, Mississippi, Louisiana and North Dakota. Each manager or owner ran his firm as a separate, independent entity.

Early in his career with Monsanto, Doering supervised several retail fertilizer operations. He felt that those businesses would have been more successful if they had been independently operated, with incentive systems for local managers. As he formed the Balcom Group, he resolved to involve others as part owners.

"People running a business should be committed," says Doering. "I wanted to have people participate as stockholders in their businesses, to be responsible for the liabilities. They're involved and they own the company; that's their commitment. If you're really part of an independent operating company, the company is where your bread and butter is."

"That was George's basic philosophy from the beginning," says Holland. "The original eight or ten companies had extremely strong managers. Nobody wanted to become just a number all of a sudden.

"Plus, you felt you retained a closeness to your customers. You've got to understand that this business is very personalized. You're dealing with rural people. They don't want to deal with some company whose headquarters is 800 miles away. They want to feel that they can pick up the phone and call the boss. A retailer dealing with Pueblo Chemical can call Tuffy Holland. Otherwise, he'd be dealing with some guy in Greeley, Colorado, who he never met. Maybe suspicious of him."

Mike Harper decided to investigate the Balcom Group.

"When people call about an acquisition, I always say I might be interested," says Harper. "Because then I get a chance to learn something outside of our normal area of interest."

Harper and Brady met Doering and James. The four reached a tentative agreement, and Harper hired a consultant for a due diligence study on their ag chemical business. No more dog food disasters or fast food fumbles; this time ConAgrans had to know what they were getting into.

"A team of people did the study," Harper remembers. "The day they made their final recommendations to us, George Doering and Phil James were waiting in the little board room in our office. The net result of the study was, 'Don't do it.'"

First advice on the ag chemical business was "don't do it".

According to the consultants, the farm chemicals business was going co-op. Co-operatives had cornered 50% of the market and were still growing. Although the Balcom Group might make money for ConAgra for a year or two, it would soon go downhill. The co-ops would dominate.

"We called a recess in the briefing and I took a walk around the block," says Harper. "As we had gone around the room, the people generally agreed with the consulting team that we should not proceed. I came back and we got the group together again — mostly management plus the consultants. I surfaced the idea that we might proceed on a 50-50 proposition,

Harper bets on buying good management people—but hedges UAP buy with a 50% option.

with an option to buy the rest on the fixed formula basis.

"The basic proposition was that we were buying management. If Doering and James were clever enough to meet all the past problems, they'd be clever enough to meet those out front. They were flexible enough and entrepreneurial enough to survive and grow. Let's bet on the people who had to operate in a very fast-changing environment. But let's not bet the whole wad."

Harper and Tom Brady walked into the board room where Doering and James were waiting, edgy. Harper informed the two that they wanted to change the deal, to buy half now with an option to take the rest later.

"George looked at Phil and said 'We were about to propose the same thing to you,'" says Harper. "They were a little worried that maybe we weren't the right guys."

In June of 1978, ConAgra spent $6.7 million for a 49% interest in the Balcom Group. The remaining stock was held in escrow at the United Bank of Denver; ConAgra had an option to buy it within five years. The escrow account was held in the name of United Agri Products.

"A bunch of people got together over a few bottles of beer to try and come up with a name," explains Tuffy Holland. "Somebody said 'If we're going to bring all these companies together, how about United Agri Products?' Until that time everyone in the industry referred to us as the Balcom Group. UAP didn't exist until ConAgra bought us."

Whatever the name of its new acquisition, the celebration marking the 49% deal became ConAgra legend.

"Balcom Group was a company, but it was a company made up of 33 very independent stockholders," recounts Jim Kennedy. "Hard playing as well as hard working. They all came to Denver's Brown Palace Hotel.

"We had put together a story of the company in one of these computerized, multi-projector deals. We set it up to show these fellows. The show was going well and then all of the sudden it went crazy. It turned out that because of the wiring in the old hotel, every time the elevator did some damn thing it affected our slide show computer. We all had to leave the room."

By the time the entire group reconvened, it was time for each stockholder to sign the required documentation. Kennedy had scheduled an evening of moderate, midwestern formalities to follow the signing. Cocktail hour from 6:00 to 7:00. Dinner from 7:00 to 9:00.

"We didn't get into the cocktail party until 7:00 because of all the signing," says Kennedy. "Didn't break it up until at least 9:00. We walked into the dining room and there was a bottle of wine at each table.

"Somebody got up to make a toast. The worst thing that could have happened did. All 33 of our guests decided 'If one person can make a toast, so can I.' I am certain the toasting took another hour."

The option for remaining 50% of UAP is exercised well ahead of time.

After dinner the celebrants adjourned downstairs to the hotel cocktail lounge.

According to Harper, "Some of these guys were hurdling tables. The police came at one point. It was a real wild western."

As with most legends, versions vary. Floyd McKinnerney, who joined the Balcom Group in 1972 and who later became president of ConAgra's United Agri Products Company, doesn't recall any visit from Denver's finest.

"The word was, it was getting a little rambunctious," says McKinnerney. "So the manager came down and told the bartender, 'Why don't you just close the door and let these folks have a good time?' I think that's the way it went. I think the manager used good judgement. Everybody had a real good time. I don't think that is an overstatement."

McKinnerney had gone to college with George Doering at Texas A & M. After graduation he went to work for a small chemical company as a salesman. When Dennison Chemical Company became a part of the Balcom Group in 1972, it changed its name to Mid Valley Chemicals and McKinnerney became president.

Harper's hunch about the Balcom Group's management paid off. The ag chemical companies' sales had grown from $3 million in 1970 to $85 million in 1975. Sales for fiscal year 1977 were $154 million. Projected 1978 sales were over $175 million; actual sales for that year were $180.5 million.

Less than a year into ConAgra's five-year option period, Harper arranged to meet Doering and James in out-of-the-way Carefree, Arizona. He and Tom Brady wanted to exercise ConAgra's option.

"We hesitated to approach Doering and James because we weren't sure what their attitude would be," remarks Brady. "We sat down with them to have a free-wheeling discussion about what it would take to build the company. We talked for 45 minutes to an hour, when George and Phil said, 'You guys ought to buy the other half of the company.'"

ConAgra purchased the remaining 51% of United Agri Products in July of 1979. Tuffy Holland admits that Balcom Group managers fretted about their futures with ConAgra. Privately, some Balcom Group members prepared to depart if their new owner grew too high-handed.

"It was a major concern when ConAgra bought us," he explains. "Here is this company that is four times bigger than we are and we don't know them. Only thing we know about them is their money is good."

Doering tried to calm their fears. Harper had repeatedly assured him that the company planned to let the Balcom Group be. Nevertheless, Holland had cornered ConAgra's top executive at the Denver signing to ask him how the company planned to manage its new ag chemical business.

"Mike answered it pretty simply," says Holland. "He got up and said 'We did a lot of surveys of this industry. Our consultants came back and said it was a crappy business but you were the best in it.' He told us ConAgra didn't know a damn thing about the chemical business, so they weren't about to come in and try to tell us how to run it. He said 'Just keep making money,' and that is kind of the way he has operated ever since."

Don Wittnam, who left Monsanto for the Balcom Group in 1973, feels that joining ConAgra helped the chemical companies maintain management flexibility and continuity.

"In a distribution company the success is based mainly on people," says Wittnam. "We were all in our 40s at the time. As long as we all had most of our net worth tied up in the company, we had less flexibility in doing some transition management. In order to maintain continuity, we felt we better get a parent in here when we were 45 years old rather than 55 or 60.

"Our basic concern was to get with a company that understood agriculture and would let us continue to manage our own company and determine its future course. It has been a godsend. For all practical purposes, within some limitations we run the company the way we did before.

"We could have been bought by a company based in Paris or New York. Somewhere you can't get to from Greeley and don't want to go if you could."

In fiscal year 1981, UAP purchased Hess and Clark, an Ohio-based animal health products firm producing items like antibiotic feed additives, livestock disinfectants and livestock dustbags. Strung between two posts, a livestock dustbag powders a cow's back with pesticides to keep the flies away. Ever since the dustbags were developed in the late 1960s, Hess and Clark had purchased them from the inventor and patent owner — the Balcom Group.

In July of 1981 UAP bought Union Carbide's subsidiary, Grower Service Corporation, another ag chemical distributor. This expanded UAP's reach into seven states, ranging from Wisconsin to North Carolina.

The ag chemical group continued to grow, both through acquisitions and internal development. By 1984 UAP was twice the size of its nearest competitor in the $4 billion agricultural chemical industry. By 1986, UAP's market share of the fragmented distribution market had climbed from 8% to 25%, its annual sales topped $800 million, and UAP companies were located in almost every state.

Successful big acquisition of UAP gives ConAgra confidence in their future planning.

One of the UAP's strong points is that its distributors formulate and sell chemicals and protect a wide variety of American crops: cotton in Alabama, Mississippi and Louisiana; citrus fruit in Texas; corn, soybeans and wheat in Kansas, Nebraska, North Dakota and Montana; potatoes in Idaho; and fruits and vegetables in California and Pacific Northwest. When crops are poor or markets slow in one region, sales in another region take up the slack.

UAP distributors sell branded products, including Lasso, Sutan, Treflan, Counter and Thimet, from major manufacturers like Monsanto, Stauffer Chemical, Dow Chemical, Union Carbide, Ciba-Geigy and Elanco Products. Distributors also sell UAP's own successful brand, Clean Crop.

Floyd McKinnerney had remained as president of Mid Valley Chemical after the sale to ConAgra, and in 1985 he was named president of United Agri Products and executive vice president of ConAgra Agri-Products Company. Two years later he was promoted to president of ConAgra Agri-Products Company and joined ConAgra's office of the president.

"UAP is probably our classic early success," says Harold Schuler. "It was a much bigger acquisition than any of the others, with top quality

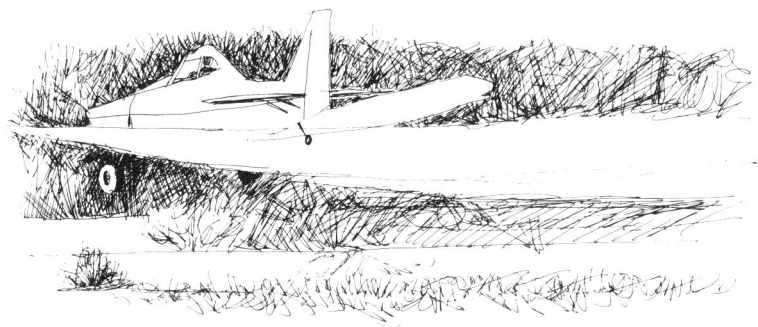

Crop dusting plane applies UAP products.

management in it. It was basically a commodity type business. We made much more than we ever projected, and early. So that gave us a lot of confidence and reinforcement. We could make acquisitions."

As financially successful as UAP proved to be, however, its contribution to ConAgra's newly developing management style was of even greater consequence.

"Our company philosophy was to build independent operating companies," George Doering explains. "Over 10 years we had accumulated about 20 different companies under different names. Our parent company owned 51% or more of each company.

"We always believed that we should have these businesses operated by independent managers. We believed that the administration part of the business should support and help, but the independent operating companies should do the real decision-making. As we became a part of ConAgra, I think that philosophy was evolving there at the same time. If the Balcom Group can take any credit, it may be that we cemented that idea and showed ConAgra that it did work. And we brought a lot of people into ConAgra who believe in and support that idea."

As Doering observes, Harper's management philosophy was developing along similar lines. Harper's vision was a corporate office that helped operating managers implement their own programs, not an office that issued edicts on flour milling or chicken raising. To help guide operating managers, however, it was essential to engage in long-range planning — the development of organized methods to help each independent operating company study its operating environment and competition, measure its results and test its strategies against those of leading competitors, and plot out its future direction.

Harper envisioned a system under which executives would meet deadlines for periodic development and review of plans and goals, but would be allowed considerable freedom on how to structure those plans and attain those goals.

"When Mike came into ConAgra he introduced a few new concepts," explains Robert White, vice president of corporate planning and development. "One was that the assets invested in the business were parcelled out to ConAgra's very competent operating managers, and that they were responsible for performance and return on investment on those assets. After that idea became imbedded, the next logical step was to begin to think forward and develop longer range plans for the business.

"In the fall of 1975, Mike had initiated ConAgra's first three-year plan. In the process he realized that perhaps planning deserved a functional focus. The job to be done was partly installation of a planning system and partly missionary work to get people to accept, become involved in and ultimately become effective at planning."

Roger "Bud" Morrison recalls the tepid reaction to Harper's first operating plan proposal. Harper set out a schedule. Annual operating plans were to be prepared in January and February. Progress under the operating plan would be reviewed at the end of each quarter. On top of that, every Monday morning at 11:00, division heads were to report their weekly progress.

"I don't think our accountants even thought they could keep records that fast," says Morrison. "But it worked. Then the next thing he threw in was 'Now we're going to do a strategic plan.' We were going to do that in the fall, to start with the beginning of the next fiscal year and cover the following three years. A couple of months after you did the strategic plan you started working on your operating plan.

"This was traumatic to people. A lot of people said 'This is impossible. Nobody can do that.' Well, the strategic plan is not that difficult if you're running a business where you know what you're doing and what you'd like to do. You're thinking strategically every day. You just don't put it down on a piece of paper."

Shortly after his arrival at ConAgra, Harper had had a wall torn out of his Kiewit Plaza office to create an alcove for a large round table.

"I had the table at Pillsbury and it was shipped down," he recalls. "Somebody said that they ought to ship it and me back to Pillsbury."

He hung corkboard on the alcove wall, and covered the board with data charts on ConAgra's various businesses. For an hour or two every Monday morning Harper updated the tell-tale charts, pacing the length of his extra-long telephone cord as he conferred with ConAgra's general managers.

"It was something like a boiler shop," says Harper. "I'd say, 'What did you make last week? What do you think you will make for the month? What are you going to make for the quarter? How's the year look?'

"I wanted them to talk to me about profit. I knew once a week they would be thinking about profit because they knew we'd be talking Monday morning."

By the time Bob White joined ConAgra, Harper had done the groundwork to develop an up-to-date annual planning system and a three-year planning process. White's task was to create a corporate department responsible for structuring and implementing the planning routine.

The former General Mills executive put together a road show for ConAgra operating managers. He taught them the elements of planning,

> "Strategic planning occurs at the intersection of information and experience"
> —Bob White.

giving examples of good and poor planning.

"The funny thing about strategic planning is that some people can do it naturally and intuitively and other people have a great deal of difficulty with it," notes White. "The best definition that I've heard is that strategic planning occurs at the intersection of information and experience. Those two elements are important in the ability to perceive a company's direction and where it ought to go next. Without an information base of some kind, a data base, an understanding of the basic analytics, any planning you develop is formless. The other side of it, experience, just helps in knowing what will work and what won't work."

According to White, the most important part of the planning process is developing the thought behind the numbers.

"First we ask for a narrative discussion of a company's strategies," explains White. "An assessment of strengths and weaknesses, vis à vis competitors and environment. Ninety percent of the benefit of the planning process is in having the company heads sit down with their people and go through this exercise. The numbers are a product of that. The numbers are important because that's how we keep score, but they are a by-product of the basic process."

White prefers simple, concise plans that address the key issues and present succinct strategies. As he tactfully observes, "Sometimes the more verbose ones don't quite have the content and substance that the others do."

Some corporate planners fashion elaborate hypothetical scenarios in an attempt to prepare for all future eventualities. White prefers a more pragmatic approach.

"Our method is to look at where we are today, and try to look out three years," he explains. "To reduce that to some sort of an actionable strategy. And from time to time to take a little bit longer look, to make certain that the assumptions that we're using on a longer term basis are reasonably sound."

ConAgra's corporate economist, Richard Gady, helps the planning department by providing economic forecasts. Gady and his small staff track U.S. and world trends in interest rates, inflation and consumer demand, as well as developments in the agricultural sector and potential changes in government policy.

As White and other ConAgra executives designed it, ConAgra's planning process is part of the everyday routine.

"I don't spend any great amount of time getting prepared for my Monday morning report," says UAP's Floyd McKinnerney. "I guess if you keep up with your business every day you're prepared for those reports."

During a plan review session, Harper presses for personal commitments to ambitious proposals. And he expects commitments to be fulfilled. Sometimes he talks over-eager executives down from lofty planning figures. Sometimes he lets a colleague aim high even though industry conditions make success unlikely, but offers to measure performance against a lower figure for incentive plan purposes. On the other hand, Harper refuses to accept a lowballing plan which is too easily achieved. And sometimes consistent lowball planners end up devising plans for some other corporation.

Once agreement is reached on the plan's figures, the company president becomes responsible for carrying out his scheme to realize his profit goals.

"Whether that takes new products, or whether that takes cost cutting, doesn't make a whole lot of difference," says Harper. "The company head knows more about that business than I do. He has the goal always ahead of him of meeting his plan — the plan that he came up with."

Once they became accustomed to their planning responsibilities, ConAgra executives realized that Harper wanted to know what they were doing — but not to make them do it his way.

Observes long-time marketing services manager Don Amsden: "If the quarterly reviews showed that a business was on or above its operating plan and was meeting the corporation's standards, then the managers were pretty much allowed to run the business as they planned, without interference. With help and suggestions, of course, but without being second-guessed or vetoed."

UAP's table-hurdling cowboys liked this philosophy. Harper knew how to offer corporate guidance without squelching the personal initiative that had created the Balcom Group's success.

"I did not believe ConAgra would leave me alone," acknowledges Floyd McKinnerney. "I was going to give them five years. The Balcom Group owners and managers all talked about it among ourselves. Wondering when the shoe was going to be dropped. At the end of the five years I looked around and everybody was still there. We continued to call all the shots."

"The best thing about UAP is that we have a lot of guys who think differently," concludes Doering. "That's okay as long as they take the responsibility and are successful. That's really the whole idea of independent operating companies. Any time you have this system you have mavericks.

There are a thousand good ways to make money and the mavericks are the ones who usually create new ideas and new opportunities.

"When we joined ConAgra we had 33 stockholders. Thirty-one of those people are still with ConAgra. The only two that are missing passed away."

CHAPTER 9

COLD CASH FROM FROZEN FOODS

AS ConAgra added new commodity-based businesses, larger U.S. corporations were selling off unprofitable food divisions. During the 1960's and 1970's, many corporate giants in non-food businesses had gobbled up food producers. Too late, they realized that low-margin food operations required management as expert as that needed for higher-margin high-tech industries. The result? Severe indigestion.

In 1970 the RCA Corporation had purchased the F.M. Stamper Company for $116.5 million in stock. To reflect its new acquisition's more familiar brand identity, RCA changed Stamper's name. Stamper became the Banquet Foods Company.

The F.M. Stamper company's history in the food business dated back to 1898 when, after teaching for 10 years in a one-room schoolhouse, Missourian Finis Stamper began to moonlight by marketing poultry and eggs. He bought his wares from country farm wives and sold them to merchants as far away as St. Louis, Kansas City and Chicago.

F.M. Stamper Company was the forerunner of Banquet Foods.

Stamper's business prospered; within five years he had moved it from Clifton Hill, Missouri, to nearby Moberly, a rail transportation center. Stamper's new plant included a picking room where the poultry was plucked, a cold storage room, a candling room where eggs were inspected and a second story feeding station capable of temporarily housing 20,000 birds.

In 1913 the company opened a creamery. In the 1920s it began processing frozen egg whites for bakeries and frozen yolks for mayonnaise producers. In 1928 it started up a mill to produce feeds for poultry, hogs, cattle and dogs.

The F.M. Stamper Co. began producing dehydrated eggs in the early 1940s. When the food shortages of World War II created a sudden surge in demand for the nutritious and relatively non-perishable foodstuff, Stamper quickly became the largest supplier. In 1943, the company installed equipment to produce canned chicken products for American soldiers' "C"-rations. Taking battlefield consumption as evidence of consumer approval, after the war Stamper kept producing canned chicken on the newly installed machinery.

During World War II, stateside demand for frozen foods had increased. Unlike the tins in which canned products were sold, the waxed paper cartons containing frozen foods didn't consume any ration points. In 1953 the F.M. Stamper Co. capitalized on this new acceptance of frozen foods, as well as upon developments in the packaging industry, by offering frozen chicken pies in newly developed inexpensive, disposable aluminum pans. Use of the "Banquet" name started around this time. According to long-time employee Don Granneman, in the mid-1950s the independent group who owned the "Minute Maid Snowcrop" brand name asked Stamper to process a meat pie under the "Minute Maid" name. Stamper was prepared to start when the "Minute Maid" group decided not to proceed.

F.M. Stamper's first creamery and egg station – forerunner of Banquet Foods.

Since the firm's production facilities were ready and waiting, Finis' grandson Howard Stamper approached the McCormick Spice company, owner of the "Banquet" brand name. Stamper and McCormick entered into a royalty agreement under which the Stamper company would package pies bearing the "Banquet" name. "Banquet" meat pies were hugely successful, and the introduction of "Banquet" frozen dinners, fruit pies and fried chicken followed. Stamper continued paying royalties to McCormick for eight or nine years, until Howard Stamper bought the brand name. Products bearing the "Banquet" label were then manufactured by the Banquet Foods Division of F.M. Stamper Co.

In the mid-50s Stamper pulled out of the dairy business. In 1958 the company moved its headquarters to St. Louis, Missouri. Five years later it stopped selling eggs. Stamper's focus had become the chicken and the meat pie business.

In 1969 Stamper acquired Batesville, Arkansas' J.K. Southerland Company, an integrated broiler producer which raised as many as 1.5 million birds a week. In 1970, the same year it was acquired by RCA, the company introduced its tremendously successful two-pound box of frozen fried chicken. The idea was to compete with the several carry-out fried chicken companies operating then, including the big one, Kentucky Fried Chicken. In 1976, under RCA's ownership, Stamper purchased the Whitworth Hatchery and Poultry Farm, Inc., operations in Georgia and South Carolina.

When RCA acquired F.M. Stamper Company, Howard A. Stamper headed the company his grandfather had created. RCA assured Howard, then in his mid 50s, that he would remain in charge at Banquet.

COLD CASH FROM FROZEN FOODS

Tragically, Stamper was killed in an automobile accident several years later. At the same time, RCA's ardor for the food business was cooling.

RCA acquired the Stamper Company in 1970, changing the name to Banquet Foods Company.

"RCA agonized over this company for the next five years," recalls Don Granneman, who became Banquet's vice president for new business channels under ConAgra's ownership. "About 1977 or 1978 they began to talk about divesting themselves of the company. They announced that to the world, and we were on the selling block for over two years.

"That was probably the most difficult time in the company's history. It was very difficult to hire people. So for over two years we just kind of marked time."

Longtime RCA executive Ed Griffiths, the company's new CEO, began paring RCA's non-electronics businesses. In previous years RCA had embarked on a buying spree, and Griffiths decided to sell such companies as Hertz, Random House and Banquet. Progress was slow, especially with Banquet.

Jim Kennedy heard about RCA's troubles from a Bow Wow dog food broker in St. Louis. After a sales meeting at which Kennedy vainly tried to drum up some Bow Wow business, the broker, who also handled Banquet products, mentioned that the frozen foods processor was for sale. Kennedy relayed the message to Harper. Harper had heard the news, too, and had been told RCA's asking price was $212 million, which was ridiculously high.

It appeared RCA had misjudged the market and would never generate any interest in the company. But ConAgra couldn't have done anything anyway.

"Two hundred twelve million dollars was a huge amount of money to us," Harper explains.

Time passed, with RCA getting nary a nibble for its overpriced merchandise. R.J. Reynolds, eager to enter the frozen food business, courted the company but was deterred by Banquet's high price.

A year after Kennedy had first mentioned RCA to Harper, Eric Gleacher called the ConAgra head to tell him the time might be right. Griffiths was getting more and more frustrated, he said. There was no connection between Banquet and anything else at RCA.

As Harper slyly speculates: "I think what originally got RCA interested in Banquet was the name 'TV dinners'."

For ConAgra, on the other hand, Banquet held a number of

By the late 1970's, RCA put Banquet Foods on the market and ConAgra was interested in the fit and possibilities.

attractions. Its chicken farms would increase ConAgra's already extensive broiler operations by one-third, in a year when poultry supplies were expected to tighten and prices rise. Even with its sales on the decline, Banquet remained the largest frozen food company in the United States, boasting well-known branded products and a significant market share in most of its product categories. Its production facilities were first-class. Finally, Banquet had the strong national distribution system and broker sales force essential for marketing success.

As Harper knew, the demand for frozen prepared foods was growing rapidly. U.S. frozen food sales had tripled since 1970. Total frozen food sales exceeded $24 billion; of that amount, sales of frozen prepared foods neared $6 billion. Demographers predicted smaller family and household units, as well as more working spouses — trends which augured well for convenience foods.

Banquet's prepared foods, which included frozen fried chicken, meat pies, dinners, family size entrees, "Cookin' Bag" single servings, and desserts, would give ConAgra some protection from wide swings in commodity poultry prices. And because many of Banquet's products were made from chicken, ConAgra could launch its expedition into the prepared foods market from familiar turf.

As he had done with the Balcom Group, Harper had commissioned a due diligence study of Banquet Foods and the frozen food industry. The study showed how Banquet had suffered from managerial neglect during its years with RCA. Harper believed that aggressive, knowledgeable top management could revive the ailing food company. By now Harper was interested. Negotiations moved swiftly.

ConAgra paid $45 million in cash and $10 million in preferred stock for something RCA had asked nearly a quarter of a billion dollars for a year earlier. Within a very short time ConAgra was earning more money than it had paid for the company. The purchase generally was called "an astoundingly good deal."

RCA's eagerness to sell and ConAgra's limited capital caused Harper to pick and choose among Banquet properties. ConAgra took Banquet's hatcheries, feed mills and processing plants in Carrollton, Macon, Marshall, Milan and Moberly, Missouri; Batesville and Clinton, Arkansas; and Turlock, California. Harper turned down four operations inconsistent with ConAgra's long range plans: Georgia and South Carolina broiler farms, a Minnesota chicken canning plant and a Minnesota frozen bread and bakery products operation. ConAgra would manage those operations until RCA could find another buyer.

"We ended up taking what we wanted out of the whole deal, and putting in the kind of management we wanted," says Tom Brady.

A year or so earlier, ConAgra had acquired United Agri Products largely to bring its entrepreneurial managers into the Omaha fold. The style of Banquet's management was 180 degrees apart from that of UAP.

"Banquet's management ran it like a quote 'corporation'," says Harper. "It was a corporate world. They had a great big building in downtown St. Louis and had board meetings with RCA and the whole ball of wax. And sales and earnings had been going down for years and years and years."

ConAgra and RCA closed the Banquet deal on November 24, 1980, Jim Kennedy's birthday. The get-acquainted activities didn't upset any birthday ceremonies, but they did interfere with a lot of Thanksgiving plans.

On the morning of the 24th, ConAgra's key executives flew down to St. Louis; their wives followed on a later flight. During the day the ConAgrans presented their company to Banquet employees, and that evening both companies' executives and their spouses celebrated with a dinner party. It was a rather dignified affair, akin to what Kennedy had planned for the Balcom Group before he met the Balcom Group.

Harper and his crew flew back to Omaha that night after the dinner. Banquet executives escorted them to the airport in the Banquet company cars — eight gleaming Toronados.

"They all lined up in front of the hotel," describes Kennedy. "I didn't know there were that many Toronados. It was like a Shriners' parade."

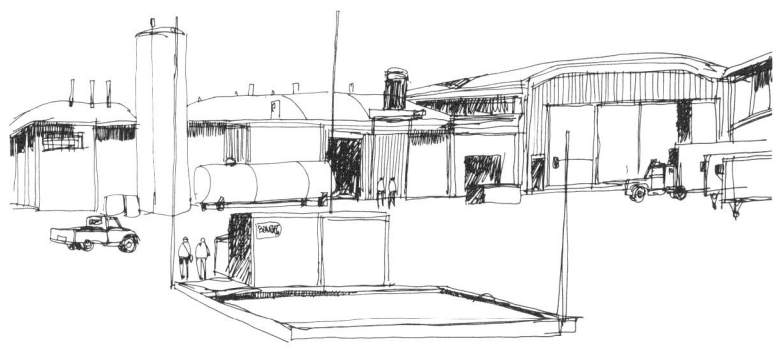

Banquet Foods Company production facility at Turlock, California.

Banquet's management "style" was too rich for Harper's taste — office hours were quickly expanded to 8 to 5.

Within a week after their illuminating day journey to St. Louis, Harper and his top managers traveled to Las Vegas to talk with a group of Banquet brokers. In conjunction with that meeting, Harper booked a hotel suite and scheduled a two-day conclave with Banquet's top executives. The purpose was to discuss Banquet's future with ConAgra.

A prime topic was Banquet's previous management style, clearly too lavish for Harper's taste. Somebody made the mistake of mentioning "country club living."

"That aroused Mike a little, and as a result of that conversation the office hours got mentioned," Kennedy remembers. "Their office hours were 9:00 to 4:30. Having grown up in the Midwest as we all had, and having worked for food companies, we had never heard of a food company that didn't start at 8:00 and work until at least 5:00. Mike wouldn't get off the subject. It was decided that beginning the next day the office hours would be 8:00 to 5:00."

Many Banquet managers, themselves old hands at the food business, liked working with ConAgra's casual, shirtsleeved executives. And the ConAgrans were Midwesterners.

"In the chicken business, that makes a difference," observes Donald Rasche, who became executive vice president for operations and administration for ConAgra frozen foods.

"Under RCA, what we could and couldn't do was pretty well dictated from New York," continues Rasche. "While ConAgra was doing its study on the company, we got to know several of the managers very well. Their philosophy about running the business sounded awfully good to us. We knew that anything was better than what we had before."

"All the ConAgra players — Mike Harper and Tom Brady and Jim Kennedy — those guys were all like a breath of fresh air," recalls Donald Granneman. "They were very heavily involved in committing themselves to the people of this company, to grow the business. For the first six months they spent so much time here, primarily assuring everybody that they were committed.

"I think everything was in place that needed to be; we just needed a leader. And a commitment from the corporate parents that they were going to grow the business."

The task of finding a leader compatible with ConAgra's philosophy fell to human resources director Harold Schuler.

Schuler had recruited Mike Harper for Pillsbury in the 1950s. In 1975 Harper turned the tables on him. Harper asked Schuler to help untangle ConAgra's labor affairs and modernize its personnel and human resources functions. Schuler, who had shared Harper's frustrations with Pillsbury's management, was looking for a change. He met with Mike on May 4, 1975, the day before the worst tornado in 62 years leveled two miles of a busy Omaha commercial area.

Harold Schuler set Mike "on fire" in his job interview — then as ConAgra's new Human Resources boss, was given the task of finding a new leader for Banquet.

"Mike and I were in his office, sitting around his round table and drinking coffee," recounts Schuler. "Our knees were almost touching. We both smoked like fiends back then. Mike had a summer seersucker suit on. An ash dropped off my cigarette onto Mike's pants and the next thing I knew he was hitting his legs. I'd set him on fire. The only thing I didn't do was pour my coffee on him."

With Harper's seersucker smoldering, the two made a deal. Harper promised Schuler involvement in ConAgra's operations, unusual for a human resources specialist.

"I came down to Omaha and just had a ball," says Schuler. "I worked harder than I'd worked in the previous 15 years, I think. But it was doing things that were almost fundamentals. There were no big inventions."

Early on, Harper and Schuler agreed on the importance of searching for the best qualified person to fill each key management slot. The foundation of a highly decentralized family of independent operating companies was the quality of leadership in each of those companies.

According to Schuler, ConAgra wanted the people it hired for management positions — as well as their counterparts in other food businesses — to know that ConAgra was in the habit of hiring the best in the industry.

That wasn't easy in 1975. ConAgra was perceived as an uninspiring commodity-based company whose stock hadn't done much except go down. And few big-time executives viewed Omaha, Nebraska, as a sophisticate's paradise.

"We tried to figure out what to do about that," recalls Schuler. "We stood back and looked at Omaha, at what its good qualities were. It's a small town. Strong work ethic. A pretty decent climate. It's not as cold in the winter as Minnesota, a little earlier spring. A good school system. At that time, taxes were relatively low.

"We put all that together, but one of the key things was housing. Housing was a very good value here."

Schuler engaged a realtor, Pat Kirk, to show homes to potential ConAgra executives. He told Kirk that her job wasn't to sell houses. It was to sell Omaha.

Kirk usually attended to the executive's wife, drawing out the couple's special needs and determining how Omaha could satisfy them. If the couple had a handicapped child, Kirk found special education opportunities. If they like horses, she came up with the right property on the edge of town. If they skied she convinced them Denver was only a state away.

"She would feed back to me with the things that were bothering the couple," Schuler explains. "Then we'd try to figure out how to meet those needs. Typically the wife was more important than the husband. And she looked for the quality of life, not the workplace."

Consequently, ConAgra enjoyed a certain degree of success in attracting people from around the country. And the company used each new recruit to help persuade the next to come to Omaha.

ConAgra's growing earnings didn't hurt Schuler's recruiting efforts, either. By 1979 or 1980, applicants started contacting the Omaha company. Schuler's mail averaged 200 unsolicited resumes a week. He had a simple formula for picking the best candidate.

"We were judging on results," says Schuler. "The results were pretty simple to judge. What commitments and plans did they lay out and how did they fulfill them? What have they done; where have they been? Did they have the kind of experience that was relevant to what we needed?

"It was more important what they had done, not what they said they were going to do. I didn't put too much credibility on what they said they were going to do."

In the fall of 1980, even before ConAgra closed the deal with RCA, Harper and Schuler had concluded that Banquet's president probably would not take the prepared foods company in the direction that the ConAgrans envisioned. But Schuler couldn't recruit since the agreement wasn't sealed yet. Maybe it wouldn't go through.

"We couldn't have any credibility recruiting or trying to select somebody for a company we didn't own yet," notes Schuler. "So we had done our research on the competitors in the industry, the different frozen food companies like Sara Lee, Campbell, Green Giant. And who the key people were. But we hadn't made any overtures yet."

Schuler was an expert at sleuthing the top people in the food business. Over the years he had developed contacts with executives, consultants, accountants and others in the food industry.

"Over dinner, over drinks, playing golf, you visit with these people about what makes the difference in a certain company. 'Well, it's this guy.' You can't accept that from just one person, but if you start getting confirmation of that from ex-employees, from consultants, from suppliers, pretty soon you start saying, 'This guy is the key element there.'"

The next step is to figure out what it takes to lure that person away.

Con Agra's philosophy of hiring the best in the industry — led to hiring John Phillips, head of Swanson Frozen Foods, for Banquet leadership.

"First you've got to make him dissatisfied with where he is," Schuler reveals. "Then you've got to make him believe that you can satisfy the things that he is dissatisfied with by a change of environment."

On the Banquet assignment, Schuler and Harper worked fast. Specifically, Harper wanted to know who ran Swanson Frozen Foods, then the leader in the frozen prepared food industry. John Phillips was the man he sought. Phillips had already been exposed to chickens and to Nebraska, in that order, during his 23 years with the Campbell Soup Company. "Through Mike's magic," as Jim Kennedy describes it, Phillips was hard at work as president and CEO of Banquet Foods by January 6, 1981. Ten days later ConAgra announced his election as a corporate vice president.

A California native, Phillips had graduated from Utah State University in 1958 with a B.A. in economics. In June of that year, he married, received his degree and started working for Campbell Soup at the company's Sacramento canned food plant.

Phillips spent six years at Sacramento, gaining experience in accounting, purchasing, industrial engineering and product supervision. In 1964, he was chosen to help start up a new plant in Texas; within five years he was the plant's assistant superintendent of manufacturing.

For the next three years Phillips served as the assistant manager of Campbell's Swanson Foods integrated poultry operations. After that he put in a stint as advertising manager in corporate marketing, then managed four Swanson frozen prepared food plants in Nebraska. Between 1975 and 1980, he managed Campbell's Pepperidge Farm subsidiary; served as corporate director of personnel; and was named vice president and general manager, and then president, of Campbell's Swanson Frozen Foods Division.

Phillips' strong background in food industry operations enabled him to quickly assess what Banquet needed after its years of benign neglect. As Harper had done when he first joined ConAgra, Phillips worked with Banquet's operations managers, reviewing the basic elements needed to improve product quality while reducing product cost.

"Banquet's biggest problem was that it was a small food piece of an electronic giant," says John Phillips. "The electronic giant had obviously become somewhat disenchanted with the food business. When RCA was reorganizing, its former chairman apparently made an interesting comment to a group of analysts. He said that while RCA was trying to learn how to clean chickens, the Japanese were developing the VCR.

"When Banquet became a part of ConAgra, what we needed to do was get down to the ABCs or the blocking and tackling of good sound business. To focus on doing what we're doing today very well, and to make sure that we have some specific objectives in front of us. There turned out to be a lot of fine people in the Banquet company, who just wanted to get aggressive and become part of a winning team again."

Banquet employee Don Rasche had moved from finance to operations in 1973. He understood the importance of being a low cost producer in the highly competitive frozen foods business.

Batesville, Arkansas frozen foods plant produces Banquet products.

"Being a low cost producer is just analyzing each step of the operation and deciding where and how savings can be made," explains Rasche. "You look at every aspect of production from beginning to end."

For example, production-driven Banquet had been wasting precious capital storing mountains of unsold prepared chicken. When Phillips took charge, Banquet had a year's worth of frozen fried chicken inventory in cold storage. Cold storage is expensive. Worse, although it retards product deterioration, it doesn't eliminate it. Both the flavor and the breading of the fried chicken had suffered from the excessively long storage period, and customer returns were all too frequent. As ConAgra's millers had done several years earlier with their grain supplies, Banquet's managers pared their chicken inventories.

Grateful to have an attentive parent at last, Banquet employees carried out Phillips' simple agenda enthusiastically.

"It wasn't three or four months after ConAgra bought Banquet that they brought in John Phillips," recalls Don Granneman, who was then Banquet's vice president of sales. "It didn't take John but about six months to get inside of the company and find out what it needed."

Although Phillips had marketing experience from his years with Campbell, he felt more at ease on the operations side of the food business. He asked Jim Kennedy to help him strengthen Banquet's ailing marketing program. For several months Kennedy commuted to St. Louis during the week and back to Omaha on the weekend. Finally, he moved his family to St. Louis.

"When I was commuting, I felt like a military advisor might — there is always a chopper around to rescue you," says Kennedy. "But the real problem was that I didn't appear as committed to the business as I was trying to get Banquet's employees to be."

Kennedy quickly discovered that under RCA's ownership Banquet's marketing arsenal consisted of one simple weapon — cutting the price.

"It was a vertically integrated operation," Kennedy explains. "The key was to keep the plants operating. The chickens were coming, the fryers were frying and the warehouses were filling up. So they would lower the price on a promotional scheme to move volume."

To unclog the jammed system, Banquet's sales department gave significant price reductions to anyone who was interested in buying Banquet products. The wholesalers and retailers packed their warehouses with cheap Banquet frozen chicken which they, in turn, sold to the consumer, passing along the savings.

"The trade would feature a product at $1.99 for a two-pound box of Banquet fried chicken when its suggested retail price was $3.49,"

Product improvement, consumer advertising, introduction of new products became Banquet's plan under Phillips and Marketing VP Jim Kennedy.

continues Kennedy. "But eventually even the consumers' freezers got filled up.

"We set about rebuilding the marketing department, reorganizing the sales department, upgrading the quality of some of the products, flushing the system of aged products, and not operating the system by how much we can produce but by how much we can sell."

Kennedy developed sales forecasts from which to set production standards. He tried to increase the company's appeal to the consumer, as opposed to the trade customer. Banquet had virtually no consumer research on hand, so a market research data base had to be built from scratch. In addition, Kennedy shored up the food company's consumer advertising budget.

Kennedy estimates that RCA had spent less than $1 million a year on Banquet consumer advertising. During ConAgra's first year of ownership, ad expense was just shy of $2 million. From there it rose to $3.5 million, then $5 million. By fiscal year 1984, Banquet's advertising budget approached $20 million.

Developing new products was a key element in attracting the potential Banquet consumer's attention. As John Phillips notes, the frozen food business is a new product world. In 1980, when ConAgra acquired Banquet, products representing 50% of the volume in the frozen food case hadn't existed five years earlier.

According to Kennedy, "There hadn't been any new products at Banquet for 10 years. They had test marketed one new product that seemed quite successful. The expense of introducing it nationally was deemed to be too much, so they pulled it off the market."

"It is very difficult to extract any marketing funds or investment from your parent who is trying to sell you," comments Granneman. "We did our best not to lose any customers, but we didn't make very much money. We had a pretty broad product line. We were trying to hang on to what we had, hoping we would be acquired by someone who would put the needed investment into this company.

"This was a time when the frozen food business was beginning to think of a lot of new products. Shortly after ConAgra bought us, the influx of new products into the field was astronomical. Fortunately, with ConAgra we had a parent that understood it was necessary to launch new products, and we became very active in the frozen food business."

ConAgra started conservatively, by adding new flavors to Banquet's existing frozen dinner line. The next step was to concoct new culinary creations. Granneman recalls how Jim Kennedy carefully mothered ConAgra's first original offering in the rough-and-tumble frozen food arena — "Saucy Chicken".

"It was a line of five or six pieces of chicken covered with a barbeque sauce flavoring, or garlic, or butter," describes Granneman. "We launched it into a dozen or so markets. The patient died. It was well received by the retail trade, but I guess it didn't deliver what the customer wanted.

Banquet earnings bound upward, ConAgra paid off its acquisition in 3 years and Phil Fletcher is hired as new president of Banquet.

"But all of us at Banquet were excited seeing someone just try to develop new products. And we all knew that if you introduce 100 new products you're lucky if 10 or 15 make it."

Kennedy stayed at Banquet's St. Louis headquarters for two years. He had struck a deal with Harper: the corporate marketing vice president would wear two hats until he had helped Banquet managers develop an effective and efficient marketing program.

"When Mike would run into a corporate problem he would get on the phone and ask if I could get up to Omaha that afternoon," recalls Kennedy. "He was very sympathetic and understanding because he really wanted to make Banquet a success. So many people said, 'This commodity company which doesn't have any trail in consumer goods, what is it doing buying a consumer goods company?' We knew the financial community would be looking at our track record on that side of the business, and it was important in all of our minds that we make a success there. Some went as far as saying we wouldn't make it. There was a real focus on wanting that success.

"I think we were all surprised that it turned around as fast as it did. It was a year. As it began to turn around we began to have a story to tell. The story may not have deserved the interest it got from the securities analysts, but it got the attention anyway. The analysts are familiar with consumer products because they partipate in them. They don't understand some of the other businesses we're in. Because Banquet had been shopped around so much, it was something that was familiar to the financial world. In a sense, this was a piece of distress merchandise."

In fiscal year 1980 Banquet's sales were approximately $350 million; pre-tax earnings were around $12 million. By fiscal year 1982, Banquet's earnings had more than doubled. In 1983 Banquet earned about

$25 million on $400 million in sales, prompting analysts to note that the acquisition had paid for itself in three years. With steady infusions of advertising money and with the cultivation of new products, sales continued to climb. Between 1982 and 1986, Banquet's sales volume increased by almost 50%.

Harper credits Banquet's employees with a major role in the company's new-found prosperity.

"They had a couple of successes with Jim Kennedy and John Phillips and their steps began to get pretty light," says Harper. "They got cocky. They got proud. Things built on top of each other and they did a magnificent job."

In September of 1981, Harper had been named chairman of ConAgra, succeeding Bob Daugherty and leaving the president's post vacant. In fiscal year 1982, ConAgra created its innovative "office of the president." Harper devised the unusual management structure to reinforce the fact that ConAgra was a decentralized organization of interrelated but independent operating companies.

Harper appointed John Phillips, Bud Morrison and George Doering as presidents and chief operating officers of, respectively, ConAgra Prepared Food Companies, ConAgra Grain Companies, and ConAgra Agri Products Companies. In their new roles, the three executives bore first responsibility to the parent corporation, but were also directly responsible for the operating results of the companies under their supervision.

As Phillips assumed his new duties in Omaha, he and Mike Harper hired Heublein executive Phil Fletcher to serve as Banquet's new president.

Sports enthusiast Fletcher pedaled his exercise bicycle before breakfast and rowed his rowing machine before bed. As a teenager, he had aspired to be a coach. When he decided the coaching life wasn't what he really wanted, he changed his college major to geology so he could still work outside. In 1954, after graduating from St. Lawrence University in Canton, New York, he interviewed with General Motors. The plant manager was a geologist, too. Phil got the job.

Fletcher worked at G.M. for four years until, like John Phillips, he joined Campbell Soup Company. He stayed with Campbell Soup for 15 years, holding various plant and production management positions and at one time working for Phillips. Fletcher obtained a Sloan Fellowship, and in 1970 he earned an MBA from the Massachusetts Institute of Technology. From 1973 to 1978 he served as general manager of operations and agriculture for H.J. Heinz, U.S.A., and in 1978 he was hired by the Heublein Company as vice president of operations for the spirits division.

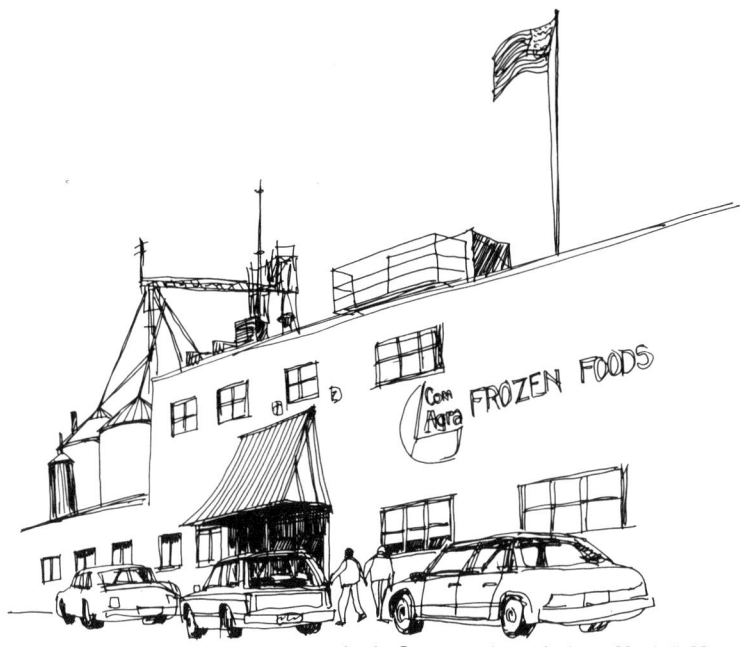

Another Banquet production facility at Marshall, Missouri.

Fletcher's primary goal was to bolster Banquet's marketing and sales strength, to get Banquet to view the market through the consumer's eyes. Like other executives transplanted to ConAgra from competing corporations, he was pleasantly surprised by ConAgra's lack of rigid management structure. As an operations expert, he had never been allowed to get involved with sales and marketing; his other employers believed that only executives with marketing backgrounds could handle the consumer side of the business. ConAgra offered him the opportunity to run an entire company.

"I have worked for other companies which would standardize the procedures and, in essence, just stifle the entrepreneurship of the individual," says Fletcher. "At ConAgra, we devise whatever we think works best for our business. To me, one of the strengths of our company is not having to force people to fit into a common system across all companies.

"I have never found a business environment like this anywhere I've ever been. Where you have the responsibility to run your business in the framework of a large company. Most large companies simply can't deal with that. Mike Harper has created a unique culture."

Early on, Fletcher learned how deeply Harper honored his commitment to the independent operating company concept. The two clashed over whether Banquet should retire its 1950s-vintage aluminum "mess kit" frozen dinner pans in favor of more modern plastic. Harper favored plastic, and insisted that Fletcher was wrong to resist the change. At a quarterly review he presented Fletcher with a beat-up World War II mess kit, and joked that if Fletcher insisted on serving Banquet dinners in them he ought to have one around.

Harper didn't overrule the new Banquet president, but during their disagreement he told Fletcher: "If you can't give me a company that will package those frozen dinners in plastic, I'll go out and buy one." Shortly thereafter ConAgra bought Armour, with its plastic-packaged Dinner Classics.

Ultimately, Fletcher decided to toss the tin and replace it with a material suitable for both conventional and microwave ovens. He chose paper.

On another occasion Fletcher doggedly pursued an advertising campaign despite Harper's predictions of failure.

"It bombed," says Fletcher. "And I lost several million dollars. I really dreaded the next quarterly review. Mike looked at me and said, 'OK, that didn't work. Now what are you doing to do?' That told me this is a different culture from any one I've ever been in before. He knew that I knew damn well that I'd screwed up. I felt bad about it. He knew that. There wasn't any 'I told you so.' He didn't waste time on that."

Banquet veteran Don Rasche asserts that the independent operating company method is the only way to run a business.

"Harper is constantly in there suggesting and badgering — and he can be a pretty strong suggester — but he does let you run your own business," says Rasche. "You're accountable for it and you have the authority to get it done. We believed in ConAgra's philosophy from the very beginning and they've proven that that's the way they operate."

By all accounts, the Banquet acquisition had succeeded. ConAgra had disproved the naysayers who questioned whether the commodity-oriented firm could prevail in the consumer market, who pointed at Bow Wow and Taco Plaza as evidence that the hayseed flour millers couldn't compete with the big guys. By their astute bargaining, Harper and his top executives had carried off a prize.

CHAPTER 10

A TOE IN INTER-
NATIONAL WATERS

SEPTEMBER 15, 1975, was a sad day for Grand Island, Nebraska, history buffs. On that day the Minneapolis-based Peavey Company announced that it had purchased the ConAgra grain elevator in Grand Island, and intended to raze the adjoining mill.

Months earlier ConAgra had closed the Depression-era plant. Its location away from major metropolitan areas left it poorly situated for milling commercial bakery flour. During ConAgra's dark days Peavey plucked the grain elevator up for a song — $600,000. The company wanted to add the Grand Island facility to the chain of elevators it operated across the nation. Specifically, the elevator would complement Peavey's grain merchandising operations in nearby Kearney, Nebraska.

For Grand Island old-timers, the demolition of the old Nebraska Consolidated Mills facility signaled the end of an era. As one Glade brother observes, "My uncle Art Glade built that mill. He turned over in his grave when they tore it down."

Grand Islanders can be forgiven if they felt a tinge of sweet satisfaction seven years later. In 1982, ConAgra purchased the Peavey Company.

Like ConAgra, the Peavey Company had a long and distinguished history in the grain business. Frank Hutchinson Peavey was born in Eastport, Maine, in 1850. At the age of 15, he left his widowed mother to strike out for the West. He found his first job in Chicago; his employer soon recommended him for a bookkeeping position with a Sioux City, Iowa, wholesale grocer. In 1868 Frank Peavey convinced the grocer and another Sioux City businessman to join him in marketing farm implements to the growing ranks of western settlers.

The business prospered — until it burned down the following year. Undaunted, Peavey found a new partner, sent for his family from Maine and took his brother into a second farm implement venture.

Long-time Peavey executive T. Truxtun "Truck" Morrison explains how Peavey's interests turned from farm equipment to grain.

"When Mr. Peavey couldn't receive cash for farm implements, he received grain," says Morrison. "That's how he got in the grain business. Sort of by default."

In the course of his bartering, Peavey discovered that few of his farmer customers had reliable markets for their grain. He started to buy it. To store that grain he built a 6000-bushel elevator in Sioux City and a series of warehouses along the railroad line. In 1874 the enterprising and persuasive young man convinced Minneapolis flour millers, who had congregated on the upper Mississippi River system, that he could supply them with grain. Peavey elevators and warehouses sprang up as each new railway snaked across the Midwest.

The Peavey Company grows in the upper Midwest by building grain storage and serving flour millers in Minneapolis.

In 1884 Frank Peavey moved his company's headquarters to Minneapolis to better serve his biggest customers. Two years later he built a wooden structure in Minneapolis that was billed as the world's largest grain elevator. In 1887, like Peavey's first Sioux City implement store, the elevator and its 1,150,000 bushels of wheat went up in flames.

That scene was all too common in an era of wooden elevators and warehouses. Frank Peavey was certain he could find a way to reduce fire's devastating toll on grain merchandisers and millers. After years of study he decided to build a concrete grain elevator.

In 1899, Peavey constructed an experimental concrete grain storage tank just outside of Minneapolis. Skeptics called it "Peavey's Folly"; the common wisdom was that only wood had enough "give" to store grain. Critics were silenced when the first grain was drawn from the tank. Instead of buckling dramatically, the tank stood tall.

A tireless dreamer, Peavey had hatched other schemes too. In 1890, his company built the first terminal grain elevator in the Pacific Northwest, near Portland, Oregon. In 1895, he devised an overland rail route through Panama, to replace the customary ocean journey from the Pacific Northwest around Cape Horn to Europe. Peavey's goal was to cut the trip from 200 to 30 days. He succeeded in drastically reducing not only travel time but profits as well. Thereafter Peavey Company grain took the traditional course to the Continent.

Frank Peavey had also cherished the idea of extending a vast system of grain elevators across Russia. In 1900 he dispatched his son-in-law, Frank Heffelfinger, to St. Petersburg to drum up some grain business with the Russian government. Heffelfinger returned to the U.S. to nix the idea. Markets were unreliable, railways poorly equipped, and government officials unwilling to relinquish operational control. But on the positive side: on his way home through Europe Heffelfinger had checked out some promising concrete grain elevators.

Later that year in Duluth, Minnesota, Peavey erected his first concrete grain terminal. The elevator had a capacity of 4,750,000 bushels. It was the largest terminal in the world. Peavey had truly become the "Elevator King of the World."

The following year Frank Peavey, always the innovator, bought the first $1 million personal life insurance policy ever written in the United States. He paid one $48,390 premium. In December, 1901, at the age of

51, he died unexpectedly of pneumonia. The policy was payable to F. H. Peavey & Company.

The firm's junior partners — Peavey's son George and sons-in-law Frank Heffelfinger and Frederick Wells — incorporated the company in 1906. In 1907 George Peavey sold his interest to Heffelfinger and Wells.

Soon after incorporating the firm, Heffelfinger and Wells signed a contract to build a string of elevators in Canada. Over the next decades, the second generation of Peavey managers continued expanding the company's grain merchandising empire. Then, in the 1920s, the company entered the flour milling, feed milling and lumber businesses by purchasing the Van Dusen Harrington Company. In 1953, with the acquisition of the Russell-Miller Milling Company and its mills in Minnesota, Montana, North Dakota, New York, Illinois and Texas, Peavey became one of the nation's top five flour millers. Fifteen years later Peavey bought the milling interests of the Colorado Mill and Elevator Company, including its Denver and Utah mills.

In early 1900s, Peavey Grain Merchandising company expands into flour milling, feed milling and lumber.

As construction boomed in the prairie states Peavey served, the company continued selling lumber to farmers and contractors.

"We actually acquired some free-standing lumber yards during the 1950s and 1960s," recalls Truck Morrison. "Then in 1972 or 1973, we acquired a company called Northwest Fabrics out of Eau Claire, Wisconsin. That really focused our retail business on retail, and not just on being part of the grain business. We separated the lumber business from the grain business out in the country, and combined it with the fabric stores to create a retail group."

In 1975 the Peavey Company sold its Canadian grain operations to Cargill. With the proceeds Peavey bought the Wheelers retail farm stores, headquartered in ConAgra's own Grand Island, Nebraska. Shortly thereafter, Peavey purchased the S & S farm stores, based in O'Neill, Nebraska, and then acquired a chain of west coast stores.

The Peavey Company had remained privately held until 1973. Within several years it was listed on the New York Stock Exchange. When Peavey put its stock up for sale on the open market, it faced problems similar to ConAgra's in attracting investor interest. It fostered its retail group in part to appeal to securities analysts and potential stockholders.

"When Peavey first went public, we were a grain and flour milling company," says Morrison. "We wanted to diversify into businesses that were related to agriculture but had higher earnings multiples than the grain and flour milling business was perceived to have."

By 1980, Peavey's principal businesses were three-fold: grain processing; domestic and export grain merchandising; and retail farm supply, building supply and fabric store operation.

A Peavey S&S store serves retail customers.

"The grain business was the biggest part of Peavey," recalls Truck Morrison. "At that time the grain group had two export grain terminals in New Orleans and one in Superior, Wisconsin. It had river loading stations up and down the Mississippi, Missouri, and Illinois Rivers. There were approximately 225 barges and six intercity tow boats, and probably 400 or 500 hopper cars."

That year grain merchandising profits were high. This fact didn't escape Mike Harper's notice.

In 1977 ConAgra had itself entered the grain merchandising business by acquiring the McMillan Company, which operated elevators in Minneapolis and Superior, Wisconsin. ConAgra opened a grain merchandising office in Minneapolis to handle its McMillan Company transactions. Later in 1977 ConAgra acquired Minneapolis' Burdick Grain Company, which supplied specialized grains to maltsters, brewers, distillers and the food industry and operated two Minnesota grain elevators.

The next year ConAgra purchased yet another Minneapolis-based grain firm, the Atwood-Larsen Company, a grain commission company which provided management services and merchandised grain for over 150 country elevators in Minnesota, North and South Dakota, and Montana. In 1979 ConAgra acquired the rights to operate Minneapolis' city-owned barge terminal on the Mississippi River. The terminal, renamed Port ConAgra, Inc., was the northern-most terminal on the river and, with its 2 million tons of commodities handled annually, the largest general commodity river port north of St. Louis.

ConAgra established a St. Louis grain merchandising office in the summer of 1979. In 1980 the company bought the Oklahoma-Kansas Grain Corporation, with its commodity handling facilities located on the

Arkansas River at the Tulsa, Oklahoma, Port of Catoosa.

That year Harper asked a mutual friend, Jim Rude, to help him contact Peavey chairman and CEO William Stocks. Rude had quit his job as a Pillsbury management information systems analyst to launch a consulting career in Scottsdale, Arizona. Five years before, Rude had helped Harper reconnect with former Pillsbury colleague Jim Kennedy, then working for Armour in Phoenix. That meeting had turned out well for both Harper and Kennedy.

This time Rude suggested to Peavey's Bill Stocks that he inquire into ConAgra, a company in a similar industry and with a similar philosophy. Harper and Stocks met. Nothing happened.

By 1982, grain merchandising profits had plunged.

Several factors had darkened the outlook for the U. S. grain merchandising industry. After the 1975 and 1980 U. S. government embargoes on grain sales to the Soviet Union, that major grain customer had sought long-term contracts with more favorably inclined suppliers. A world recession and strong U. S. dollar had weakened foreign demand for U. S. grain. The governments of other exporting nations were paying farmers ample subsidies to produce grain, while the U. S. government paid farmers not to produce.

But Harper still thought Peavey's operations might dovetail nicely with his own company's. ConAgra had recently acquired or leased rail and river storage and loading facilities in Arkansas, Indiana, Kentucky, Oklahoma and Wisconsin. By fiscal year 1981, ConAgra grain merchandisers had a handling capacity of 400 million bushels, and commanded a fleet of over 100 leased barges and nearly 1000 leased railcars.

That year ConAgra had sales of $1.4 billion and net income of $27 million. The 5500-employee Peavey Company had sales of $821 million and net income of $23 million. ConAgra had more than 200 operating locations; Peavey had 135 grain-handling facilities and 224 retail locations. Peavey's comprehensive domestic grain elevator system, combined with its several export elevators, neatly filled the gaps in ConAgra's domestic grain merchandising operations and opened the door to export merchandising. And joining forces would enable both companies to stay in the running against top grain merchandisers Cargill and Continental Grain Company.

Meantime, ConAgra's grain merchandising interests were expanding; Harper began developing an interest in a Peavey acquisition.

Early in 1982 Rude hosted the two CEO's in his Scottsdale home.

Nothing happened again.

"Then we met again and Bill began to move a little bit, meaning it might be possible," recalls Harper. "We talked about how we might get some investment bankers. I called him after that second meeting and he said, 'OK, let's get together.' We met Bill and his investment banker in a Minneapolis hotel room. We hammered at that damn thing and got to the point of the handshake."

Stocks had found that he liked Harper's way of running a business.

"We both strongly believed in independent profit center operations with responsibility," explains Stocks. "Peavey didn't call them independent operating companies, although we had the same idea. Mike had advanced it into the IOC concept and was, frankly, somewhat ahead of us in terms of that philosophy and the degree of sophistication with which it operated."

Peavey's public ownership heightened the demand for security regarding the potential deal. A leak could result in a stockholder's suit from an investor claiming that those in the know used unfair advantage to buy or sell stock. To keep to a minimum the number of people apprised of the upcoming deal, Harper dispensed with the company's usual extensive due diligence study.

"In acquiring public companies the rules of the game are slightly different," says Tom Brady. "You sit down with the chief executive officer and his financial guy and that's about as far as it goes. You deal with the public documents, and with the projections and commitments of the CEO and financial officer."

The weekend after developing their "agreement in principle", Harper and Stocks traveled to New York City to meet with the requisite batteries of lawyers and investment bankers. They had to fashion the broad agreement into a final, detailed accord.

Harper and Stocks had already met with their respective boards to inform them of the agreement in principle. Each CEO had confided in a few top executives before leaving for the East Coast. Board members and executives alike were sworn to secrecy.

The meetings in Jim Rude's Arizona home had been polite enough affairs. The New York assemblage was another story.

"Eric Gleacher was there and Stocks' investment banker was there," Harper explains. "We were fighting, and the deal fell apart. The word 'deal-breaker' is used all the time in those kinds of negotiations. Somebody will throw up his hands and cry, 'Ah, hell, that's the deal-breaker!' Then you get up and you leave, and you caucus and things get settled.

"It's sort of fun. In fact it's exciting. It really is exciting. Your heart's in your mouth. That's true with most people. At least I hope it's true with most people."

Through hours of haggling, the final agreement took shape. On Sunday evening, after the long weekend of negotiations, Stocks and Harper returned to their home towns. Each man intended to publicly announce the merger on Monday morning.

They didn't know that all hell had broken loose in Minneapolis. On April 18, 1982, the Sunday *Minneapolis Star-Tribune* printed the scoop: the city's own Peavey Company had agreed to merge with Omaha-based ConAgra, Inc.

Peavey employees were stunned. Bill Stocks felt lousy. On Monday morning he assembled the entire Minneapolis staff — over 400 people — to officially inform them of the deal and to apologize for their having learned it first from the press. Because of Peavey's long history of family involvement and stock ownership, many Peavey employees remained shocked and dismayed after the merger. One particularly stone-faced listener was Peavey executive Truck Morrison.

The Peavey/ConAgra merger was hammered out over the weekend; announced prematurely by the Minneapolis Star-Tribune.

In the spring of 1982, Morrison was occupied with developing plans for a new grain export terminal in Kalama, Washington, about 50 miles down the Columbia River from Portland, Oregon. Morrison had delivered his presentation on the Kalama project to the board immediately before Stocks unveiled the ConAgra-Peavey agreement in principle.

"We were excused from the board meeting after our presentation," says Morrison. "The meeting didn't let up and it didn't let up. Board meetings are generally about three hours long and this went on for five or six hours. I still wasn't suspicious.

"Then things started to leak, not about ConAgra, but that Peavey was considering a sale to somebody. Two days after the board meeting the

Export grain terminal at Kalama, Washington.

rumor came out of our flour mill in Alton, Illinois, that ConAgra was acquiring Peavey."

Over the weekend, under the insistent questioning of a *Star-Tribune* business writer, a Peavey family member broke. Sunday's headlines trumpeted the deal. Morrison was outraged.

"On Monday, Bill Stocks called top management into the board room," he recalls. "I know where he was sitting, and I know exactly where I was sitting. As far as I was concerned, he had sold my company to the enemy. I mean I was so mad that if looks could kill he would not have lived. I didn't say anything and I walked out. George Gosko, the president of Peavey, knew what had to be going through my mind, because it was written all over my face. He called me in his office right then and I spent three hours with him."

Gosko's attentions cooled Morrison down but they didn't convince him to stay on. As Truck recalls, the executive headhunters went to work as soon as the proposed merger was announced. The Pillsbury Company set its sights for Morrison.

"I almost went to work for Pillsbury," says Morrison. "Mike Harper got wind of this through Bill Stocks, because I wasn't hiding it. Maybe I should have, but I'm not that kind of person. Mike came up, and I remember we had lunch at the Minneapolis Club. We had lunch at 12:00 and at 2:00 or 2:30 the restaurant was empty and we were still talking.

"I was obviously intrigued with Mike, and intrigued with the management philosophy which he had and which ConAgra supposedly operated under. I say 'supposedly' because I didn't know any better."

Harper persuaded Morrison to stay.

"You can't promise anybody anything under pressure," observes Harper. "But you can help an individual think it through. Talk about what might happen someday in terms of our commitment. To build the company, not just to buy Peavey and then dismantle it. We would try to build Peavey. Truck thought about that for a bit and then he decided to stay with us."

"It was a fantastic decision," Morrison acknowledges. "If I had left I would have been part of Pillsbury's flour milling and grain business. Pillsbury is a restaurant business. Then it's a food company. And then the third leg of the the stool is the ag business. I mean it's a poor third. So it wouldn't have been a very glamorous job for me."

Not that Morrison had sought glamour at Peavey. His mother's grandfather was Frank Peavey, the grain firm's founder. When Truck joined Peavey in the early 1960s, he became the last family member to go to work for the company. But he didn't advertise his mother's maiden name.

"Most people didn't know that Truck Morrison was a Peavey," he explains. "I had some advantages in that. I had the right to act with the freedom which comes from not being a member of the family.

"And my father was the chairman of Cargill. So I was viewed in the trade as the son of the Cargill chairman who went to work for Peavey."

After the Minneapolis fiasco and before the final signatures by the parties, Peavey's management and board of directors insisted upon a thorough investigation of ConAgra. The Minneapolis firm dispatched its investment bankers to Omaha to carry out the inquiry.

"They sent two young guys, probably 25 years old, in conservative pinstriped suits with vests," says Mike Harper. "Nothing looks more conservative than a really young guy in a vest and blue pinstriped suit.

"They called in each member of management and were very serious. Didn't smile until it was lunch."

At lunchtime Harper found out the reason for his guests' wary approach. The young bankers had flown into Omaha's Eppley Airport that morning. A model of the city's new Twin Towers building was prominently displayed in the airport concourse. ConAgra was slated to move there from its Kiewit Plaza quarters; as the model showed, the company logo was already emblazoned across the structure.

"These two young guys with their briefcases walked through the airport, saw the model, got in a cab and were heading toward town," describes Harper. "One asked the the cab driver, 'Does it take long to get to ConAgra?' The other young fellow piped up 'It's that building right there.' And the cab driver says 'Oh, there's nobody in that building'."

His passengers

Marine leg unloads grain shipment from river barge.

blanched. About that time an enterprising soul had rented space in a downtown Chicago office building, set up a dummy office for a fictitious company and bilked a number of unsuspecting investors. If this Omaha food firm were trying to pull the same scam, the earnest junior bankers wouldn't be so easily fooled.

A few words from Harper convinced them of ConAgra's solvency. The Federal Trade Commission, however, was more persistent with its concerns.

FTC takes an interest in the proposed ConAgra/ Peavey merger; consent agreement is signed and Peavey finally acquired for $180 million.

To the FTC the fit between the two grain companies apparently seemed too comfortable. Bill Stocks recalls that one FTC employee in particular developed a keen interest in whether a ConAgra-Peavey merger violated federal antitrust laws.

Stocks flew to Omaha to review the antitrust issue with Harper. As the two men conferred in Harper's office, they received an urgent call from their Washington attorney.

"I believe that there was a rapidly scheduled hearing coming up, and the attorney thought it would be to our advantage to be there," recalls Stocks. "This was late in the day. We got on the plane and flew to Washington. I had no extra clothes with me because I had just come from Minneapolis for the day."

Harper and Stocks booked themselves into a Washington, D. C., hotel. Stocks headed out to buy some shorts, socks and toothpaste. The stores were closed. He trudged back to his hotel room to wash out his shorts and socks before bed. But Washington, D. C.'s infamous hot, humid weather left Stocks' clean underwear still dripping the following morning.

"We got up in the morning to attend the hearing," says Stocks. "I squished down the hallways in my wet socks and wet underwear."

And in a beige suit exactly like Harper's.

To speed the merger along, ConAgra and Harper signed a consent agreement with the Federal Trade Commission. ConAgra and Peavey agreed to sell four flour mills in Salt Lake City and Ogden, Utah, and Billings and Great Falls, Montana. The companies also agreed to sell related warehousing and distribution facilities in San Francisco, Oakland and Los Angeles, California. The sales, required by the end of the fiscal 1984, would reduce milling capacity by about 28,000 hundredweight a day.

The total value of the ConAgra-Peavey merger was approximately

$170 million — $53 million in cash and the rest in stock. Peavey stockholders who accepted ConAgra common stock in payment, and who held it for six years, saw their investment appreciate fivefold. Red Thomas explains that ConAgra issued stock to finance the deal because it couldn't have stayed within its long-term debt ratio had it financed the deal entirely with cash.

Referring to ConAgra's annually reported public commitment to its financial standards, Thomas points out: "The amount of equity that was a part of that transaction was designed to make sure the business could fit within pages four and five."

While they insisted upon adherence to the company's long-term debt ratio, ConAgra managers eased the company's financial standard prohibiting short-term debt past the end of the fiscal year. Because of the nature of Peavey's business, ConAgra executives revised the standard to allow short-term debt at the year's end, if it financed cash or hedged commodity inventory. To enhance the company's ability to obtain credit if tough economic times occurred, the allowable long-term debt ratio was reduced from 40% to 35%.

The Peavey Company had been in the grain merchandising business for over 100 years when it joined ConAgra. Only in the previous decade, however, had Peavey experienced its greatest surge of growth in export grain merchandising. During the 1970s total U. S. grain exports increased by 250%; Peavey's rose by 400%.

One-third of that volume passed through Peavey's New Orleans facility, completed in 1979. The Kalama, Washington, elevator approved in 1982 would enable the company to compete in the Pacific Rim countries, projected to have the world's highest grain import growth rates in the 1980s.

In addition to transporting grain, Peavey maintained around 100 commodity brokerage offices nationwide. These offices carried out Peavey's grain hedging activities and served public traders in commodity futures.

The acquisition of the Peavey Company increased ConAgra's grain merchandising capacity by 150%. Soon after ConAgra and Peavey merged, Mike Harper told Lewis Remele, group vice president of Peavey grain operations since 1975, and Roger "Bud" Morrison to figure out a way to split up the combined Peavey and ConAgra properties. The grain merchandising operations of the two firms were taken by Peavey Grain Companies, headed by Remele, with Truck Morrison second in command. The milling facilities went to ConAgra Grain Processing Companies under Bud Morrison.

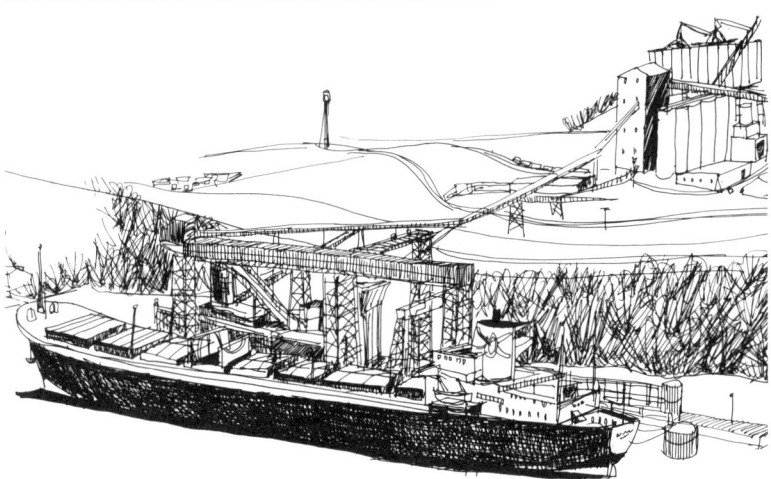

Loading grain shipment at New Orleans river terminal.

The consolidation of ConAgra and Peavey mills gave ConAgra's Grain Processing Companies more than 20 mills in 15 states.

The newly formed Peavey Grain Companies operated 80 grain elevators in 14 midwestern and western states, and ConAgra became the nation's largest publicly-held grain merchandiser, better able to compete with the privately-owned giants.

In fiscal year 1983, to complement the operations of its recently completed New Orleans elevator, Peavey Grain increased from 38% to 100% its interest in another Gulf of Mexico facility, the New Orleans Public Grain Elevator. Peavey Grain expanded ConAgra's Tulsa elevator and relinquished operation of Port ConAgra in Minneapolis. Peavey's Kalama facility approached completion, and the company anticipated that it would help bring a coveted 10% of the U. S. export grain market.

By the spring of 1984, ConAgra's annual grain merchandising operations totalled around one billion bushels of grain. About half of that grain was exported. ConAgra operated 150 country elevators, five export elevators, 400 barges, eight towboats and 1,500 railroad cars.

Unfortunately, industry overcapacity caused grain merchandising losses in the mid-1980s. The weak world economy, high Third World debt and strong U. S. dollar continued to constrain world demand for U. S. grain. In 1984, the United States' share of the world grain trade fell below 49% — 10 points lower than in 1980. ConAgra's export operations felt the pinch from reduced commodity flows.

When ConAgra acquired Peavey, each company operated between 200 and 225 barges to transport its commodities. According to Don Stone, now ConAgra's vice president of transportation, the major commodities moved by barge are wheat, corn and fertilizers. Wheat and corn float downriver; at the Gulf of Mexico fertilizers are loaded for upriver traffic. Grain is the driving force.

"Peavey owned part and leased part of its barge fleet," says Stone. "ConAgra leased all of its fleet. Those two businesses were merged into Peavey, and a profit center was established which operates out of Alton, Illinois, as the Peavey Barge Company."

Like Peavey's grain merchandising operations in general, the Peavey Barge Company saw lean years through the mid-1980s.

"There have been some years when business was terrible," says Stone. "The rail sector as well as the barge sector became overbuilt in 1979 and 1980, for a number of reasons. There were shortages which brought investor groups into the railroad and barge markets. At that point grain export markets fell substantially."

Because of the sluggish grain merchandising industry, for several years Peavey Grain failed to meet ConAgra's stringent return on equity standards. The Minneapolis-based company suffered sizable losses before its fortunes improved. Aggressive managers like Truck Morrison, former Cargill commodity trader Robert Peyton, Thomas Racciatti, from Continental Grain, and others whom they attracted helped the company withstand the economic turndown until, in fiscal year 1988, the grain operations attained ConAgra's ROE standards. Harper views the Peavey acquisition as a strategic, if not tactical, success.

"Peavey represented our first toe in the water trying to become an international company as well as a domestic company," observes Harper.

"We realized that the grain business was depressed when we purchased Peavey," comments ConAgra economist Dick Gady. "I think perhaps we expected the business to turn around a little quicker than it did. But exports kept dropping for a couple of years after we bought Peavey, creating a real tough environment for that kind of business.

"Peavey represented our first toe in the water in trying to become an international company" — C.M. Harper.

"I think in retrospect that will serve to be a blessing. A company that has to operate in that type of environment does things to really make management tough, to streamline the businesses. As a result Peavey is probably a lot stronger today than it would have been if we had bought it when things were good and then had to go through the problems."

The Peavey deal coincided with doldrums in the flour milling, as well as the grain merchandising, industry.

Merging with Peavey increased ConAgra's potential milling output

Northwest Fabrics retail store in shopping mall.

from 95,000 to almost 200,000 hundredweight per day. ConAgra became the largest flour miller in the U. S., as well as the leading supplier of wheat flour to commercial bakers and durum semolina flour to pasta makers.

In addition to the mills targeted for sale under the consent agreement, Peavey had flour mills in Denver, Colorado; Hastings, Minnesota; Superior, Wisconsin; Alton, Illinois, and Buffalo, New York, and a mill under construction at Phoenix, Arizona.

Unfortunately, excess industry capacity had weakened the flour milling business. In January of 1983, the U. S. government announced an agreement to export to Egypt, during calendar year 1983, one million more metric tons of flour than usual. The added subsidized flour production needed to fulfill this contract equalled about 8% of the industry's volume, and nearly doubled U. S. flour exports. Even with this agreement, U. S. flour milling production barely exceeded 90% of capacity in 1983.

Joining forces with Peavey, however, allowed ConAgra to improve its position as an efficient, low-cost producer. For example, ConAgra had developed its system of destination mills ever since R. S. Dickinson pioneered the idea with Nebraska Consolidated Mills' Decatur, Alabama, plant. Locating newer mills near metropolitan consuming areas had saved transportation costs, because grain costs less than flour to move.

Conversely, the Peavey Company had several of its mills situated near rural grain-producing areas and transported flour from those mills in bulk railcars. Peavey brought to ConAgra its bulk flour railcar fleet, consisting mainly of small 100,000-pound cars. ConAgra soon began to trade up, trading three or four 100,000-pound cars for one 180,000-pounder eligible for cheaper lease and freight rates.

Railroad deregulation brought new rate structures, lowering the price of transports from the Peavey origin mills. Soon ConAgra was shipping grain a short way to its Peavey-era origin mills and a long way to its ConAgra-era destination mills. Stone contends that having both arrangements gives balance to the company.

"The flour mill at destination is obviously focused on a relatively small marketing area," he observes. "No matter how intense competition may get in that area you are pretty well locked into that situation.

"If you come back to a flour mill that is located near the wheat-producing area you have market flexibility. If the market in Philadelphia becomes too intense and you can make more money selling flour in Atlanta, you can just readjust your marketing efforts. You can't do that with destination flour. There is something to be said for both."

By 1985, ConAgra's milling capacity had grown to twice that of 1980, when Harper first approached Stocks. The company's production: nearly five billion pounds of flour a year.

The Peavey Company's grain merchandising and flour milling businesses harmonized with and enhanced ConAgra's own grain and flour operations. Peavey's retail operations were less familiar.

Peavey's building supply centers provided farmers and other rural dwellers with the materials for do-it-yourself home construction and repair. Its country farm stores furnished personal goods from cowboy boots to lawn mowers. Home seamstresses could shop at the company's fabric stores, again principally located in smaller agricultural communities.

By 1985, ConAgra milling capacity grows to 5 billion pounds a year; Peavey Retail operations, less familiar, are reorganized.

"The notion was to serve the farmer with all of his needs," explains Bill Stocks.

The Peavey Company had formally organized its retail group in 1974. Between 1974 and 1983, retail sales grew from $50 million annually to over $200 million.

At the time of the merger, Peavey had 110 farm supply stores, operating under the names "Wheelers," "S & S", "Big R", and "Peavey Mart". It had 73 Northwest Fabric stores, and 34 building supply centers called

Wheeler Farm Store, one of Peavey retail chains.

"Peavey", "Fish" or "Peavey/Thunderbird".

Peavey's retail operations were added to ConAgra's "Agriculture" segment, along with formula feeds and additives, fertilizers, and UAP's agricultural chemicals. ConAgra sold Peavey's building supply stores and its Canadian retail stores. Despite trying times for farm communities, in fiscal year 1983 Peavey's retail stores generated almost half of the "Agriculture" segment's profits. ConAgra's intensive marketing efforts coaxed farm and fabric store earnings higher still.

Because of ConAgra's successful integration of its own operations with those of its former rival, both the company and its leader earned top marks from Peavey veterans.

"I'd rate Mike Harper very highly," declares Bill Stocks, who retired from ConAgra in 1987. "He's not just a manager, he's a strong leader. What are his strong points? I'm trying to think of what his weak points are."

Truck Morrison is convinced that Harper aptly described ConAgra's management philosophy that afternoon at the Minneapolis Club.

"There's a term now used — it's 'intrapreneurial' — which means an entrepreneur in an organization," says Morrison. "I think that really applies to ConAgra. And sometimes for better or worse.

"There are days maybe I wish I were back in the old system. I feel totally accountable for the businesses I'm responsible for and I have never, except for having a farm, worked for myself. There are advantages to working for yourself and advantages to working for a corporation. ConAgra tries to create an environment where you have the advantages of both.

"The challenge in ConAgra is to manage what you have and to grow. It's constantly looking over your shoulder at all those wolves biting at your rear end. And yet you're looking forward at the mountain that you've got to climb."

The grain business continued to improve, and in 1988 ConAgra added more mountains to climb. The company acquired eight flour mills from International Multifoods Corporation, as well as the grain merchandising division of Pillsbury.

Bud Morrison engineered the Multifoods deal. He got wind that Multifoods wanted to dispose of its flour mills even before the company started looking for a buyer. Buying the mills was cheaper than constructing new facilities. The mills' daily capacity of 80,000 hundredweight raised to 22% ConAgra's portion of the flour milling industry's total capacity.

It was Bud Morrison's final acquisition negotiation for the company he had joined in 1969. In January 1988 he was named senior vice president of ConAgra, Inc., and he retired in August 1989. His 20 years with the company's flour milling operations had seen exceptional growth. The number of mills increased from 15 to 29, daily hundredweight capacity rose from 68,400 to 266,000, and sales skyrocketed from $77,770,188 to $860,727,000.

"Bud Morrison built the largest and most successful flour milling business in the nation," said Mike Harper in ConAgra's 1989 annual report.

The acquisition of Pillsbury's grain merchandising division was engineered by Thomas Racciatti, president of ConAgra Grain Companies. Pillsbury operated 48 grain elevators and grain-handling facilities in the Midwest, owned or leased five towboats, 53 barges and 888 rail cars.

Pillsbury's grain division merged with Peavey Grain Company, giving Peavey more than 110 grain-handling facilities in 14 states and a storage capacity exceeding 160 million bushels.

As a result Peavey Grain Company will handle over 1 billion bushels of grain and flour a year.

CHAPTER 11

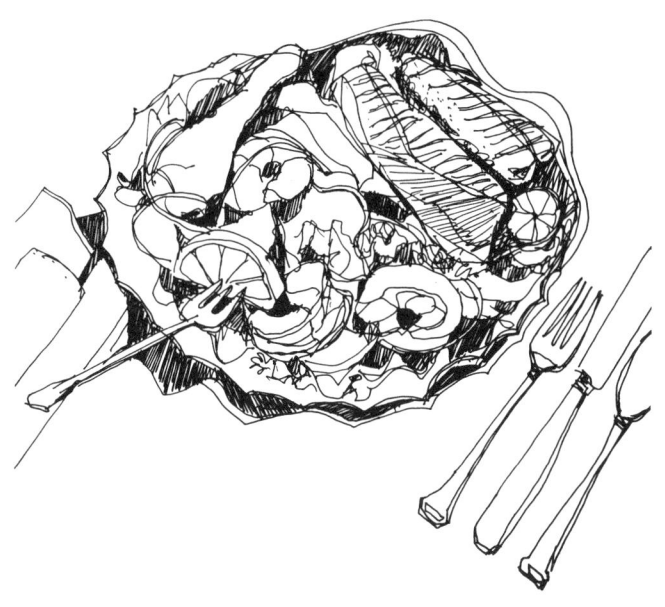

THE CENTER OF THE PLATE

TO Mike Harper, the "center of the plate" is the real power in the food industry. The term refers to the protein element of the meal, the entree. And Harper never overlooks the opportunity to add another helping to ConAgra's center of the plate. Scaling unsteady mountains of grain and flour hadn't entirely diverted his attention from other food industry opportunities.

In September of 1982 ConAgra entered into a joint venture with England's Imperial Foods Limited. The two companies combined their poultry operations — ConAgra's Country Skillet and Imperial's Country Pride — to create Country Poultry, Inc.

The name "Country Pride" had been developed in 1975. Imperial Foods adopted it because the right to use the poultry operations' previous name — "Pillsbury Farms" — ended that year. That was part of the deal Pillsbury executive Mike Harper had struck with Imperial's managers in 1974, when he sold them Pillsbury's poultry division. Now the poultry unit that Harper had vainly urged Pillsbury to keep had found shelter under ConAgra's welcome wing.

"That was a great coincidence," declares Harper. "Good company, good people, and by God, they thought they had gotten rid of me. Almost ten years later, old Baldy shows up again. Small world."

ConAgra and Imperial Foods had each invested $18 million to form the new Country Poultry, Inc. ConAgra took over the management of both Country Pride and Country Skillet, and obtained a five-year option to buy 100% of Country Pride.

With annual volume exceeding 1 billion pounds and sales nearing $1 billion, Country Poultry became the United States' largest poultry business. Using both the "Country Skillet" and "Country Pride" brand names, the company marketed broiler chicken, turkey, table eggs and processed poultry products to retailers, distributors and food service operations across the U.S.

When Country Poultry was formed, ConAgra's Country Skillet company primarily produced "ice-packed" poultry, while Imperial's Country Pride used the newer "chill-pack" method. "Chill-packed" poultry is rapidly deep-chilled in a blast tunnel where 40-below-zero temperatures and 45 mile-per-hour winds prevail. After its brief arctic immersion, the poultry is held to an internal temperature of 28 degrees. The chill-pack method reduces water pick-up during processing, keeps the chicken drier in the package and extends shelf life.

In June of 1984, after Harper and his executives determined that they could safely expand ConAgra's commodity poultry operations, ConAgra exercised its option to buy Imperial's 50% interest in Country

"A small world" — Harper reacquires the poultry unit he once tried to persuade Pillsbury to keep when ConAgra buys Country Pride.

Poultry. ConAgra had grown to the point where the poultry industry's cyclical low points wouldn't seriously jeopardize the company's overall profitability. And the large number of value-added products that ConAgra now produced further shielded the company from periodic poultry losses.

Once again, Harper pulled off a deal just in time to profit from a market turnaround. Fiscal year 1984 brought a surge in broiler markets.

"Country Pride gave us some poultry processing plants that were better than ours," observes Tom Brady. "They marketed their chickens a little differently than we did, and the integration of Country Pride and Country Skillet made for a very strong company. The poultry cycle went in our favor shortly after we bought Country Pride, and we were able to pay it all back pretty fast."

Eric Gleacher compares the Country Pride acquisition to the Banquet deal. He recalls that Imperial Foods, like RCA, had recently restructured under a new CEO who wanted to jettison all of the firm's commodity business.

"The English company had put in a tremendous amount of money, they had built and modernized plants," says Gleacher. "Mike bought the business back at about half of what Imperial had put into it, and he made a fortune in the chicken business.

"The Banquet deal is more noteworthy because people see it in stores. But the Country Pride deal has been an astonishing money maker."

George Haefner has been an integral part of that money maker for 35 years. He joined Pillsbury in 1954, and worked in Pillsbury's poultry division when Mike Harper sold it to Imperial Foods. Haefner remained with the chicken business when Imperial sold it back to Harper. Today he is president of ConAgra Poultry Company and a member of the office of the president.

Clyde Sasser, president of ConAgra Broiler Company, works with Haefner in El Dorado, Arkansas. Like Haefner, Sasser is a veteran of Pillsbury and Imperial. Sasser signed on with ConAgra before the Omaha company acquired Imperial.

Neither Haefner nor Sasser is intimidated by the fact that their boss, Mike Harper, knows something about the poultry business.

Points out Haefner, "Anyone who has a choice would rather have a boss who knows about his business."

Catfish are harvested from growing ponds by nets.

Poultry wasn't the only product that bore the "Country Skillet" name. In the late 1970s, ConAgra had started to market its grain-fed catfish under that label.

ConAgra had continued to expand its catfish operations ever since Allan Mactier purchased the Stral Catfish Company in 1970. By 1980, ConAgra owned fish processing and fish meal plants in Isola, Mississippi; a processing plant in Tippo, Mississippi; two catfish hatcheries; and six catfish farms. The company produced more than 10 million pounds of catfish in 1980, about 30% of the total U.S. farm-raised catch.

By 1981, the Nebraska-based firm had to hire a private detective to investigate livestock rustling of a different sort than that practiced on the western plains. The booming catfish business had attracted a new kind of cat burglar. These outlaws netted $1 million worth of catfish from Delta farmers and processors, before the law reeled them in.

Recognizing seafood's growing popularity with a diet-conscious public, in 1979 ConAgra had joined an east coast investment group in a $2 million shrimp aquaculture venture in Honduras. Trawlers dragged the coastal waters for pregnant female shrimp, which were returned to sea after spawning from 200,000 to 400,000 eggs aboard ship. The shrimp fry were held in tanks for three weeks, released to 268 acres of ponds dredged from an undeveloped mangrove swamp, and harvested after a four-month grow-out.

ConAgra learns to swim in aquaculture with farm-raised catfish operations. Then dives deep into ocean seafood with Singleton and Sea-Alaska acquisitions.

ConAgra dove whole-heartedly into the growing seafood market in 1981. In February it acquired Singleton Seafood Company; in January it bought all of Sea-Alaska Products, Inc., except its interests in a fleet of fishing vessels. Harper named as head of the company's seafood and aquaculture businesses Willard Adcox, the Southern gentleman who came to Nebraska Consolidated Mills in 1963 as manager of Dalton Poultry.

In the early 1950s, Henry "Booty" Singleton had expanded his shrimp trawler business to include frozen shrimp processing. Within 10 years he had sold his boats and opened a processing plant. By the late 1970's Singleton Seafood was the nation's number one shrimp processor, with annual sales of $100 million. Booty Singleton sold his company to ConAgra, but not before extended negotiations.

"Bob White, our vice president for corporate planning, was our man in charge of negotiations," recalls Harper. "He spent so much time at Singleton that he wound up in their company film."

Jesse Gonzalez, then Singleton's executive vice president, led the negotiations for the seafood firm. After the sale, he became president of Singleton Seafood Company and, ultimately, ConAgra Shrimp Companies and O'Donnell-Usen Fisheries Corp.

Singleton purchased shrimp from independent fishermen at waterfront facilities, including Singleton's own docks at Key West, Florida, and

Dockside processing plant for Singleton seafood products.

Shrimp boats at a Singleton dock.

Freeport, Texas, and processed the catch at its Tampa, Florida, plant. In addition to being the U.S.'s top shrimp processor and commanding 15% of the breaded shrimp market, Singleton sold scallops, oysters and flounder.

The seafood firm marketed nearly 80% of its product through food service channels, like Long John Silver's, Denny's Restaurants and Ponderosa chain restaurants; it sold the remainder in retail grocery stores. With ConAgra's encouragement and financial backing, Singleton increased its retail involvement and quickly became a market leader.

Not so with Sea-Alaska, which fell victim to tough conditions in the crab and salmon industries. Founded in 1972 by Robert Resoff, who had previously established and sold two other seafood firms, the Seattle-based company processed Alaskan king crab, snow crab, salmon and herring at its Dutch Harbor, Alaska facilities. When ConAgra acquired it, Sea-Alaska was one of Dutch Harbor's top three crab processors.

Sea-Alaska's operations occurred aboard its three processing ships. A 500-foot Vietnam-era cargo carrier remained permanently docked at Dutch Harbor, its engines replaced with refrigeration equipment for use in crab processing. The company's two mobile vessels docked at Dutch Harbor for crab season. During salmon season they journeyed to the Bristol

Bay and the Bering Sea, there to anchor and process fish bought from commercial fishing boats.

At the time of its acquisition, Sea-Alaska met ConAgra's stringent performance standards. But within a year, industry conditions took a disastrous turn. Massive overfishing had caused concern about future world seafood supplies, and the Alaskan government slashed the allowed king crab catch by 60%.

ConAgra quickly tried to secure its position as a seafood processor. It purchased certain assets of Alaska Packers Association, a processor of herring and frozen and canned salmon, from the Del Monte Corporation in April, 1982. The following year brought a fisherman's strike and a weak salmon run.

Harper knew it was time to cut his losses. In fiscal 1984 ConAgra discontinued Sea-Alaska's frozen salmon business and cut back assets committed to the king crab business. A slimmed-down Sea-Alaska concentrated on the canned salmon business and the more limited opportunities in the crab business.

While ConAgra executives strengthened the company's poultry and fish operations, they remained alert for opportunities to compete in yet another arena — the red meat industry.

The meat-packing business was no way to get rich quick. The industry was plagued by out-of-date facilities, high labor costs, a production-oriented outlook and growing competition from poultry and fish. Historically, meat-packing companies had handled all aspects of production "from squeal to the meal", from slaughtering to processing. Because of the industry changes, over the years meat companies had begun to specialize in either slaughtering or processing.

ConAgrans were familiar with the industry's troubles. In 1978

Sea Alaska's processing ship and plant at Dutch Harbor.

ConAgra had nearly acquired MBPXL, formed in 1974 by a merger between Missouri Beef Packers and Kansas Beef Industries. The Wichita, Kansas, firm was the nation's number two beef producer, second only to Iowa Beef Processors of Dakota City, Nebraska. In the previous fiscal year MBPXL had recorded income of $5.7 million on sales of nearly $1 billion, compared with ConAgra's income of $15 million on sales of $544 million.

After trimming and strengthening poultry and fish businesses, ConAgra begins to look at the red meat industry. A first attempt goes awry.

The merger would have given ConAgra $60 million in capital at a time when the company was worth a grand total of $39 million. Instead, MBPXL was snatched from Harper's grasp through a series of events that left him bitterly criticizing MBPXL, Cargill and the Nebraska judiciary.

In October of 1978, MBPXL and ConAgra board members signed an agreement to merge. MBPXL directors were to present the terms — a one-for-one exchange of common stock — to their stockholders for ratification. But after signing the binding agreement with ConAgra, an MBPXL director invited an offer from Cargill, which already had shown an interest in the beef processor.

Cargill responded enthusiastically. The huge privately-owned competitor of ConAgra bought up one-fourth of MBPXL's stock at $27 per share. ConAgra's stock was selling at $20.75 per share. Cargill paid cash to MBPXL stockholders, who in turn had to pay a 25% capital gains tax. ConAgra stock was on an uphill climb, and its one-for-one exchange would have been equal to or better than Cargill's offer after taxes. Cargill made it known that if MBPXL's stockholders rejected ConAgra's offer, Cargill would most likely make an offer to buy the beef packer's remaining 2 million shares, giving stockholders a total of about $68 million in cash.

ConAgra sued. Within two weeks the MBPXL board recommended that shareholders accept the Cargill proposal. The board also canceled the December 15 stockholders' meeting at which it was to present ConAgra's proposal.

In March of 1979 Cargill merged with MBPXL, which is now known as the Excel Corp. The loss stung Harper. He was determined to obtain recompense for what he viewed as Cargill's unlawful interference with a binding agreement between ConAgra and MBPXL.

In 1980, a Douglas County, Nebraska, judge held that Cargill had

Is a contract a contract? Nebraska Supreme Court says "maybe not": in ruling against ConAgra's merger agreement with MBPXL.

indeed interfered with ConAgra's attempt to merge with MBPXL.

In 1982, hearings were held on the issue of damages. On October 4, 1983, nearly five years after the meat-packing company slipped through Harper's fingers, the Douglas County District Court ordered Cargill to pay ConAgra $15,996,000 in damages. The judge had subtracted the $21 value of ConAgra's stock on the day MBPXL board members decided not to recommend acceptance of ConAgra's offer from the $27 price that Cargill paid, and had multiplied the $6 difference by the number of MBPXL shares outstanding.

The *Omaha World-Herald* reported that Warren McCoy, by then a retired consultant to ConAgra, said ConAgra officials welcomed the decision but doubted the ruling would be the final chapter. They were right.

In March of 1986, in a four-to-three decision, the Nebraska Supreme Court reversed the lower court's award. The majority held that even though MBPXL had signed an agreement with ConAgra, the meat packer had a duty to consider Cargill's offer. However, the Supreme Court did not deal with the question that the MBPXL board also had the duty to present both offers to its stockholders.

Harper was incensed. Always outspoken, he publicly questioned the "quality of justice" in ConAgra's home state. Didn't this mean a contract wasn't a contract in Nebraska? If signed merger agreements could be undone at will, the door was open to any promoter looking to earn a fat fee by offering a competing offer. As suggested in the dissenting opinion, "the law of the jungle" would truly be the doctrine governing corporate mergers in Nebraska.

"What Mike was saying is that if the boards of directors of two companies, both of which have enough money to buy the best legal counsel, if they agree on a merger with the understanding that the merger will be submitted to their respective shareholders, it ought to be enforceable," explains ConAgra legal counsel Jack North. "You can understand how the little guy on the street can make a mistake in a contract. But a Cargill or a ConAgra, with all their legal staff, if you can't enforce their agreements, whose can you?"

"The agreement ought to be submitted to the shareholders," adds North's colleague, attorney Bruce Rohde. "They could vote it up or down. And they were never given that opportunity. At the time the Supreme

"Mike's attitude was that ConAgra was going to enter into a lot of merger and acquisition transactions, and he wanted everybody to know that ConAgra's word is good," continues North. "And on the other hand, when anybody makes a deal with ConAgra, ConAgra will expect their word to be good. So throughout the lawsuit it was really just a basic philosophy. 'Whatever we say we'll do, we'll do. And whatever you say to us you'll do, you'll do.'"

ConAgra's arguments were offered in vain. Later in 1986 the Nebraska Supreme Court turned down ConAgra's final request for a rehearing of the case. But by that time the company had entered the red meat business by another route.

Armour Food Company, with a long and distinguished history in the meat packaging industry and now a Greyhound subsidiary — comes to ConAgra's attention.

In 1983, executives at the Greyhound Corporation launched a study of other companies' planning procedures, visiting four or five firms known to have first-rate planning departments. Their goal was to implement new procedures in Greyhound's subsidiary, the meat processor Armour Corporation. The executives contacted ConAgra, whose management reputation had improved considerably since Mike Harper first asked his managers for annual plans.

ConAgra executives said Harper would be pleased to conduct a short course on efficient planning for Greyhound — as long as CEO John Teets attended. Harper and Teets had never met.

By 1983, Greyhound was more than a busline. It had diversified into the food, consumer product and financial services industries. Greyhound had acquired Armour in 1970, as a friendly suitor rescuing the company from a takeover attempt by General Host. At that time Greyhound was valued at $798 million compared to Armour's $2.1 billion.

Teets had joined Greyhound in 1964. He left in 1968, but returned eight years later as a group vice president in charge of service companies. In 1980 he became head of Armour, and in 1982 he was promoted to Greyhound CEO.

"Shortly after that we determined that, with the labor situation, we were going to be unable to be competitive in the meat industry," recalls Teets.

Armour had a distinguished heritage in that industry. In 1867, Philip Danforth Armour started a pork packing business in the Chicago stockyards. In the early 1870s, P. D. Armour designed and built the first chill

First Armour slaughter facility — at Chicago about 1867.

room for refrigerating meat products. In 1878 he helped develop the first refrigerated railroad cars for cross-country transportation. Continuing its string of firsts, Armour became the first food company to establish a research and development program; by the mid-1880s Armour chemists were busy thinking up uses for animal by-products.

In 1884 the Omaha Union Stock Yards Co. was established to serve as a collecting point for livestock raised by Nebraska and western Iowa farmers and ranchers. Thousands of the Belgian, Bohemian, Czech, German, Latvian, Polish, Swedish, Ukrainian, and other immigrants arriving at Ellis Island flocked to the plentiful jobs in Omaha's new packinghouses. In 1885 Omaha's population was 60,000; two decades later it had doubled.

Armour's first venture in Omaha was an 1887 partnership with brothers Michael and Edward Cudahy. Three years after opening the Armour-Cudahy Packing Co., Armour sold out and returned to Chicago. But the opportunities in Omaha were too good for Armour to resist for long, and in 1897 the company opened a new plant there, joining Cudahy and Swift. By the time Wilson & Company moved to Omaha in 1938, the city could claim the distinction of hosting the four meat packing industry leaders.

In the heydays of the late 1950s the industry was Omaha's largest employer, providing jobs for nearly 15,000 people. The city's 19 packinghouses slaughtered more than 1.5 million head of cattle, nearly 3 million hogs and over 500,000 sheep a year. The heart of this industry were the Big Four — Armour, Swift, Cudahy and Wilson — all located within a six-square-block area in South Omaha.

"There was just a mass of people on Q Street," recalls Elsie Irvine, a forty-year veteran of the Omaha packing industry. "The four plants each had from 2,000 to 5,000 people. 75% to 80% of those people lived within walking distance of the plant. Most of the employees during my time were immigrants or first generation. I'm one of the Belgians. I live near the Belgian Curve, between Q and L Streets.

"It was a place where an inexperienced person could get a job. It didn't take any training to get your first job there."

But in the 1960's new competitors brought upheaval to the industry. Independent packers, led by Kansas Beef Industries and Iowa Beef Processors, built new plants far superior to the two- or three-block-long monsters that lined Q Street.

Their new, smaller, more efficient facilities were located out in rural communities, close to the feedlots and the farmers who supplied their animals. Cattle did not have to be shipped long distances to the packers, shedding precious pounds on the journey. The new plants had cement floors cleaned with a daily hose-down, instead of wooden floors spread with sawdust to be swept away when it got too wet. They had convenient truck loading access; Armour's plant, built to accommodate rail shipping, used elevators to hoist its meat four stories up to the truck docks.

The new meat-packers could also pay lower wages to their rural, generally non-unionized employees. The Big Four, with nationwide union "master contracts", could not compete.

Armour gave up most of the ghost in Omaha in 1968, retreating to its Chicago headquarters. When Swift closed in 1969, the packing industry ceased to be a major employer in Omaha. Wilson and Cudahy tried to hang on, but they drastically cut back operations, employing fewer than 1,000 workers each. After several temporary closings, Wilson shut down for good in 1976. The Cudahy plant closed in 1978, leaving only a small sausage operation. In the mid-1980s, 10 small packers employed just 1,300 Omahans.

By the time Teets considered selling Armour, the meat packer's costs, particularly for labor, were well above those of competitors like IBP.

"Iowa Beef Processors was the low cost producer — setting the price of beef — and many times that was below what we could manufacture it for," Teets says.

"The Armour situation was a bad one for John Teets," observes Eric Gleacher, who was a friend of both Teets and Harper. "I told him he ought to sell Armour and he agreed."

Gleacher knew Harper was interested in expanding in the food chain, saying he'd be interested in any deal on the right basis. Teets, for his

In 45 minutes of talk and with a handshake, ConAgra's Harper and Greyhound's John Teets reach a deal. part, realized the subject of an Armour deal might come up when he went to Omaha with his executives for the planning seminar.

"When we met in the morning, Mike showed us openly and candidly how they go through their planning process — computerization, how they automate everything, how they handle their organization," says Teets. "It was very enlightening. Then we got into the discussion. He approached me about whether we would be selling Armour. I said, 'Let's talk about it'."

As Mike Harper recalls, once they started talking it took 45 minutes to reach a deal.

Harper had raised the issue of price. The ConAgra executive had done his homework, studying what public information he could find. Teets' quote was considerably more than book value.

"It was obvious that the price he wanted would not be justified by earnings," says Harper. "There were some additional earnings that could come through productivity improvements, but even so it didn't look like it could work. Then I surfaced an idea with him."

Harper had already given thought to how ConAgra might finance a deal with Armour while avoiding a shaky balance sheet. ConAgra could sell stock on the open market and combine the proceeds with cash on hand, to come up with a book value price. But another idea occurred to Harper during his brief conversation with Teets. The Greyhound executive had been highly complimentary about ConAgra's stock performance.

"I suggested to John that, instead of our selling the stock on the open market, he take that common stock plus cash," says Harper. "At book value. Our common stock had been appreciating and he knew that. He might come out a lot better off if he took our stock, held onto it for a couple of years, and then sold it.

"And that's the way it turned out. That bridged the gap. He had to have more than book value, and he was willing to take a risk on it. John is a good risk taker."

Teets agreed to take 3,400,000 shares — 15% — of ConAgra's common stock, worth $92 million. In addition, ConAgra would assume $90,370,000 in Armour obligations. Greyhound signed a "standstill agreement" prohibiting the sale of any major block of stock without prior notice to ConAgra. The deal restricted Greyhound from accumulating more ConAgra stock, and allowed ConAgra to require Greyhound to sell its ConAgra stock after three years if Greyhound could get at least $35 per share.

"It worked out well for us," concludes Teets. "Three years later we sold the stock for a profit of $85 million, more than I had ever dreamed."

As in previous acquisitions, the agreement in principle was the easy part. The agonizing work of crafting the definitive agreement fell to the two companies' accountants, attorneys and financial experts.

"We ran into problems; you always do," acknowledges Harper. "The lawyers are fighting over something and protecting their clients. Every now and then John and I would call each other. No matter who initiated the call, the guy on the other end would say, 'Yeah, that's the way I remember, too. I'll straighten my people out.' John kept his word. There isn't anything you cannot accomplish in the terms of a complex deal if the guy you shook hands with will keep his word.

"That is one thing I really look for. It's the most valuable thing in business. I guess some people call it integrity. They don't begin to vacillate. Or try to change the deal somehow to their advantage. The phrase 'a deal is a deal' in principle is very important."

The Armour deal brought ConAgra 19 meat processing plants, one beef slaughterhouse and one pork slaughterhouse. The two slaughter facilities were the only ones left to the former meatpacking giant; in the previous 10 years Armour had sold or closed 40 more. The meat company employed 6,500 people, of whom 4,500 were production employees. Half of the production employees worked under the master labor contract with the United Food and Commercial Workers Union.

Industry analysts greeted the acquisition favorably.

They noted that to build from scratch a brand name as strong as

Armour plant at Kansas City in the early 1900's.

With Armour, ConAgra acquires a strong brand name, good production facilities, new consumer products and some union problems.

Armour's would be prohibitively expensive for ConAgra. Armour plants were among the meat industry's best-equipped; Greyhound had invested more than $100 million in capital improvement. The acquisition would add Armour's production facilities for refrigerated processed foods — ham, bacon, hot dogs, and lunch meats — to the frozen food plants ConAgra had acquired with Banquet and Singleton. Collaboration between ConAgra's poultry and fish experts and Armour's lunch meat specialists could result in new refrigerated processed poultry products, canned poultry and canned fish.

Within the frozen food category, the meat processor's premium-priced "Dinner Classics" frozen dinner would nicely complement Banquet's moderately priced offerings. Armour had a loyal food-service clientele; in fact, the "Dinner Classics" line had evolved out of Armour's airline meals. Armour's extensive and efficient distribution system could transport any of ConAgra's growing catalog of consumer products. And, of course, those new consumer products would further insulate ConAgra from cyclical changes in the commodity markets.

The sticking point was the cost of labor. In June of 1983 5,000 Wilson Foods Corporation employees ratified a pay reduction from $10.69 to $8 an hour. Harper was willing to assume Armour's master labor contract if the company's union employees accepted a similar reduction. He believed that Armour couldn't compete against non-union and lower-wage packers paying less than half what Armour's master contract provided.

Union members refused, voting down two separate proposals supported by union leadership, in the fall of 1983. As a result, on December 17, 1983, as it had announced six months earlier, Greyhound closed the 13 Armour plants covered by the master agreement. On December 18 ConAgra reopened 12 of the 13 Armour plants with employees earning wages and benefits totalling $10 to $11 an hour, rather than the previous $17 to $18.

Harper knew the move was controversial. But he felt that the only alternative to reducing labor costs was a drastic one — the demise of the company. And, by the mid-1980s, that alternative had become all too common in the meat industry. Harper wanted Armour to live to see a 20% return on equity.

John Teets, who joined the ConAgra board in 1984, noted the

ConAgrans' intense commitment to achieving their stated financial goals.

"Mike Harper talks about 20% ROE and it comes out of all his management people," observes Teets. "They all believe it and understand it and achieve it — 20% return on equity. I was walking to my first ConAgra board meeting, and I mentioned to one of Mike's managers that it appeared to me that everybody had that stamped on their buttocks. '20% ROE.' Seemed to me they were tattooed with it.

"At the next management meeting Mike presented me with a pair of shorts with '20% ROE' on them."

The joke didn't die in the boardroom.

"Somehow *Fortune* magazine got wind of this and took a picture of me holding these shorts," says Harper. "This went throughout the country thanks to the wire services, and we got a very dignified spread nationwide. There were headlines like 'Undercover Story Breaks at ConAgra' and 'ConAgra Executives Carry Deep-Seated Goals in Their Underwear.'"

With the secret revealed to corporate America, Harper threw discretion to the wind. He hung the white boxers from the flagpole out at ConAgra's Omaha airplane hangar.

"We brought a new level of sophistication to our city," concludes the midwestern executive.

All kidding aside, Harper expected Armour to start contributing to that goal of "20% ROE". And ConAgra was ready to help. Don Wallen, who became Armour's marketing vice president, remembers the first time he met his new boss.

"We were told that representatives from the new owner were going to come in and introduce themselves," says Wallen. "Mike Harper came in and he had about three people with him. We introduced ourselves, and Mike said he had a little film about ConAgra. I had never heard of ConAgra. I don't think anybody had.

"I was really quite amazed that he probably talked for no more than 10 minutes. And we were used to chief executives who would talk for an hour. So that was a very pleasant introduction."

A month or so later, Harper and several top executives flew back to Armour's Phoenix headquarters. They spent two days in a hotel with a number of Armour managers, getting acquainted.

"I was very impressed with that," recalls Wallen. "Here is a chairman and his top people willing to take two full days to come to learn about Armour, about how we saw things, what our dreams and aspirations were, and to kind of let us get to know them. Mike sat down next to me and said, 'I hope you all don't mind if I take off my shoes here and get comfortable.'"

Armour retail meat delivery truck — circa 1930.

Determined to put the group at ease, Harper continued, "You'll notice that I st-stutter a bit. I never st-stutter over the w-w-word 'profit'. But occasionally I have trouble with the word 'l-l-loss'."

Wallen left that meeting with confidence in Armour's future.

"We could come away and tell the people who worked for us that these guys are regular people, they're interested in us, they're successful people," he explains. "We felt we knew them."

ConAgra's first move was to reorganize Armour by product groups. That way managers could focus on the production and marketing techniques appropriate for each type of product.

"ConAgra's management team agreed that Armour was more than just one company," says Rod Stephens, a retired 45-year Armour veteran. "What they chose to do was to restructure Armour into Armour processed meat company, Armour fresh meat company, Armour dairy company, Armour frozen food company and Armour transportation company. That way they broke them all out as independent operating companies."

The processed meat, dairy, and fresh meat companies were headquartered in Omaha. The frozen food company was combined with Banquet Foods in St. Louis to create the ConAgra Consumer Frozen Food Company, or CCFFC. ConAgra established CCFFC so that Armour and Banquet could share support functions while retaining separate sales, marketing and R&D operations.

All that reorganization meant a lot of cross-country moves for Armour employees. Many managers had followed Armour from Chicago to Phoenix in the early 1970's. Jim Kennedy worked for Armour back then, and he recalls what happened shortly after Greyhound acquired the company.

"In an effort to make those two big corporations one, it was decided that something major had to happen to reduce duplication and to create one culture instead of two," says Kennedy. "While they made a major show of it and evaluated 15 cities, there was no question that we were eventually going to Phoenix. That was where the chairman's wife wanted to go. So 565 families moved to Phoenix. It was really a traumatic situation."

Kennedy was wooed back to the Midwest after his 1975 meeting with Harper in Jim Rude's house. After ConAgra's 1983 acquisition of Armour, however, many long-time Armour employees were more reluctant than he had been to move from sunny Phoenix to blizzard-prone Omaha. Especially in December.

Armour families move from sunny Phoenix to Omaha (in frigid December) but compassion from ConAgra executives and red carpet welcome from ConAgra employees help.

At that time Rod Stephens, who had started his Armour career as a $15-a-week sausage maker, was Armour's southwest regional vice president, in charge of the Decker Meat Company. When ConAgra acquired Armour, Stephens was named president of Armour Processed Meat Company. One of his responsibilities was to shepherd the 85 families who trekked from the Phoenix area to the Omaha corporate headquarters in 1984.

"The Armour people had been in Arizona 14 years with Greyhound," says Stephens. "Their kids had gotten 14 years older, they'd had some new ones in the meantime, and it was a great change for the family. But ConAgrans went out of their way to make Armour welcome. They had welcoming parties, they had picnics, they assigned a senior executive to each employee to work with and answer questions."

ConAgrans in Omaha commissioned 18 billboards spelling out a welcome in Armour in hot dog link letters. They assigned each arriving family a host family with matched employment and interests. They distributed coupon books, city guides and state driver's information. They created two "hot lines" for questions about the company and the community, respectively. With the help of the Omaha Chamber of Commerce, they held receptions to present an Omaha orientation film — with wine and Armour cheese to feast on while viewing.

"They just rolled out the red carpet," says Stephens. "There was not anything left undone. They went the extra mile to make the Armour people feel comfortable."

Harper admits that moving several hundred people across the

In the meat business, ConAgra learns competition is widely scattered; market shares very splintered. Armour develops bright new product ideas to compensate.

nation can create big headaches for all concerned. "It disrupts the life of the employee, the spouse and the kids," he says. "The problem is that you have to decide for the long term what is in the best interests of your company. You have to make a disruption like that as easy as possible, and to deal with compassion. But at the same time, unless you're competitive you lose the game."

Once the Armour families had renewed their acquaintanceship with mittens and jumper cables, the real work began.

As with Banquet, ConAgra needed to steer Armour from a production-driven to a market-oriented philosophy. But ConAgra's success in boosting demand for poultry and fish had helped to shrink the market for red meat as industry capacity held steady. Between 1970 and 1980, per capita beef consumption in the U.S. had dropped from 84 to 78 pounds. And falling demand caused producers to bring fewer animals to market. This pushed raw material prices up and profits down, particularly for Armour's largest segment, the processed meat company.

Although Harper was confident that a consumer preference swing would eventually materialize, Armour's red meat operations faced difficult times in the interim. Rod Stephens stressed the importance of ConAgra's staple ingredients for success — low-cost production and innovative marketing. But marketing in the meat industry is a tricky proposition.

"It's an interesting thing," comments Don Wallen. "I was trained as an economist and I took a lot of marketing at the same time, so I'm familiar with many different industries. There's a tremendous difference between candy or cigarettes or food, depending on the kind of market that's evolved over time.

"For example, in cereal the market is an oligopoly; there are a few very large competitors. In the meat business, we have over 300 brands competing against us. Probably the largest market share of an individual company is about 10%. And we're in essence number two, with about 4% or 5%."

Armour's marketing department, led by Wallen and marketing services director Don Tamsen, generated bright ideas to increase consumer interest in Armour's products.

Armour introduced a new line of "lower salt" ham, luncheon meat, hot dogs, sausage, and cheese, made with one-third less salt than usual. The company's lower salt bacon and hot dogs both ranked number one among their lower salt competitors. In 1986 and 1987 a new Armour package, designed to preserve processed meat freshness while increasing customer convenience, garnered "package of the year" awards from Packaging Institute International and *Food Processing* magazine.

The "Vin Fiz" promotion commemorates a pioneer aviation milestone — and gets Armour meats a whirlwind of product publicity.

In 1987 Armour helped raise funds for the Special Olympics as national sponsor of the organization's "Law Enforcement Torch Runs". Armour also donated $16,000 worth of food — 5,600 pounds — for a reception and luncheon enjoyed by Special Olympics participants and their families. The following year Armour sponsored an Olympic volleyball exhibition between the U.S. and the Soviet teams. The featured food item was the "Russian hot dog": Armour's best, topped with caviar.

Sports car driver Jerry Miller traveled the country, racing the Armour Star Z28 Camero IROC and making promotional appearances. He starred in a TV public service announcement sponsored by Armour and the National Council on Alcoholism to point out the dangers of teenage alcohol and drug use.

But Armour's boldest marketing exploit had to be the flight of the Vin Fiz — the third Vin Fiz, that is. The original Vin Fiz was a carbonated grape drink Armour developed in 1911. The second Vin Fiz was an experimental Wright Brothers fabric and wood biplane which Calbraith Rodgers flew from New York to California in 1911, in a grand scheme to promote the drink. The third Vin Fiz took flight in the fall of 1986, on the 75th anniversary of Cal Rodgers' record-setting transcontinental trip.

In 1911, William Randolph Hearst offered $50,000 to the first person to fly from coast to coast within 30 days. The dashing young Rodgers, a lover of fast horses, yachts, motorcycles, automobiles and, finally, aeroplanes, wanted to win the prize money. J. Ogden Armour, whom Rodgers met at an international air show, agreed to finance his venture if along the way Rodgers would promote Armour's new soft drink with leaflets and personal testimonials.

Seventy-five years later, IBM materials scientist James Lloyd, Jr., approached ConAgra with the idea of re-enacting the journey of the Vin Fiz. He felt that Calbraith Rodgers' skill and daring had gone unrecognized. Although Rodgers failed to nab Hearst's cash prize because his flight took too long, he succeeded in becoming the first pilot to fly from coast to coast. Four months later, however, the adventurous young man perished in a plane that plunged into the Pacific Ocean. Armour's Vin Fiz soft drink was hardly more successful; it fizzled in less than four years. Only the Vin Fiz plane remained, on permanent display in the Smithsonian Institution.

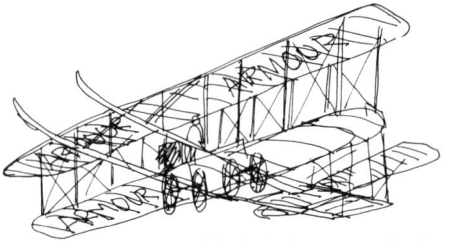

The original Vin Fiz biplane sponsored by Armour.

ConAgra gave the go-ahead for the project, so ground crew mechanic Jack McCornanck designed and built a prototype biplane. With its fabric and aluminum construction and 26-foot wingspan, the modern Vin Fiz was smaller and lighter than the original. And, presumably, safer. Cal Rodgers sat on a corduroy seat so he wouldn't slip off into the clouds. Jim Lloyd got to use a seat belt.

Rodgers had flown 4300 miles in 82 hours over a period of 49 days, suffering some 20 crashes. Partly because Jim Lloyd regularly stopped for gas rather than letting the plane run out like his predecessor, the IBM scientist's trip took 98½ hours over 56 days — with only one precautionary and two forced landings.

Rodgers navigated by the "iron compass", following the railroad tracks across the country. Lloyd traced the original route as closely as he could, though it led him over cities and power lines where pastures and open farmland had stretched 75 years before.

In 1911, Cal Rodgers' Vin Fiz flight cost Armour $180,000, equivalent to over $2 million in today's dollars. Don Wallen paid $100,000 in 1986. That covered the whole works: the plane, Lloyd's and his crew's expenses, spare parts, and promotional brochures and posters.

In return for that $100,000 ConAgra received an immeasurable amount of free publicity. Live coverage from "Good Morning, America" and a front-page spread in *USA Today* kicked off the Vin Fiz's journey. Local and national newspapers, wire services, radio stations and television networks reported on the flight as Lloyd made his way to California.

One hundred and forty people who had witnessed Rodgers' original flight autographed the wings of the modern biplane. A 97-year-old Indiana resident recalled pushing Rodgers' craft, powered by two propellers attached to the engine by a bicycle chain, to help coax it off the ground. Jim Lloyd rode the firetruck in Middletown, Illinois, and got his hair cut in a 1911 barber chair in Kent, Ohio. Nebo, Illinois, named a street after the Vin Fiz.

On November 11, 1986, Lloyd and the Vin Fiz glided into Long Beach Municipal Airport with a bandaged propeller, a loose muffler and a deflated tire. Hundreds of people, a presidential telegram, and a buffet luncheon of ConAgra provender awaited him.

After the hoopla, Jim Lloyd returned to his job at IBM. The Vin Fiz replica soars from the ceiling of "Western Heritage – Omaha's History Museum", located downtown in the former Union Pacific railway passenger terminal.

Even with such intrepid marketing, Armour's processed meat operations have yet to satisfy ConAgra's exacting financial return standards. But acquiring the meat company brought other benefits to ConAgra.

Armour's diverse and popular products help make ConAgra a complete and major provider of "center of the plate" protein items for foodservice and retail customers.

Armour had been a leader in the food service business for 25 years, since the company first sold boil-in-the-bag entrees to that market. By the time ConAgra acquired Armour, the firm offered food service products like frozen entrees in disposable aluminum steam-table trays, five-pound boil-in-the-bag entrees, low-sodium bland diet frozen entrees for hospitals and nursing homes, and airline in-flight meals.

In 1979, Armour's frozen food division had successfully launched

Turn of the century Armour branch – at Lexington, Kentucky.

"Dinner Classics," the nation's first line of premium frozen dinners; later the company unveiled "Classic Lite", the first complete calorie-controlled frozen dinner. By 1985, Armour offered 16 varieties of "Dinner Classic" and nine of "Classic Lite", and held the number one spot in national sales of premium frozen dinners.

Armour's dairy product company marketed cheese, butter, spray-dry products, eggs and food oils. Workers at Armour's Kentucky spray-dry plant processed the dehydrated cheese, butter, eggs, shortening, cream and chicken fats increasingly sought by national packaged foods manufacturers. Armour Star produced the country's top-selling lard, that traditional pie crust ingredient. And statistics showing that between 1960 and 1985 the average American's annual cheese consumption jumped from 8.3 to 22 pounds gave plenty of incentive to focus on cheese marketing.

In the fall of 1984 ConAgra acquired Northern States Beef, Inc., an Omaha-based boneless beef and hamburger processor that supplied fast food restaurants, school lunch programs and the federal government. In the Armour Fresh Meat Company, ConAgra combined Northern States Beef with Armour's Nampa, Idaho, cattle processing plant and its Dixon, California, lamb processing plant.

Armour's Pfaelzer Brothers Company marketed premium meats and gourmet foods by mail. Pfaelzer's full-color catalog offered mouth-watering items — including seafood, smoked salmon, cheeses, fruits, and elegant hors d'oeuvres and desserts — for birthday, anniversary, wedding and holiday gifts as well as for business gifts and employee incentive awards. A pioneer in the use of dry ice to ship beef, Pfaelzer used careful, labor-intensive packaging and freezing methods to ensure that customers enjoyed the full flavors of the company's fine meats and foods.

In all, Armour brought a diverse lot of popular products to the ConAgra inventory. Moreover, its acquisition enrolled the company in the ranks of the big-time meat processors, although half a decade later than ConAgra had planned when it negotiated with MBPXL. ConAgra had become a provider of all the major protein foods dubbed "the center of the plate" — chicken, turkey, fish, pork, lamb and beef.

CHAPTER 12

MIKE HARPER:
HARD-WORKING
AND HIGH-FLYING

MIKE HARPER: HARD-WORKING AND HIGH-FLYING

HE woke up in the morning with heartburn," recalls Josie Harper. "He took some bubbles for it and it seemed to go away."

It was September 14, 1985. Mike Harper had been in San Francisco on business, and he and his wife, Josie, stayed over the weekend to visit his mother. On that Saturday morning they planned to take her to lunch at a restaurant 10 minutes from their hotel.

"Mike's mother wanted to stop at the drugstore, so we did that on the way," Mrs. Harper continues. "As we were walking to the restaurant this heartburn came back. His mother and I went into the restaurant and he went back to the drugstore for something for the heartburn. We had lunch and his mother had another little errand; Mike said the heartburn was really getting bad.

"So we took him back to his mother's apartment and that's when he started perspiring. We could tell that this was something more than just an upset stomach."

Harper remembered that on the way in from the airport he'd seen a hospital off the freeway. Josie rushed him to the emergency ward.

"It happened to be a heart center," says Josie. "The doctors said 'You're having a heart attack'."

Harper's doctor chided him for not having come in first thing in the morning. But at least medication, rather than corrective surgery, was the only treatment he needed.

Harper stayed at Mary Seaton Hospital for 10 days. ConAgra dispatched a company plane to fly him to the Mayo Clinic, where his son practiced medicine, for additional tests. From Rochester, Minnesota, it was home to Omaha.

"I think he was home a week or two, and then he sort of had an office in the living room for a couple of hours each day," explains Mrs. Harper. "It was a month to six weeks before he started going back downtown."

"All the presidents kept their parts of the company going," recalls Mary Robbins, Mike Harper's administrative assistant. "But he was always available to chit-chat. He was raring to go again."

Con Agra's chief executive's heart attack causes him to change some habits — operating company presidents keep things going without change.

According to Josie Harper, her strong-willed spouse became a model patient. Before his heart attack, Harper smoked heavily. Many times he had quit for months only to start again; if he picked up one cigarette he was right back to his daily 2½ packs.

Harold Schuler joined Mike Harper in his periodic attempts to kick the habit.

"We'd find ourselves going to other smokers' offices and smoking their cigarettes until it got to be so embarrassing we had to go buy some," Schuler confesses. "Until Mike's heart attack, he didn't quit smoking with any conviction. He'd do it because he knew he should and the doctor would nag him about it."

According to Schuler, Harper's disposition used to suffer mightily when he tried to go cold turkey.

"Nobody wanted to be around him," says Schuler. "And very few people could tell him 'You're being a miserable horse's ass, Mike.'"

Schuler appointed himself to the task. When Mike's temper frayed, Schuler would knock on his door and announce that he needed to talk to him for a few minutes.

"He'd say 'Yeah, you're going to give me a horse's ass lecture again'," quotes Schuler. "I'd tell him he was right. 'He'd say I know it, but I really wasn't a horse's ass because that guy deserved it.' I'd agree, but I'd point out that he wouldn't have behaved the same way if he had been smoking. And he'd say 'Got any cigarettes?'"

Harper's San Francisco experience cured him. Observes his wife: "That was his last cigarette." He quit for good and, according to Schuler, stayed pleasant while doing it.

Harper took up walking and stationary bike-riding, in addition to the skiing, tennis and golf he already enjoyed. The 6' 6", 245-pound executive passed up many of the rich, heavy foods he liked and reduced his weight to 220. He took a few three-day weekends in Aspen, Colorado.

Harper also eased away from his hectic travel schedule, reduced his attendance at civic events and cut back on speechmaking. "Most people who have heard me speak probably will think this is a good idea," he told a reporter from the local daily.

He even slowed his pace at work — a little.

"He's definitely a Type A personality," observes Mrs. Harper. "He has to try to change that. I think it makes it worse if you think about that too much."

After 35 years of marriage, Josie Harper was accustomed to her husband's high-gear personality. The couple met in 1949 on the South Side of Chicago, where Josie vacationed with her aunt and uncle. Josie was lazing on the beach of Lake Michigan when a friend introduced her to a young University of Chicago MBA student. Like Josie, he was from South Bend, Indiana.

"It was odd that we hadn't met there because South Bend isn't that big," comments Josie. "But I'm two years older than Mike. At that time I wouldn't have looked at somebody two years younger."

She did look in Chicago, and the two were married the following year. Mike had just finished his graduate program and the Harpers immediately moved to Lansing, Michigan, where he worked for General Motors. Josie kept the books at the Michigan State University student bank — for 9½ months. She quit when eldest daughter, Kathy, was born. Carolyn and Charles Michael Jr. arrived in quick succession.

In 1955 Harper joined Pillsbury and the family moved to Minneapolis. After Elizabeth was born in 1959, their St. Louis Park house seemed a tad small, so they bought a home in the village of Excelsior, at Lake Minnetonka.

Harper, a fairly active member of the Republican Party, served as an Excelsior village councilman for five years. Then a group of neighbors, concerned about a rumored lakefront condominium development, drafted him to run for mayor. He held that position for one year. He resigned it to come to Omaha.

"I knew he wasn't happy at Pillsbury," says Josie Harper. "He had the feeling that he was going to go sideways or not have any kinds of a challenge at Pillsbury. He had always liked challenges, and I was sure that if anybody could help ConAgra he certainly could. I think Mr. Daugherty gave him all the confidence in the world. He knew that there were good people there.

"Financially, we knew that it could only go up. It could go either up or just out."

Uprooting the family after 19 years in Minnesota was no small task. Josie stayed in Excelsior for nearly a year after Mike started at ConAgra, organizing the household as well as helping two of her daughters plan their weddings. When she finally moved south, Omaha more than fulfilled her expectations.

"Mike always liked challenges... I was sure that if anybody could help ConAgra he certainly could" — Josie Harper.

"Our impression of Omaha was that it was like the plains," she recalls. "We were quite happy to see that it was hilly and that it really was a pretty city. There are awfully nice people here. Just lovely, nice people who make you feel welcome and include you.

"It's actually much easier to get acquainted here than in Excelsior. We lived there at least 8 years before the house that we lived in was called 'the Harper house' instead of 'the Bidwell house'."

Consultant Jim Rude recalls flying into Omaha shortly after Harper joined ConAgra, to inspect the company's management information system. Josie hadn't arrived yet, and Mike invited Jim out to his new home in Omaha's wooded Ponca Hills.

"He had two lawn chairs in the family room and that was it in the house," says Rude. "We sat there and had a couple of drinks and talked about what he'd gotten himself into."

That night, Rude's accomodations at the Blackstone Hotel were considerably more inviting than Harper's stark quarters. On later visits, the consultant frequently bunked at the Harpers'. But being Mike's houseguest had its drawbacks.

"You get awakened at 5:00 in the morning," Rude complains. "I never could understand it. Josie would get up and have breakfast ready by 6:00 and by 6:15 we'd be on our way downtown. And that was a late morning."

"Mike and I both happen to be early risers," says retired ConAgran Harold Schuler. "We used to have coffee almost every morning, for 20 or 30 minutes. Usually I would get to the office about 6:30 and Mike would be there when I got there."

Harper's heart attack curtailed his marathon coffee drinking. He now drinks sugar-free hot chocolate, hot tea or diet caffeine-free cola instead. And he no longer arrives at the office quite as promptly as in the past.

"Some mornings I look at the first notes on his computer and the times on them are 6:00, 6:15," explains Mary Robbins. "But then I've noticed lately he's coming in later. Around 7:00 or 7:15."

Mike's up-at-dawn habits are part of a generally conservative lifestyle, far from the jet set existence of some internationally renowned chief executive officers.

"Mike tends to be an early-to-bed kind of guy," says Harold Schuler. "His style of living is basically not too different now than it was when he moved to Omaha. The shoes he's wearing are probably from J. C. Penney. He gets a haircut when there's a board of directors meeting. He'll say 'I haven't got that much hair, and those haircuts cost four bucks!'"

"He has always been relatively conservative in his personal finances. He cringes if he has to pay over $100 for a sportcoat. Well, $100 sportcoats disappeared five or 10 years ago. I kid Mike occasionally about when he's going to start spending some of his money and indulging himself. He says 'What the hell. I've got everything I want'."

Schuler thinks Harper's distaste for pomp and ceremony operates as a plus on Wall Street.

MIKE HARPER: HARD-WORKING AND HIGH-FLYING 209

"Wall Street analysts see Mike Harper sit up there and cross his legs, and there will be a hole in the bottom of his shoe or the heels will be run down," he comments. "Here's a guy who is very eloquent and knowledgeable talking about business, and who is so unimpressed with himself that he doesn't worry whether he's wearing the latest tassel loafers."

Harper's nonchalant approach to fashion — as expressed in his penchant for short sleeves — nettled an unidentified public relations specialist, however. At a board meeting, a photographer took a series of candid shots for the 1985 annual report. When the report was published, it contained the obligatory page of directors' pictures. But the photo of Harper looked strange. Closer scrutiny revealed that a vigilant artist had inserted a white band around Harper's wrist, to fill in the undignified gap between hand and jacket sleeve.

"Someone drew cuffs on the picture," recalls Mary Robbins. "All the others had their sleeves sticking out of their jackets by just the appropriate amount. We laughed about that."

With his Husker-sized frame it's just as well that Harper is no clotheshorse.

"I don't select his suits," explains his wife. "I do buy just about everything else for him and it isn't easy. Everything is a big and tall size, so it's hard to dress him."

Hence the short sleeves and practical shoes. For some occasions, however, Harper just can't get away with wearing them.

"Mike is obviously not comfortable in a tuxedo," observes his friend Schuler. "But he can put one on and go to dinner with some of the top senators in Washington or at the White House. He cleans up pretty nice."

In an effort to trim his figure from "big and tall" to just "tall", the newly health-conscious Harper has reduced his breakfasts since the days when Josie used to head for the kitchen by 5:30 a.m. These days he favors juice and toast in the morning.

"He's a very easy person to feed," says Josie. "He likes all the casseroles that you could throw at him. Pasta, chili, Mexican food. In fact I have to be careful because those are the things he likes best."

At lunchtime, Harper usually retreats to his office for a meal prepared by cook DiDi Graves in her nearby kitchen. If guests are visiting, DiDi may serve lunch in Harper's executive conference room, which doubles as a dining area. Both host and guests know they'll be served the best: ConAgra products, like Singleton shrimp, Banquet chicken and Armour meats.

"Right now Mr. Harper is on a turkey kick," Mrs. Robbins says. "He eats turkey sausage whenever there's a breakfast. For lunch he eats lots of turkey. Ground turkey patties. Turkey sandwiches. Even chili with turkey."

Having a little fun is part of ConAgra management's style — peanut butter for breakfast with Willie Nelson is a case in point.

In July of 1987, CEO Harper hosted an impromptu breakfast meeting with pony-tailed Willie Nelson. The celebrated entertainer had flown in to sign an agreement with the University of Nebraska to hold the FarmAid III concert in Lincoln's Memorial Stadium.

Word of Nelson's visit to ConAgra headquarters didn't reach Harper until 15 minutes before the singer arrived. Harper scurried to the kitchen to scout out some Peavey's Home Brand peanut butter. The result: a feast of peanut butter, toast, orange juice and coffee for Harper, Nelson and several businessmen including Bob Kerrey, Nebraska's former governor and current U. S. senator.

"Mike enjoyed doing that kind of thing; he's a real person," says corporate communications vice president Walt Casey. "He's not a bit pretentious. And we have a lot of fun. That's part of our style and I think it comes through.

"A typical image of a corporation is stuffy and big, overbearing. A lot of them deserve to be thought of that way. I sure as hell think we're not that way and I hope we never get that way."

It's not likely, given Harper's well-known ability to laugh at himself. Harold Schuler recalls how Harper ended up with a fireman's hat on his head, and egg on his face.

"Six or seven years ago there was a fire in a grain elevator in North Omaha," says Schuler. "It turned out that the elevator belonged to another company, but Mike saw it from the airport and was absolutely convinced that it was ours. He got in his car and rushed over there. Mike is very much of a take-charge guy. He knocked on a nearby resident's door to use the phone and called Bud Morrison to tell him his elevator was on fire."

Morrison reassured Harper that the elevator didn't belong to ConAgra. Mike energetically insisted otherwise. Morrison called Bob Newman, ConAgra's head of flour milling operations.

"They drove over to their elevators, which obviously were not on fire," explains Schuler. "Mike was pretty embarrassed because he had really been very intense, raising hell about it. Six months later at one of our big management meetings Morrison presented Mike Harper with a fireman's helmet, since he's 'the guy in charge of fire alarms'.

"Mike took it beautifully, and he wore the hat around at the meeting. He was demonstrating to people that they could needle him too."

Harper's work hours reveal him to be hard-working, but appreciative of his time at home. On weekdays, he generally arrives at his downtown office by 7:00 a.m. and leaves by 6:00 p.m. Once in a great while he'll duck out for the golf course at 4:00, but on most late afternoons he takes 30 minutes to review his schedule with Mary Robbins. On Saturday or Sunday — but not both — he goes in early and finishes by midmorning.

Although he often dictates from his home or his car, he tries to leave his briefcase at the office. Evenings are reserved for dinner, relaxation and a comfortable chair with the evening paper or an absorbing war novel. Unless there's a computer problem gnawing at him.

"If he has a problem on his home computer, nine times out of ten he'll work on that," says Mrs. Harper. "I guess if he's thinking about anything to do with figures, he'll put it on there to work it through. On a Saturday he can sit there for eight hours."

Jim Rude swears that Josie Harper wasn't always so sanguine about Harper's hours at the computer.

"She told me once if I didn't get that damn thing out of the house she was going to burn it," he says.

Harper's interest in home computers is matched by his fascination with employing computers in the business world. According to Rude, no chief executive officer in the country uses the computer to assist him as effectively as Harper does. The ConAgra CEO learned the value of a well-organized and responsive information system while still at Pillsbury.

"We had a very sophisticated management information system at Pillsbury," observes Rude. "Pillsbury was one of the first companies in the country to use what they call 'time-sharing', where you use the terminal in your office. And Mike was one of the two or three executives able to write his own programs and run his own system."

"Whoever controls the information controls the company" — Terry Hanold's philosophy at Pillsbury guides Harper in shaping ConAgra's computer system for the future.

"When Terry Hanold was president at Pillsbury his philosophy was that whoever controls the information controls the company. Harper has followed that."

Even in the early days of computers, when the printer would spit out a yellow sheet of paper about as glamorous as a teletype, the complex machines — and those who understood them — wielded a certain clout. Harper recalls a Pillsbury manager who brought a computer printout to a meeting to bolster his position. Impressed by the data and models he presented, the other executives agreed to his recommendations.

"After the meeting I found out that this guy had typed that sheet out on the computer," relates Harper. "It had never been a model or anything. He just typed out the answer he wanted and put it on computer paper. That really made it important."

ConAgra — Nebraska Consolidated Mills, actually — had bought its first computer back in the 1960s.

In 1962, Earle Olson, a production manager at the Puerto Rico flour mill, and Marv Wilkening, a Decatur animal nutritionist, asked the NCMCo. board of directors for a computer to do least-cost poultry feed formulations for the company's feed mills. They assured the board that with the 20K memory of an IBM 1620, they could create and solve eight formulas a day.

By 1969, NCMCo. was using computer programs to store broiler production records, catalog fixed assets, record sales analyses, evaluate new business ventures and select plant sites. In 1971, the newly named ConAgra inaugurated a computerized record system and cost performance analysis service for Puerto Rican dairy farmer customers.

Under Harper's patronage, ConAgra's computer system took giant steps forward.

Shortly after Harper joined ConAgra, he met with Jim Rude and Joe Petty, now vice president of management information systems, to outline the data needed to carry out his new duties. In order to understand the company, Harper felt it was essential to have certain information almost immediately.

"But he said 'There's one problem you two have, and I'm glad it's not my problem'," says Rude. "'You can't spend any money to do this, because we haven't got any!'"

Ultimately, with Harper's input, ConAgrans Joe Petty and Rita Albers designed the company's new management information system. An indispensable part of that system is the executive information system, or EIS, which supplies top management with up-to-date information. Harper set down two criteria for the EIS: it had to quickly provide a broad spectrum of information, and it had to be easy to use.

Information available on EIS ranges from personal memos and news announcements, to commodity market quotations, to financial models and sales figures.

"At our Monday morning meetings, we project every company's numbers up on the computer screen," says Harper. "It's fascinating. Some of the top officers in the company don't know what is going to come up there. Some of their businesses, whose headquarters are out in the boonies, have sent in their data remotely. The computer adds it up and projects it on the screen.

"Most of the guys out there are smart enough to call their boss here and whisper 'Hey, I'm going to change my estimate.' But there have been a few surprises."

Harper's computer can graph the profit curve for each IOC over any given period of time. It can give him the numbers that each company sent in with its strategic plan. It can provide an up-to-the-minute report on ConAgra's borrowing costs. It can also deliver the mail.

Harper receives at least 70% of his internal correspondence on the computer. ConAgrans call their computerized communications system "the tube".

"The computer is just fantastic," says Mary Robbins. "All of those little notes that we used to type out, maybe two lines on a sheet of paper, Mr. Harper does on the computer."

"I hardly ever dictate an internal letter any more," says Harper. "Once in a blue moon. But I will peck out something short on that darned tube. I don't put in a lot of adjectives because I don't want to type them. I use a lot of abbreviations because I can't spell very well and I can't type fast.

"That gets you to the essential elements of a message. At most two or three sentences. These messages are funny to look at sometimes, because they're written by guys like me."

"If you want to ask something you just type a short question on there or phrase a couple of paragraphs," adds Bud Morrison. "You know, if you call somebody up and say 'What would you do if we could get some corn at 20 over?', sometimes the first answer you get is going to be wrong.

"If Mike or I call someone and ask a question, it puts the other person under a lot of pressure. After he gives an answer and hangs up he might say to himself, 'That isn't quite right. I wish I'd thought of this or that.' Sending a message over this tube system gives a way to do that. It gives a little more time to think about the response."

Using the tube does away with wasteful "telephone tag" and makes time zone differences irrelevant. It allows a traveling ConAgra executive to pick up messages by stopping in at any ConAgra office with EIS access.

It also eliminates what Harper terms "a hierarchical phenomenon".

As he explains it: "I call another ConAgra executive and the secretary says 'He's in a meeting. Who's calling?' I say it's Mike Harper. 'Oh, I'll get him!' I beg the secretary not to interrupt the person, but by God you cannot stop her, because her boss has left some standing instruction that if the baldheaded old guy calls, to come get him.

"If you write a note instead, it's not disruptive. If it's urgent, you call. But if you just want some information or have a question that can be answered at some point in time, you put it on the tube."

Even years after Harper first asked Jim Rude to help design an information system, the budget-conscious chief executive retained his dedication to getting the most computer power for his money.

When ConAgra purchased Banquet the company had 11 months to transfer off of RCA's New Jersey-based computer network. Rude and his colleagues started developing the operational plan in February, and by the end of May they had it ready. It scheduled the move two months early — by November 1. Rude presented the proposed plan to Harper.

"We made a damn good plan and a damn good presentation," declares Rude. "When we got all through Harper just said 'It's not good enough. We're going to cut over on August 1st.'"

Rude told Harper there was no damn way to do that.

Harper replied, "August 1st is the date and that's when it's going to be done."

It was. ConAgra rewired its computer building, added power, rebuilt the data center, changed operating systems and absorbed Banquet's operations. Rude gives the credit to Joe Petty and his staff.

"Joe was against the decision, but once it was made, he told me to give him the plan and get out of the way," says Rude. "That's a typical Harper story. However, too many people take Mike too literally when he makes those kinds of statements. He also is a very logical and rational man. If you ain't going to make it and there are good reasons why, he ain't going to question it."

When ConAgra and Peavey combined their computer systems, Rude helped develop a plan that saved $2.7 million in the cost of collecting information. Harper wouldn't accept any savings under $5 million.

"No matter how long we kept saying 2.7, he kept saying 5," recalls the systems consultant. "So we came in at about $4.3 million. And he was plenty happy.

"He pushed for $5 million, because if he hadn't we might have gotten $2 million rather than $2.7 million. And as it was, because he pushed we got $4.3 million."

For an early-to-bed, conservative, logical, rational kind of guy, Mike Harper has one interest that might seem out of character. He flies. He learned at age 56.

"He has always been fascinated by airplanes, and always wanted to learn how to fly," says Josie Harper. "Finally one day he said to himself 'This is ridiculous. If I want to learn how to fly, why don't I do it?' And so he did."

Harper signed up for flying lessons at Omaha's Sky Harbor Air Service, and studied on the weekends and in his spare time for several months. Josie took a "pinch hitter's" course. Together they occasionally travel in a Cessna 182 four-seater.

"I was not nervous about his first solo flight," Mrs. Harper says. "I was nervous on my first flight with him. Since then I took the 'pinch hitter's' course so that I can fly the airplane and probably land it once. That's all that's necessary, and I'm not so sure I wouldn't bend something. But I have all the confidence in him. I enjoy it."

Harper approached his aeronautical studies with his characteristic self-discipline and wholehearted attention.

"He went at it just like he goes at everything else," observes Harold Schuler. "He just became an absolute student of it. He wanted to know all about navigation and radio, not just about flying the airplane but about all that's involved with it.

"Our company pilots tell me he is the most thorough, careful, meticulous guy about all the pre-flight steps, following all of the safety regulations. That's typical of Mike. If he does something he's going to do it very, very well."

In 1978, Harper had hired chief pilot Jim Hollenbeck to establish a corporate flight department. While commercial air service from Omaha's Eppley Airfield to certain of the nation's major cities was relatively convenient, flights to many other destinations involved time-consuming layovers. Out of necessity, ConAgra had sold a Lear Jet in the mid-1970s; the company replaced it when Hollenbeck started.

Now, ConAgra's Omaha hangar houses three jets: two Lear 35s and one Gulfstream II. Two Citations and a Cessna are kept in Greeley, Colorado. Seven or eight pilots and three maintenance workers staff the Omaha facility; a proportionately smaller contingent operates out of Greeley.

"The pilots will fly four days a week, on the average," says Hollenbeck. "They average six days a month overnight, but they fly some really odd hours. The four days is deceiving. For each day you fly you might have to get up at 3:00 a.m. It sounds like — and is — a really good life, but the pilots give five and a half days to the company every week.

"Typically I schedule pilots a week in advance, but we always have late changes. After all, the whole reason for the corporate flight department is to be responsive to the needs of the corporation. About 80% of our flights are booked one to two weeks in advance; it's the other 20% that changes everything."

The Gulfstream II is a 62,000 pound craft with room for 12 passengers, three crew members, a full galley and a lavatory. Half of ConAgra's G-II flights are international, primarily to Europe and South America. Often an international flight will carry eight to ten passengers heading for different destinations in the same general area.

At 18,000 pounds, the Lear 35s are significantly smaller than the Gulfstream II. Where the G-II flies about eight days a month, the eight-passenger Lears are busy running shorter trips five or six days a week.

The "computer age" at ConAgra also becomes the "jet age" and the corporate flight department grows with the company's operations.

In 1985, at the urging of Harper and several other Omaha businessmen, the Omaha Airport Authority provided land for improved corporate flying facilities. Formerly, the rather spartan facilities were crowded on the west edge of the airport, near the public terminal. Now, a series of new, well-appointed private hangars stands on the east side of the airport, between the main runways and the Missouri River.

Harper considers it important to have a first-class hangar and private lounge, because they shape a visitor's first impression of the community.

"The first thing seen by any visitor we bring in on company business is the airplane," comments Hollenbeck. "We try to keep them in absolutely top-notch shape inside and out. Actually one plane does not quite measure up to our standards yet. We need to put some paint on it.

"The second thing is when they walk in the door of the hangar. Whether or not they like these two things leaves an impression in their minds, so they'll remember us."

The flight lounge located in ConAgra's 150 x 100 foot hangar stands out from the ranks of conventional, pleasant, corporate reception areas.

"We were working with a designer to get a comfortable place with nice rest rooms, a kitchen, a place where we could have a bite to eat and drink," recalls Hollenbeck. "I drew up the basic design and wanted the designer to finish up. When she did, it looked like a very nice reception room just like any other corporate reception area."

Hollenbeck met with Mike Harper, Jim Kennedy and vice president of public affairs Marty Colladay.

"Mike said 'Why don't we do something different?'" he continues. "'Why don't we make it a World War I ready room?' I asked Mike if he had any idea what that looked like. He said 'No, but I'm sure you will get the idea.'"

Hollenbeck knew his air lore, but he had no notion of what a WWI-vintage flight room looked like. Nor, understandably, did the designer.

Retired Air Force Lieutenant General Colladay came to the rescue. A designer friend of his raided her father-in-law's attic to assemble an impressive collection of World War I era memorabilia: photographs of airplanes and French airfields, as well as several air corps recruiting posters. Added to those were artifacts purchased from a collectors group the Con-Agrans tracked down.

Now the glassed-in corner room is truly one of a kind. A leather davenport, leather chairs and a fireplace invite relaxation. A map used by French pilots is displayed in the seating area and an autographed picture of Captain Eddie Rickenbacker hangs behind a dark oak bar. Lamps made of WWI-vintage shells light the room. Draped on a coat rack are an authentic World War I blouse and a well-worn leather flight jacket. The final touch is a big brass spittoon.

During sensitive acquisition negotiations, Harper may use the flight lounge for meetings with publicity-shy executives. With the telephones turned off, the perimeter gates locked, and catered food left in the refrigerator, privacy is guaranteed. Sometimes the fewer Omahans who take note of a visiting CEO, the better.

"I try not to know who I've flown in," confides assistant chief pilot Roger Haney. "The less I know the less I can let slip."

Despite his keen interest in and extensive knowledge about aviation, when Harper is an airline passenger he refrains from backseat driving. Instead he reads, dictates, or chats, often while downing an Armour sausage or a diet soda.

"He will absolutely not tell another pilot how to fly," states Schuler. "And he would be very

Harper's personal passion for flying leads him to attempt a cross-country flight record to celebrate his 60th birthday.

critical of any member of management who would attempt to override the pilot's judgment. He believes that if you've got a pro, you follow the pro's advice."

Harper's passion for flying led him to do something a little different for his 60th birthday. On September 26, 1987, he flew from San Francisco to New York, setting a world time record for a piston engine plane in the Cessna 182 weight class. Roger Haney describes the adventure.

"Mike wanted to do something having to do with aviation for his birthday," he recalls. "Originally Jim Kennedy, Jim Hollenbeck and I met with Mike and kicked around some ideas. They found some cities named Charles, and one name Mike, and there is a Harper, Kansas. But flying to those towns didn't really appeal to Mike. He liked the idea of flying across the continent."

Haney did preliminary studies on a transcontinental flight. The weather posed a problem. Since Harper is not instrument rated, he would need help if he ran into foul weather. He could fly above a solid layer of clouds, but he couldn't descend through them; he would have to stay "on top" until he found clear skies. Harper and his pilots decided he should have an instrument-rated airman along. Haney got the nod.

"I was more or less a passenger," says Haney. "My only job was to sit there and shoot an approach should it become necessary.

"It was something Mike didn't want publicity on, although there was a story in the *Omaha World-Herald*. I don't know how that leaked. It was something personal."

The Cessna 182 was modified in preparation for the flight. A "speed kit" adjusted the ailerons and flaps, in order to eke out another 10 to 15 miles an hour. The back seat was removed and an auxiliary gas tank installed in its place. And unlike Calbraith Rodgers and Jim Lloyd, Mike Harper planned his trip from west to east coast to take advantage of the prevailing winds.

Haney and Harper arose at 4:30 a.m. to be off at first light. They wanted to cross the mountains in daylight.

"With a single engine airplane you don't want to lose an engine at night," says Haney. "We picked our way through the valleys in the Rockies, at an altitude of 11,500 feet. We used a computer-generated flight plan to pick our winds and altitudes."

The two pilots' California weather service had chosen a splendid day to fly. But as Harper and Haney neared Sioux City, their refueling stop, Haney considered cutting the trip short.

"We had a small electrical problem about 100 miles from Sioux City," he explains. "The amp reading was 22 volts and it should have read

26. The alternator had kicked off."

Haney's first thought was that the alternator had quit or that its belt had been thrown off. Even the 30 minutes needed to put on a new belt would probably have blown the chance for a world record.

"I mentioned to Mike that if we weren't going to make the record, why go on," comments Haney. "He didn't share my opinion. He said 'We're going to New York today.' While we were sitting there Mike decided to try and recycle the switch. He did, and that reset it."

The airport at Sioux City had fuel trucks out on the runway so Harper didn't have to taxi in and waste time. Refueling took 14 minutes.

"We would have made the stop in less than ten," Haney notes. "We had to wait for two National Guard F-4s to take off. Just bad luck."

Harper crossed the country in 16 hours and 11 minutes, with a weak tail wind and his one fuel stop. Haney never touched the controls.

"What Mike did is considered a pretty good accomplishment among private pilots," observes Haney. "It would be an accomplishment for any pilot, amateur or professional. And it would be tough for anybody, amateur or pro, to do it better than he did it."

That doesn't seem to surprise Haney.

CHAPTER 13

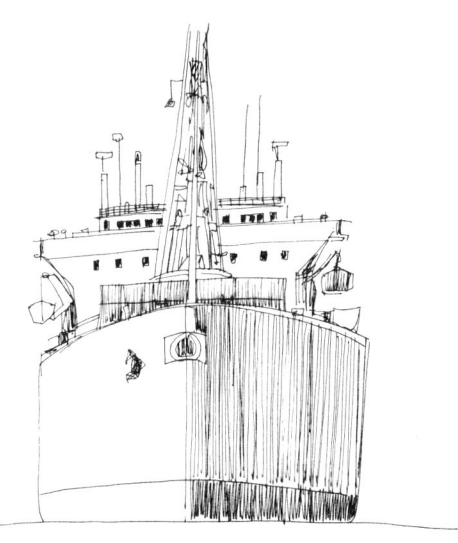

TOWARD NEW
HORIZONS

L ONG before pilot Mike Harper crossed the continental United States in record time, ConAgra had stepped beyond America's shores for new business ventures.

In the 1960s Nebraska Consolidated Mills had dipped a toe into international waters with a series of ventures, some — Puerto Rico, Spain and Portugal — successful, and some — Australia, the Dominican Republic — not.

The successes remained a part of ConAgra, although by the mid-1980s they constituted a relatively small part of the company's operations. By that time, however, an increasing number of American businesses were becoming aware of the potential for big profits, as well as big headaches, in overseas markets. ConAgra was not to be left out.

"The first step in getting a corporation into the international business is management's decision to do it," says George Doering. "That happened in 1983. Management made the commitment, and said that it was something ConAgra needed to make plans for."

At a meeting held in Omaha, top executives agreed that ConAgra could benefit by expanding upon the Peavey Company's experience in international grain exports. According to Doering, three factors stimulated ConAgra's increased involvement in the international marketplace.

"I'd say the number one objective was to protect the security of the company," Doering observes. "ConAgra was basically a domestic business, but the world was rapidly changing into one market. To protect ourselves we had to learn to sell, trade, market and develop our company internationally.

"Number two, we thought there was a tremendous amount of growth possibility in things that we like to do. The basic food business is tremendous worldwide, compared to just domestically. And three, we thought that sourcing materials and products, and developing resources outside of the country, were critical to the company's future growth and profits. So in the long term it just made sense strategically for us to be international."

"The food business has become a worldwide business," says Mike Harper. "In the late '50s and early '60s, if you thought about the food business you thought of it as a U.S. business. You couldn't afford to run a plant in Indiana just for the sake of the people living in Indiana; you had to think of all 48 continental states. Now it would

The food business has become a worldwide business. ConAgra makes a commitment to international business in 1983.

be just as ridiculous to think about the food business in the continental U.S. and ignore the rest of the world.

"Worldwide events have a significant impact on the food businesses in this country. Foreign government subsidies and the price of the dollar have an enormous effect. A drought in Ethiopia can affect the price of edible beans in the U.S. and other countries. The food business truly is a worldwide business. How do you live in a world like that? You have to be commercially involved in it, or read books. If you read books, it's going to be way too late to act."

Distinguished Nebraska native Clayton Yeutter, Secretary of Agriculture in the Bush administration, joined ConAgra's board in 1980. At the time, he was president of the Chicago Mercantile Exchange. He resigned from both the Merc and the ConAgra board in 1985, after President Reagan appointed him United State Special Trade Representative, a position with the rank of ambassador. Yeutter had urged Harper to move into international trade.

"Mike was hesitant to do so because he didn't feel the organization was quite ready to take on that ambitious challenge," recalls Yeutter. "As it turned out, with exchange relationships being what they were, it was probably wise that ConAgra did not start earlier.

"My point was that it takes preparation time. You can't wait until the opportunities are there and then begin to establish an international organization. You have to get it in place, and have it poised and ready when the opportunities present themselves."

When the time was ripe to commence ConAgra's global onslaught, Harper looked to Peavey Company officials as the resident authorities on international trade.

"We had just bought Peavey the year before, and we had those folks in the board room because they had done more international business than anybody else," explains Mike Harper. "But not much, just exporting. We had their management there, and we talked about this subject. We asked for a volunteer to operate a company that we named in that meeting: CTC, standing for ConAgra Trading Company. Truck Morrison made the mistake of volunteering. That started his international career."

Morrison was named president of ConAgra Trading Companies, the new organization formed to expand the scope of ConAgra's overseas grain trading. He spent the next few months scouring the industry to find the world's top traders — experienced people familiar with international markets — and to hire them away from the world's top companies. In the fall of 1983 he hired Robert Peyton.

"I worked for 17 years for a small company — called Cargill," jokes

Peyton. "We started ConAgra's international operation by setting up trading offices. That's the least expensive, most cost-effective way of getting a foothold in a foreign country. Once we establish a trading office we discover opportunities for acquisitions, for business development, for processing."

CTC opened its first trading offices in Geneva, Switzerland; Rotterdam, the Netherlands; and Buenos Aires, Argentina. As it established those offices, ConAgra also embarked upon a quest for international trading companies available for purchase, complete with experienced staff and overseas locations.

The new ConAgra Trading Company opens its first international trading offices. This foothold helps the company uncover opportunities for further development and acquisitions.

In April of 1984, ConAgra acquired 49% of the Glendon Corporation and its principal operating company Woodward & Dickerson, a 111-year-old international trading firm based in Bryn Mawr, Pennsylvania. Woodward & Dickerson specialized in trading fertilizers, agricultural and industrial chemicals, cocoa, coal, sulfur, and other commodities. The firm had offices and associated companies scattered around the world — in Australia, Canada, England, Hong Kong, India, Japan, Jordan, Korea, Malaysia, Pakistan, the Philippines, and Singapore — and agents stationed in yet another 50 nations. Eighteen months after acquiring its minority interest in Woodward & Dickerson, ConAgra purchased the remaining 51% of the company.

In March of 1985, ConAgra bought Berger and Company, an international trader of pulses, birdseeds, fertilizers, chemicals, and metals. Pulses — edible legumes like beans, peas and lentils — are the second most-used food product in the world, trailing only wheat. Berger operated offices in Argentina, Canada, Chile, Cyprus, England, Switzerland and Taiwan. Later that year, Berger bought the Pillsbury Company's Edible Protein Division, adding domestic bean originating, processing and packaging to the company's international operations.

Kurt A. Becher, an international grain and feed ingredient merchandiser, entered a 50-50 partnership with ConAgra in the summer of 1985. One of the world's largest merchandisers of fishmeal, Becher maintained headquarters in Bremen, West Germany, and offices in Hamburg, Munich, London, Paris, Sao Paulo and New York.

ConAgra was rapidly establishing strongholds around the globe. In June of 1985, the Nebraska-based agribusiness firm formed a new

ConAgra International in 1985 incorporates CTC and the several worldwide trading and marketing activities the company has developed or purchased. company — ConAgra International. Created to strengthen and build ConAgra's worldwide trading and marketing activities, ConAgra International combined Peavey Grain Companies, CTC, Woodward & Dickerson, Inc., and Berger and Company.

ConAgra International laid claim to 35 trading offices in 22 countries, as well as to extensive merchandising facilities and transportation assets in the United States. Its annual invoiced sales exceeded $5 billion although, since most trading transactions report only gross margins, ConAgra reported substantially less in net sales. George Doering was named chairman of the new company and Bill Wurster, the former head of Woodward & Dickerson, became president and chief operating officer.

"Honestly, I have no idea how I was selected to head ConAgra's international operation," states Doering. "Part of that was just the evolution of the company. I was involved in the acquisitions of Woodward & Dickerson and Berger and Company. I think that the experience of knowing these people, getting them to come into the company and being able to work with them during the acquisition phase likely just made a normal extension, because we had to bring a lot of different types of people, cultures and companies together."

By 1986 CTC, the internal development project started in 1984 to expand grain trading overseas, had added trading offices in Tokyo, Sao Paulo and Mexico City, and had formed a new business to import and distribute bulk and processed foods. Geldermann, Inc., a Chicago-based commodity futures brokerage business which Peavey Grain acquired in 1984, had in turn purchased commodity futures brokerage Agra Gill & Duffus, Inc., as well as the Heinold commodity futures brokerage and fund subsidiaries of the DeKalb Corporation. ConAgra had acquired Camerican International, which marketed food products and ingredients to processing, foodservice and retail markets through its headquarters in New Jersey, its international offices in Japan, Taiwan and Thailand, and its representatives in numerous other countries. And ConAgra had bought Squillante and Zimmerman, Inc., a New Jersey-based international marketer of fresh fruits and vegetables, which became an independent operating company under Camerican.

ConAgra's Caribbean Basic Foods Company built upon the Puerto Rican operations Nebraska Consolidated Mills had developed in 1959.

Feed, flour, brewers grits, and corn meal from Molinos de Puerto Rico remained market leaders in Puerto Rico, while ToRicos ranked among the island's top poultry producers. Spanish basic food companies Bioter-Biona, S.A., and Saprogal, S.A. — one half- and the other wholly-owned by ConAgra — were major feed and poultry producers, meat processors, and hog breeders. ConAgra also controlled a majority interest in Sapropor, S.A.R.L., a profitable Portugese company engaged in feed production, hog breeding and trout aquaculture.

Fertilizer distribution and marketing are developed into a major ConAgra business—it complemented company's feed and grain operations.

In the fall of 1986, Woodward & Dickerson's operations were restructured; the firm's international fertilizer trading operations were combined with the domestic operations of ConAgra Fertilizer Company, headquartered in Knoxville, Tennessee. This independent operating company brought together fertilizer buyers and sellers in domestic and overseas retail and wholesale markets; retailed feeds and fertilizers; and marketed fertilizers to dealers and blenders.

ConAgra got its start in the fertilizer distribution business when it acquired Montana Flour Mills in 1969. Montana Flour Mills sold around 35,000 tons of fertilizer that year. By 1984, ConAgra's annual volume in U.S. fertilizer sales had reached 1.5 million tons. When Woodward & Dickerson's fertilizer operations were moved, ConAgra Fertilizer Company had already expanded rapidly in the domestic market by acquiring Pacifex Fertilizer Company, Boyer Valley Fertilizer Company, Cropmate Company, Agribasics Fertilizer Company (initially a joint venture formed by ConAgra and the Scoular Company), and CCS Fertilizer. Under the leadership of top executives like company president Jack Farmer, who died in May of 1987, and his successor Jack Satterwhite, the fertilizer merchandising and marketing firm became one of the top three in the United States.

"In 1982 we really decided to get serious about the fertilizer business, and that is when we started beefing up our organization," recalls Satterwhite. "That is when we became a marketing, distribution and transportation company, and the entire U.S. was our marketing territory.

"Jack Farmer and I saw a window where we could expand into fertilizer, and it complemented our feed and grain operations. When we looked into our crystal ball, we could see five, eight, ten years ahead that fertilizer manufacturers would stick to manufacturing, and that we could

By 1987, ConAgra International and ConAgra Grain Companies encompass a variety of different businesses, serving a variety of different cultures.

develop a marketing company for these basic products. We take products from major producers, and then we distribute them through wholesalers, distributors, retailers, and producers."

In January of 1987, Woodward & Dickerson's nine-member international fertilizer division relocated from Bryn Mawr to Knoxville. As part of ConAgra Fertilizer Company, the international division marketed nitrogenous, phosphatic, potassium, and many other fertilizers worldwide. The combined annual fertilizer sales of Woodward & Dickerson, Petrosul International, Ltd. (formerly a Canadian subsidiary of Woodward & Dickerson) and the domestic operations of ConAgra Fertilizer Company exceeded 4 million tons.

By 1987, ConAgra International encompassed eight different businesses: Berger, Camerican, Geldermann, Woodward & Dickerson, Petrosul International, Caribbean Basic Foods Company, ConAgra Europe, and ConAgra Grain Companies. ConAgra Grain Companies in turn included Peavey Grain, Atwood-Larsen, Burdick, Alliance Grain Company, Agricol, Agro Canada Ltd., CTC, and Kurt A. Becher.

On January 2, 1987, after 37 years with Woodward & Dickerson, Bill Wurster retired. The following June, Truck Morrison was named president and CEO of ConAgra International, with Bob Peyton as executive vice president and risk officer.

ConAgra's newly global businesses brought their own unique headaches.

"It seems like there are continual mini-crises going on, and they're in parts of the world that we, who are from the Midwest, aren't very familiar with," says Truck Morrison. "You have all sorts of ethical, moral, and legal issues that are different than we would perceive them to be here. And so you're constantly trying to manage all those interests of the people from different cultures in a business that is, by nature, risk-taking and therefore risky."

Morrison explains that the most basic American notion of a legal right or responsibility may be irrelevant in an international transaction.

"A debt in our terms is not always a debt in other parts of the world," he states. "The market for the things we sell goes up and down. If a person chooses not to take the product that he contracted for three months ago, because he can now buy it cheaper, he would owe you the difference

TOWARD NEW HORIZONS

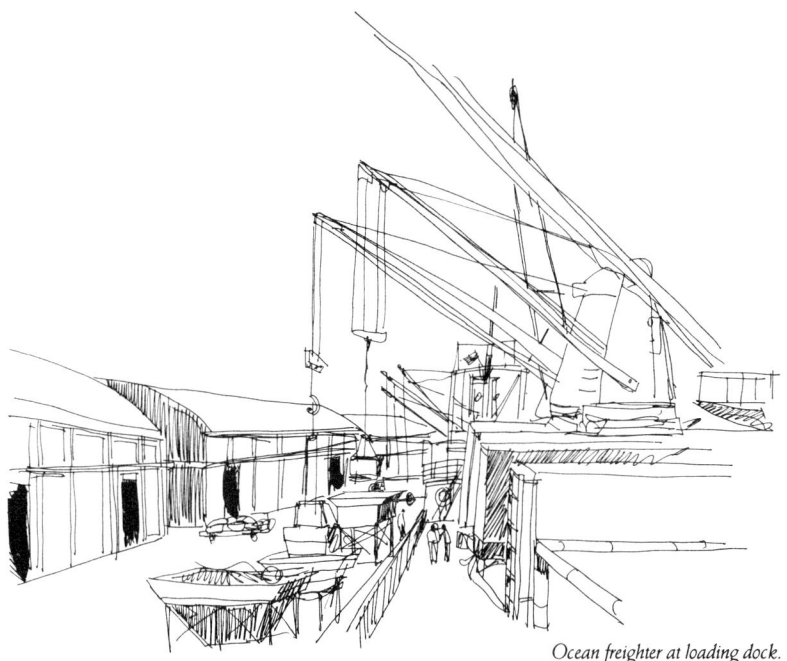

Ocean freighter at loading dock.

in the United States. In Brazil, he may not."

Sometimes the products that U.S. consumers clamor for fall with a dull thud upon foreign markets.

"In international business you have to learn what those people want and what their needs are, and produce the products that they will want to sell," explains Doering. "That means that a lot of our products developed in the United States just don't fit the market."

For example, ConAgra entered into a partnership with a Japanese distribution company that shepherds Banquet's frozen foods through Japan's complex distribution system. But American processed foods taste salty to the Japanese palate, so Banquet adjusts to fit the modified taste specifications. And, while Banquet's miniature chicken wings and chicken nuggets are well-received in Japan, its domestically popular two-pound box of fried chicken is much too large for Japanese consumers.

"Other American companies had broken ground in Japan, in terms of American chicken products," notes Phil Fletcher, now president of ConAgra, Inc., and president and chief operating officer of ConAgra Prepared Food Companies. "But we did have to change flavor profiles and quantities in packages. In Japan, both the size of the appetite and the size of the home freezer are much smaller."

In international dealings, language barriers can increase the opportunity for misunderstanding — and demolish a developing business relationship.

"In other parts of the world, the spoken word is not what the written word may say," continues Morrison. "Then when the written word comes, it may not be actually what they want to do.

"I've had seven or eight years of Spanish, but it was a long time ago. If I ever got back into it maybe I could speak it again, but right now I can't do more than order a meal in Spanish. And that's a typically American problem, so business is generally conducted in English. Yet English as spoken by a foreigner and as thought by a foreigner does not have necessarily the same meanings that it would have to you or me. If I drop a word you'd know what I was going to say. If that happened and you were Brazilian, we would have to be very explicit and further define the conversation so we both know what we really meant. And the trouble is that I'm the one making assumptions because you're speaking English, but you're thinking in Portugese and you may not be saying to me what I think I'm hearing."

To help navigate around such cultural obstacles, ConAgra developed the practice of hiring foreign nationals to head or staff its foreign offices.

"Experts who have grown up in foreign countries, have been educated in those countries and understand the needs of their people have been the backbone of our international business," asserts George Doering.

"We don't rely on interpreters overseas," notes Bob Peyton. "We look for people who are native to the country to manage the business. They have to understand the business, they have to understand the industry, they have to know where the acquisition candidates are."

"The neat thing about our overseas offices is that when we travel we always have someone from that country or area," says Doering. "They're able to help us, to translate, and to get us where we're going. Having overseas offices, which really came from our acquisitions, has been a big advantage for us in getting into the marketplace."

ConAgra's technologically advanced communications system helps bring its farthest-flung outposts closer together. In 1988, ConAgra connected major offshore offices to its computerized executive information system, to reach nearly 1000 locations worldwide. ConAgrans in the U.S. can communicate with their counterparts in Asia, 12 hours opposite in time, by leaving a message on the computer screen. It takes a few seconds — a boon when, in Peyton's words, "ConAgra has people who are into tomorrow already."

"We're pretty well scattered around Europe," adds Truck Morrison.

"We have offices in Latin America: Sao Paulo, Buenos Aires and Santiago. And Mexico City. We have offices in Asia: Tokyo, Seoul, Taipei, Hong Kong and Singapore. And joint ventures in Bangkok and Kuala Lampur.

"I think we have offices in about 25 countries. It's hard to keep track."

ConAgra now trades upwards of 80 different commodities through its international offices and agents.

> **International business for ConAgra today means: Offices in about 22 different countries trading upwards of 80 different commodities.**

Berger and Company markets to canners, packers and other buyers in the U.S. and over 60 foreign countries. The edible protein division, with its 40 bean processing plants and its packaging operations for 27 varieties of beans, peas, lentils, rice and popcorn, is one of the nation's largest packagers of beans and other dry products. The company's customers include Campbell Soup, H.J. Heinz, Pillsbury and Quaker Oats, as well as foreign governments like Angola, Algeria, Brazil, Colombia and Mexico. Berger also serves the American and International Red Cross, the European common market, and religious groups working to alleviate food shortages in various countries around the world.

Woodward and Dickerson obtains bulk commodities, food products and machinery from many lands. Its former subsidiary, the Canadian company Petrosul International, converts molten sulfur extracted from natural gas into a dry fertilizer ingredient to market to the world.

Jesse Gonzalez, president of ConAgra Shrimp Companies and Singleton Seafood Company, explains that Singleton sources 85% of its shrimp from overseas. The tender crustaceans arrive from around the globe: from Ecuador, Venezuela, Costa Rica, Guatemala, French Guiana, Guyana, India, Pakistan, and Taiwan.

Camerican imports crushed pineapple from Thailand; tuna from the Philippines; apple juice from Argentina, Austria and Hungary; quick-frozen broccoli from Mexico; mushrooms from Taiwan and the People's Republic of China; and green beans from Belgium. It also trades tulips, pectin, honey, fruit juice concentrates, cheese, anchovies, oysters, and shrimp. The company brings fresh fruits and vegetables to the U.S. during periods when American-grown products are not available. Many of these "counter-season products" are imported from South America, where the growing season is the opposite of the Northern Hemisphere's.

"The food is primarily for the industrial user, for the Banquet Foods and the Stouffers and the Stokeleys of this world," explains Truck

Morrison. "We sell to our competitors a lot."

ConAgra's operating companies in Spain and Portugal produce and distribute feed, chickens, hogs, trout, and processed meats, along with more exotic fare: Portugese eels, for example, to sell to the Dutch.

ConAgra sends about $750 million worth of exports to Japan annually. United Agri Products buys agricultural chemicals from Denmark, Israel, Italy and West Germany. Peavey Grain Companies trade grain worldwide; in a typical month, the business may lease 24 ocean-going vessels out of its West Coast and Gulf of Mexico terminals, to deliver 900,000 tons of grain overseas. And the ConAgra Flour Milling Company annually sells 4% to 5% of its product to foreign countries, including major customers Egypt, Iraq, and Saudi Arabia.

ConAgra is in the first stage of forming an organization for originating grain in South America — wheat, corn and soybeans from Argentina and soybeans and soybean meal from Brazil. ConAgra companies also bargain with the Soviet Union.

"The Russians are tough people to do business with," says Doering, who has traveled twice to their sprawling land. "They're tough bargainers. They're very good traders and they're very smart. They can make fairly rapid decisions when they need to. They're hard to reach an agreement with, but once we do so they're pretty good about living with their agreements.

"One other thing I'd like to say about the Russian people: of all the people we've dealt with there's not any of them that I haven't liked. As individuals they're very personable, very good to international people."

ConAgrans are quick to point out that ConAgra International companies don't just broker transactions.

"We find a product and we source that product and we find a customer and we deliver that product to him," states Doering. "That's much different from what a broker does."

"We deal in the physical property," states Bob Peyton. "We buy it from the producer, put it in hopper cars, load it on a vessel and ship it to the consumer."

As risk officer, Peyton analyzes the commodity positions in ConAgra's various international companies. He establishes the parameters within which to assign each company its own risk limit, and monitors each company's position with respect to that limit. One object is to avoid a disaster like the one that preceded Harper's arrival at ConAgra.

"Whenever we have a discussion about position limits we've always set everything up on the basis of a worst case scenario," explains Peyton. "Which is 1973."

Under Harper's stewardship, the excesses of that year are unlikely. He and his executives have rapidly transformed a successful domestic business into an ever-growing, internationally-based powerhouse.

"They've done a magnificent job of developing the international entity," says Secretary Yeutter. "An international trading organization has to be able to go where the demand is and the purchasing power is. That changes constantly, so the organization has to be very flexible. Mike's strategy of having an entity and a system that can be responsive anywhere at any time is a sound one."

"Mike Harper's commitment to build the international business has been very important," says George Doering. "Some of the contacts he has gained over the last 10 to 15 years have given us entrees in the international area. He's always had a good feel for the agricultural industry in the United States. He's been able to participate on some important committees at different government levels and upon request from trade groups. So we've always felt like he understands the ag business, the economics behind the business, and their importance to a food company.

"And I think Mike has grown to have a real feel of business internationally. He believes very strongly that this is one marketplace; it's the world."

For the future, ConAgra International targets specific markets for expansion. Company executives see tremendous growth potential in Japan, Hong Kong, Korea, the Philippines, Singapore, and other highly developed Asian locations with strong consumer demand. In addition, South American countries like Argentina,

Loading grain sacks for export.

Risk in dealing in international commodities, as in other company businesses, gets viewed in relation to a worst case scenario — which is 1973, the year of ConAgra's trauma.

Brazil and Chile are high-consuming areas whose low-cost agricultural producers use advanced technology.

"We see the international business becoming more involved as a processor and producer of a finished or value-added product," forecasts Doering. "ConAgra will not just export. We may produce in different countries for sale in other countries."

Doering points out that the prospect of growth has never frightened ConAgrans.

"As we grow internationally, one of our most important advantages will be that we just don't get into situations that we can't control," he comments. "We're not going to do some crazy wild things to grow, without having our risk manageable and the growth under control from an accounting and financial standpoint. Because there is a lot of international business that is risky.

"We would never tell anybody that we are not going to have any more surprises. We're always going to have country shocks, political barriers, changes in political stability, economic changes that occur because of the wilder swings in the international market. We are also going to have some good things happen on the up side because of that. The good and the bad will more than balance out. We feel that we have a lot of profit opportunities."

"As we get more and more involved with other countries, we become less parochial," adds Truck Morrison. "I am and will always be an American, but when the Argentine corn crop fails I used to be totally centered around saying 'Hooray! It's good for us'. Now I say 'Oh, my God,' because we're an exporter of corn in Argentina.

"We have a definite strategy of spreading our political and environmental risk. We are now in almost all the origin countries in the world for grain and pulses."

Morrison notes that Cargill and Continental are currently the two large international grain houses. ConAgra is the challenger.

"Cargill has been overseas since the Second World War, building an infrastructure for 30 years," says Morrison. "We've been doing it for three or four years. They're way ahead, but we're growing. If you look at who's growing the fastest, it will almost always be perceived as ConAgra."

"At this point I guess the grain business is our primary thrust, but

Traditional granary for farm storage in Spain.

secondarily Berger and Company will become a big company worldwide for us," predicts Peyton. "Longer term, the products that Camerican deals with have a lot of potential. Tomato paste, olives, fresh and frozen fruits and vegetables."

Clayton Yeutter expects a worldwide increase in food production to heighten ConAgra's trading opportunities.

"Some of those countries that have been major importers may not be major importers in the future, if their own food production rises," he explains. "At the same time, that's simplistic. A lot of countries will begin to import more, even as they produce more, because their standards of living rise and they try to upgrade their diets.

"All in all, what we're likely to see is that some countries will reduce and others will increase their level of imports in the coming years. But there ought to be a substantial amount of business out there."

Yeutter also offers a novel solution to the United States' international trade deficit: mass-producing ConAgrans.

"If we could clone Mike Harper in the

Cargill and Continental Grain are currently the two largest international grain houses. "But...if you look at who's growing fastest, it will almost always be perceived as ConAgra"
— Morrison.

American business community, our trade problems and a whole lot of other economic problems would be over," claims Yeutter. "I truly believe that Harper's performance at ConAgra may well be the most impressive executive performance of anybody in the U.S. business community over the last decade.

"And a lot of it was just done with sheer people skills. He surrounded himself with very talented people, gave them a sense of direction, provided the minimum levels of supervision required and turned them loose."

CHAPTER 14

STAKING A CLAIM IN
CATTLE COUNTRY

A CLAIM IN CATTLE COUNTRY

CONAGRA'S interests run the gamut of the food industry, but because the home office is in Omaha, ConAgra's executives are easily reminded that meat is an important contributor to the company's resources. A drive of less than a dozen miles from the office can take those executives past cattle grazing in green pastures or standing head to head in giant feedlots, or hogs rooting on the rolling prairie hills.

The meat industry surrounds Omaha, and ConAgra has steadily increased its stake in that industry by purchasing red meat processors that offer good profits and good management. One of the first important acquisitions was E.A. Miller, Inc., of Hyrum, Utah.

"I think there were two or three things that made us attractive to ConAgra," speculates beef processor John Miller. "One was the fact we were profitable. And another was that they recognized we had a lot of management talent. Third, I think ConAgra saw a need to integrate into the beef business and felt we would be an important component in that process."

In 1936 John's grandfather, Utah rancher E.A. Miller, decided to go into the meat packing business to supplement the meager earnings from his cattle operation. He constructed a small building, with a 20- by 30-foot cattle kill floor and a 12- by 14-foot cooler, to slaughter three or four of his cattle a day for sale to local merchants. Even by Depression-era standards, it was a humble undertaking.

Nine years later E.A.'s two sons, Lynn and Earnest Jr., became full partners in E.A. Miller, Inc., the family meat business. E.A. died in 1954, his company's first $1 million sales year. In 1956 federal inspection was established at the plant, enabling the company to ship meat out of Utah, largely to the West Coast.

In 1973, at the beginning of his son John's college career, Lynn Miller had a heart attack and died unexpectedly. Four years later, John graduated from Utah State University. He had majored in the humanities and

E.A. Miller beef plant at Hyrum, Utah.

ConAgra saw a need to integrate into the beef business and recognized broad ranged management talent in E.A. Miller, Inc., a family controlled high-growth business.

planned to obtain his MBA from Harvard University before returning to the family meat business. But a tragic airplane crash that killed seven more company employees, including one of his cousins, prevented John from attaining his educational goal. Instead of hitting the books in Cambridge, Massassachusetts, he headed to Hyrum to help his family.

John joined the company as an assistant manager to American Commodities, a hide and rendered products division. In 1979 he was named general manager at E.A. Miller; in 1981, at age 28, he became its chief executive officer. In 1977 the meat company recorded about $70 million in sales. By 1981, sales had jumped to $200 million; five years later, to $1.2 billion, in part through several plant acquisitions.

"In the late 1970s and the 1980s we simply revised our marketing and changed our strategic plan," John explains. "We made a commitment to build a business that could compete with the major packers in the country."

During this period a number of major meat packers were courting the E.A. Miller company. ConAgra was, too. Unlike its rivals for Miller's attentions, however, ConAgra had only relatively modest fresh meat operations. The company's Omaha-based Northern States Beef processed cows and marketed ground beef, beef cuts and trimmings. A plant in Dixon, California, processed lamb and cattle, and a Nampa, Idaho, facility processed cows, steers and heifers.

E.A. Miller's growth had not been without financial risk for the Miller family, and ConAgra offered desirable opportunities for growth as well as a management philosophy compatible with that of the Utah company.

"We were not looking to get out of business," says John Miller. "It was important to me personally that I understand ConAgra's desire to grow the business, because I've still got a lot of years that I want to work."

ConAgra purchased E.A. Miller's packing plant, its transportation facilities and its 25,000-capacity Idaho feedlot. The Miller family kept the Hyrum, Utah, feedlot. Through its new acquisition, ConAgra slaughtered about 7,000 cattle a week, and processed around 10,000.

Even those numbers were to soar. In March of 1987 ConAgra announced its intent to merge with Monfort of Colorado, Inc., a vertically integrated company that produced, transported, and distributed beef and lamb products.

Monfort of Colorado, based in Greeley like United Agri Products, was the nation's largest lamb processor and fourth largest beef processor. At over $25 million, its net income for fiscal year 1986 was almost one-fourth of ConAgra's. Monfort processed about 2.5 million cattle and from 500,000 to 1 million lamb a year. The company's two Colorado feedlots fed 180,000 cattle annually, and its third, under construction, would accommodate another 100,000.

Monfort operated beef- and lamb-processing plants in Colorado, a beef-processing plant in Nebraska, and a lamb-processing plant in Kansas. Its 380 refrigerated trucks transported beef and lamb across the nation. Beef products were shipped to international markets, too. The company produced food service and retail meat products like pre-cooked roast beef, pork pizza toppings, sauces, soups, marinated items and barbecued ribs.

ConAgra purchased E.A. Miller plant and facilities — next step, sought a merger with Monfort of Colorado that would make ConAgra the third largest U.S. meat packer.

Merger with Monfort would boost ConAgra to third place in the U.S. beef-packing industry, behind undisputed leaders Iowa Beef Processors and Excel Corp.

Like E.A. Miller, Monfort of Colorado began as a family firm. In the early 1930s, Warren H. Monfort started a cattle feeding enterprise. In 1960, his son Kenneth opened the company's first meat processing plant, a 500-head-a-day operation. Monfort of Colorado created the world's first 100,000-head feedlot in 1968, and was among the first companies to produce boxed beef at its packing plants.

"Boxed beef" was one of the major innovations to emerge from the 1960s and 1970s, turbulent years for the meat packing industry. Traditionally, whole beef carcasses were shipped to retail and food service markets. After a carcass reached its destination, the butcher divided it into smaller cuts. In the late 1960s, meat packers began portioning beef carcasses into primal or sub-primal cuts at the plant, rather than shipping whole carcasses. (Primal cuts include chuck, loin, rib and round; a sub-primal cut is a smaller portion of a primal, like a chuck roll.) Primal and sub-primal cuts were individually vacuum-packaged, and cuts of the same kind were boxed together, in units of approximately 40 pounds, for shipment. This is "boxed beef".

One of a fleet of Monfort semi's serving U.S. grocery chains.

Boxed beef reduces the meat processor's shipping costs by removing excess fat and bone before the meat is shipped. It also reduces the retailer's costs: the retailer who purchases boxed beef need not maintain as extensive an in-store butcher shop, or pay for fat and bone to be trimmed off and tossed out.

"The supermarkets are starting to concentrate more and more on being first-class merchandisers, movers of product," says John Phillips. "They're getting out of the concept that they were going to be totally integrated. It stands to reason that, for instance, trimming steaks and roasts should be able to be done better at the manufacturing level than at the store level."

Phillips uses the lamb industry as an example.

"Most of the lamb in the country is shipped as whole swinging carcasses, which means the butcher shop gets a lamb," he explains. "So they've got to take care of the hocks and the loins and the racks and the shoulders and everything. Well, the vice president of meat procurement in a grocery chain located in southern California will tell you that's not the way lamb is consumed. He's got stores in Fresno and down in the San Joaquin Valley where they sell a heck of a lot of lamb shanks, but they don't sell many loin chops and they sure as heck don't sell many racks of lamb. On the other hand, in Beverly Hills they sell lots of loin chops and lots of racks of lamb, but not many lamb shanks.

"So when he gets that whole lamb, he's got to merchandise the whole thing, where if we were packaging that lamb for him in our plant, we could mix those things up in the boxes any way he wanted them. Ship full boxes of shanks to Fresno and racks to Beverly Hills."

In the mid-1980s, lamb and beef producer Ken Monfort heard Mike Harper deliver a speech at a cattle feeders' convention in Colorado. At Harper's request, George Doering introduced him to Monfort, a fellow Greeley resident. Harper suggested that ConAgra might contemplate merger with the Colorado company. Ken Monfort wasn't interested.

Mike Harper meets Ken Monfort. Although not interested in a merger at first, a later contact in 1987 leads to a "done deal."

Early in 1987, Doering called Monfort again. Would he like to have lunch?

"I had lunch with him at the Red Steer Cafe, and we talked about everything but merger until the last minute," recalls Monfort. "Then he said, 'Would you be interested in talking to Mike about something?' I told him I wasn't particularly anxious to do so but my wife, Myra, who was our legal counsel, warned me that if anyone made any overtures I should at least talk to him."

Ken and his son Dick, then Monfort's executive vice president and chief operating officer, met Doering and Harper at Doering's Greeley home. Two weeks later they met again to cement the deal.

"It was probably one of the quickest, easiest negotiations Mike ever had," Monfort observes. "We were a public company. We had current audits. We weren't a very complicated company. Maybe I didn't ask for enough."

Ken Monfort liked ConAgra's reputation for letting its IOC managers run their own operations. He also believed that investment in a diversified company would benefit Monfort of Colorado's stockholders. And he knew that Mike Harper didn't like to be fourth or fifth in any business he entered; that meant that ConAgra's red meat operations were destined to grow.

Monfort acknowledges that he and Dick pondered the consequences of merger. After all, Ken's father had started the company as an independent farmer; Ken was raised working every job on the feedlot.

"I had a little concern about losing the independent image," Monfort acknowledges. "But most of our company's growth came about after my father was no longer active. And Dick and I are used to buying cattle. Once you make a decision you forget about it. After we decided that we would do it at a certain price, why, we quit worrying about it."

"When Ken and I first got together it was pretty general, a light conversation," Mike Harper remembers. "ConAgra was heavily engaged in our lawsuit against Cargill over MBPXL at that time. We did not want to get into anything that would complicate that suit.

"A number of years later, I had a little program I built on a personal computer. I take 'Value Line' information for a fairly wide-ranged list of food companies I make up. I run the information through this program I wrote. It generates certain ratios, things like that."

Administrative secretary Mary Robbins had assembled the "Value Line" data for her boss before he embarked on a European business trip. On his return journey, Harper entered the information into a personal computer stowed on the ConAgra jetliner. One name that appeared on the screen: Monfort of Colorado.

"When I got back George Doering set up the meeting at his house," says Harper. "We talked not bluntly, but openly. People who try to beat around the bush and sneak up on somebody's blind side — that doesn't work. Get it out on the table."

Ken Monfort named his price. It was more than Harper wanted to pay, but it would still make ConAgra's numbers work.

"George and I walked out in the kitchen for a while, and Kenny and Dick walked outside the house for a while," recalls Harper. "I asked George what he thought. Would Monfort take less? Should we lock our heels, or pay him what he asked?

"We both agreed that we didn't think he'd take any less. There was no reason he had to sell. And lots of reasons why he possibly wouldn't want to sell. So we agreed to pay the price, and came back into the living room. Ken said that after his walk with his son, who was running a good share of the business — a sale would change that young man's life to some degree — they agreed it would be a good thing."

"Originally Mike said something to me about being on the board, because our family members were going to be significant stockholders," Ken Monfort recalls. "I had looked at the annual report, and I knew Mike was the only management person on the board. I said I didn't need to be on the board, because that kind of sets you aside from the other management people. That was all we talked about. I figured he'd use me in what way he wanted."

In the summer of 1987 Harper appointed Ken Monfort to ConAgra's office of the president. Monfort's fellows in that office were Philip B. Fletcher, president and chief operating officer of ConAgra Prepared Food Companies; George R. Haefner, president and chief operating officer of ConAgra Poultry Company; Floyd McKinnerney, president and chief operating officer of ConAgra Agri-Products Companies; and

A CLAIM IN CATTLE COUNTRY   245

T. Truxtun "Truck" Morrison, president and chief operating officer of ConAgra International and ConAgra Grain Processing Companies. Monfort served as president and chief operating officer of the newly-formed ConAgra Red Meat Companies, which included Monfort of Colorado (later shortened to Monfort, Inc.), E.A. Miller, Inc., and ConAgra's Omaha-based fresh meat business.

Ken Monfort did not move to Omaha after his company joined ConAgra, preferring to remain a resident of his longtime hometown, Greeley, Colorado. The lifestyle compensated for the inconvenience of living 518 miles from his corporate office.

"I get up early in the morning when I fly to Omaha for an 8 a.m. meeting," he notes, wearing just what he might wear in his environs: tan jacket, brown sport shirt, yellow pants, yellow shoes and red suspenders. Ties are reserved for occasions when they're absolutely necessary: formal dinners, stockholders meetings and funerals.

Cowboy boots were a part of Monfort's office uniform until he developed foot problems. He still pulls them on to tramp the Monfort feedlots in Greeley and Yuma, Colorado.

"I was raised on a farm," he explains. "And I feel like a farmer when I'm in the executive suite."

Ken Monfort attended Colorado State University for three years, seeking a degree in animal nutrition. He left to get married and to return home to the family business. In the mid-1960s he took a fling at politics, and was twice elected a state representative.

"I was going to save the world," he says.

His mission ended abruptly in 1968, when former Colorado governor Steve McNichols defeated him in the Democratic primary for U.S. Senator.

The meat packing industry has a long history of labor unrest, and Monfort of Colorado was no exception. During a 1980 strike this unrest reached the boiling point. Police told Monfort there was a contract out on his life. For over two months Monfort had 24-hour police protection; for two more months the police were never far away.

Notes Monfort: "I learned to drive a little better, with a policeman tailing me all the time."

Planning chief Bob White describes the Monfort acquisition as one more case of ConAgra's "planned opportunism".

"Through the strategic planning process, we want our businesses and the corporate entity to be attuned to thinking about those things that make sense from a strategic standpoint," White says. "Then when the companies are available or offered for sale, we are in a position to move

The Monfort acquisition can be described as one more instance of ConAgra's "planned opportunism" — boosts annual red meat sales to nearly $2.5 billion.

rather quickly to get something accomplished. "The election to sell is oftentimes purely in the hands of the owner, but the awareness of whether acquisition would make sense to ConAgra is within our control. We looked at Monfort over several years and said to ourselves, in effect, 'That would make sense at the right time and in the right place'."

According to White, planned opportunism has been a keynote of ConAgra's success in ensuring that its many companies fit into a general scheme.

"That fit is a little bit ectoplasmic, in that it's evolving as the company changes with each additional acquisition," explains White. "The more things we've been able to do, the more things become possible to do. That has extended our boundary limits in the whole foods spectrum, so that we're now spread reasonably well across the food chain. And as we successively make acquisitions we open up additional opportunities."

The acquisitions of E.A. Miller and Monfort had boosted ConAgra's annual red meat sales from about $200 million to nearly $2.5 billion between fiscal years 1986 and 1987. Then, directly on the heels of the Monfort deal, ConAgra further advanced its goal of success in the meat industry. In autumn of 1987 ConAgra purchased a 50% interest, with an option to buy the remainder within four years, in the Dallas-based Swift Independent Holding Corporation. The Swift corporation was the parent of Swift Independent Packing Company (SIPCO) and Val-Agri, Inc. — beef, pork and lamb processors with annual sales of around $4 billion. ConAgra paid $51.5 million for its half interest. Instead of waiting four years, ConAgra completed the purchase of SIPCO and Val-Agri in July 1989 for another $51.5 million. Mike Harper said ConAgra decided to proceed earlier than necessary in order to save some expense, specifically interest costs.

To nail down the original SIPCO deal, Harper met repeatedly with chairman and CEO Edwin L. Cox, Jr.; the two dickered in a Chicago hotel, in the ConAgra airplane hanger reception room, at Cox's Texas ranch. Pilot Harper had to envy Cox's Texas air facility: a private airstrip stretching across the businessman's Lone Star land.

SIPCO was the United States' second largest pork processor and third largest overall meat processor; annually, it processed about 6 million hogs, 3 million cattle and 500,000 lamb. The company operated beef-processing plants in Iowa, Kansas and Texas; pork plants in Iowa, Missouri and Minnesota; and a lamb plant in Texas. And during fiscal 1988, SIPCO announced plans to expand its three pork processing plants, raising its annual pork production to nearly 12 million hogs and its national market share from 7% to almost 14%.

Newest acquisition in red meat — SIPCO — further improves ConAgra's market position to second in beef and pork, first in lamb.

No less important, SIPCO operated the largest food distribution and sales system of any U.S. meat processor. Its 50 food distribution branches served 18,000 retail grocery chains, independent retailers, wholesalers, hospitals, schools and other food service institutions.

The combined production of ConAgra Red Meat Companies and ConAgra's interest in SIPCO yielded these gratifying market positions: second in beef, second in pork and first in lamb.

When Harper and Doering had negotiated with the Monforts, the potential for acquiring an interest in Swift wasn't mentioned.

"Mike said that ConAgra didn't like to be fourth or fifth in size in any business," says Ken. "He told me that they liked to be first or second, and that he would want to grow the company. I said that was fine.

"I didn't have in mind growing it this fast."

Though Harper vigorously sought a leading role for ConAgra in the meat business, he was hardly blind to the industry's new challenges. The 1980s had brought changes as significant as those occuring 15 to 20 years earlier. In the 1960s, innovative meat packers had marketed packages of pre-cut "boxed beef" to retailers. In the 1980s, meat processors wooed busy, health-conscious consumers with leaner meats and increasingly creative value-added products.

This intensified courtship sprang largely from market statistics showing the customer's waning desire for red meat. Increasingly, consumers were purchasing and preparing poultry and fish instead. Homemakers seeking low-calorie and low-fat meals looked askance at red meat, with its higher fat and cholesterol contents. They also looked askance at its higher price.

In addition, poultry and seafood processors like ConAgra were aggressively marketing their products, offering novel value-added items and educating the public on tasty ways to prepare chicken, turkey and fish. Newly popular ethnic cuisines, like Oriental and Indian cookery,

New developments in the industry and new consumer concerns lead ConAgra to value-added products, prepackaged and brand-labeled meat products.

introduced Americans to meals other than the familiar meat, potato, and vegetable.

To counter the decline in meat consumption, meat processors responded to consumers' health concerns. In many supermarkets, the hefty slab of steak ringed by an inch-thick margin of fat and streaked through with white became as scarce as the pickle barrel. Instead, packing plant workers trimmed the fat to half- or quarter-inch depth before shipment.

Moreover, ConAgra tried to buy cattle that provided the right quality of meat with just enough fat. In the past, meat packers had bought lots of 100 or more cattle, paying the same price for all animals even though they would vary in fat content and beef yield. Now, many packers were seeking consistently lean or high-yielding cattle. Industry experts expected such cattle to command a higher price, leading to standardized feeding methods designed to produce cattle of uniform quality.

In addition to providing consumers with leaner red meat products, meat processors introduced new value-added products to accommodate busy lifestyles. Following the lead of poultry processors, meat packers increasingly applied consumer marketing techniques to sell their traditionally unlabeled, undifferentiated "commodity" product. Portion-sized cuts; marinated, seasoned, stuffed or breaded meats ready for the conventional or microwave oven; fully cooked gourmet meats for purchase at the supermarket deli counter all boosted meat's appeal to the active — or tired — diner, while offering price stability to the processor.

Monfort test-marketed one of the meat industry's newest developments: vacuum-packaged, brand-labeled meat. Besides encouraging brand loyalty, the airtight plastic package extended the product's shelf life and allowed the processor to control product quality from the packing plant to the consumer's refrigerator.

"I think we're going to see the beef industry moving toward a differentiated product with brand name advertising," predicts former ConAgra board member Earl Butz. "The poultry industry has done a tremendous job of merchandising. That's one of the reasons that we now eat more poultry meat than we eat beef or pork in this country.

"Poultry's cheap, to be sure. But they've made it easy to serve. And it lends itself to brand promotion. If you go down to buy beef, what do you buy? If you buy a standing rib roast, you just buy a cut off a chunk of beef. You don't know where it came from. We're just before the move into a differentiated market, where you can begin to promote brand names."

Ken Monfort contends that red meat demand hit bottom around 1986, and has enjoyed a steady recovery ever since.

"Beef has regained some positive appeal," he asserts. "The price level and the quantities we have indicate that demand has switched around. Not knocking our own poultry people, but I think consumers are getting a little tired of bland foods. At least once in a while they want a good steak."

Adds ConAgra economist Dick Gady, "The meat industry, and particularly the beef industry, has gone through a kind of wringing out, with a drop in cattle numbers and a drop in red meat demand. We see the beef industry trying to produce a leaner product, one that the consumer is going to desire more. It looks like beef demand is stabilizing, so the environment may be a bit better out in front than it has been.

"I think, too, that there are some advantages of being in beef, poultry and hogs as a group. We can't predict what's going to happen to demand five years out in front. It's possible that poultry demand would drop and beef demand would increase. If that's the case, then ConAgra is in a beef market that would be an offset to weakness in poultry."

Mike Harper observes that trendlines never go on forever.

"One can only eat so much chicken — you get to 100% and the trendline flattens out," he explains. "The same thing is true for the declining trendline in beef consumption. It can't go on forever to zero."

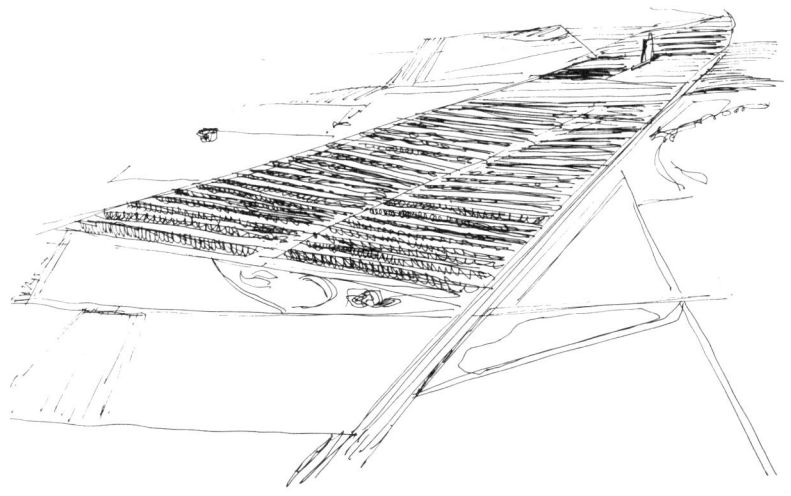

Vast Monfort feedlot near Greeley, Colorado.

Harper points out that the very existence of those ominously declining trendlines brought about changes in the beef industry. "The industry is coming up with products that are more desirable from the consumer's standpoint," he says. "That is because of that trendline. Remember back in physics they told you every force has an equal and opposite force. Or every action has a reaction. Or something like that. That is true in business, too."

As beef demand has risen, so have beef prices, leading farmers and ranchers to withhold cows and heifers from the market to rebuild herds. This in turn has caused tighter cattle supplies, bringing about a price cycle similar to, but longer than, Harper's familiar poultry cycle. For ConAgra's meat companies, managing the supply stream for its processing plants became a high priority as the cattle supply shrank. Contract arrangements with cattle feeders, as well as company-owned feedlot operations, supplemented cattle purchases on the open market.

"The availability and quality of supplies are vital to the success of our processing operation," explains Ken Monfort.

"If we have a certain percentage of our production in feedlots, then we are assured of a certain percent of our production requirements," says Harper. "It is very helpful in case there is a shortage at some point over time. It is important as an insurance policy for us."

Ken Monfort reassures independent feedlot operators who might fear the company's intentions. "Monfort of Colorado started as a feedlot that expanded into the packing business," he explains. "Feedlots are a part of our heritage. But we feed mostly near our western processing plants, where the supply of cattle is limited. We don't always have cattle in sufficient numbers to guarantee efficient processing operations. We feed less than 15% of the total cattle we need, and our goal is never to exceed 20%."

In addition to helping ensure steady supplies for company processing plants, ConAgra's feedlot business is a good earnings contributor, stabilizing red meat earnings over time.

"As a general rule our processing business has stronger results when feeding margins are bad, and vice versa," says Monfort. "I was supposed to say 'skinnier.' I should never say 'bad'. When our feeding margins are skinnier. It also works that way when they're bad."

In large part, ConAgra fulfills its supply requirements by purchasing cattle on the open market. The company buys cattle from almost every one of the cattle producing states.

"At certain times of the year most of our cattle come out of Texas, Oklahoma and Kansas," he says. "Other times of the year they'll be northern cattle, from Colorado, Montana and Wyoming."

"We buy lots of cattle in Nebraska, the Sand Hills. Other than the Pampas in Argentina, I think that's the best cattle producing country in the world."

According to industry analysts, in the summer of 1985 ConAgra slaughtered less than 1% of all cattle slaughtered in the United States. By January of 1988 the company stood second only to IBP and led Excel by a slim margin in cattle slaughtering. In the fall of 1988 ConAgra acquired Cook Family Foods Ltd., a Lincoln, Nebraska-based smoked ham company with annual sales of more than $160 million, and Monfort announced a $41 million campaign to expand and modernize plants in Colorado, Iowa, Kansas, Nebraska and Texas, as well as a Colorado feedlot.

While ConAgra's growth in red meat sales was phenomenal, the company continued to develop the other "center of the plate" categories — fish and poultry.

And ConAgra was second in the nation in total red meat sales.

Two years after his appointment, at the end of June 1989, Ken Monfort retired and was succeeded as president and chief operating officer of ConAgra Red Meat Companies by his son Richard L. "Dick" Monfort, who also joined the office of the president.

"We picked Dick because he was the best candidate in the industry," Harper says. "The only problem was his last name."

At about the same time Phil Fletcher was promoted to a position that had been vacant since 1976 — president and chief operating officer of ConAgra, Inc., making him Harper's No. 2 executive. Fletcher remained as president of ConAgra Prepared Food Companies and was named to the board of directors. Ken Monfort was named to the board, too, and because he was no longer in management, he accepted.

Michael L. Sanem replaced Dick Monfort as president of Monfort, Inc. Nearly two years earlier John Miller had assumed the top spot in Armour Food Company. His brother, Ted A. Miller, later became president of E.A. Miller, Inc.

While ConAgra's phenomenal growth in the meat industry may have been its most publicly noted feat of 1987 and 1988, the company continued to develop its other "center of the plate" categories — fish and poultry — as well.

In March of 1987, ConAgra's Sea-Alaska Products independent operating company merged with Trident Seafood Corporation, a leader in the Pacific Northwest seafood industry that resources, processes and markets crab, salmon, herring and bottomfish. ConAgra acquired a 45%

interest in Trident, and Charles H. Bundrant remained as president of Trident.

Before that merger, Sea-Alaska had purchased Bristol Monarch Corporation, a processor of herring and salmon for expert markets.

Two months after acquiring its 45% interest in Trident, ConAgra bought O'Donnell-Usen Fisheries Corporation, a source of cod and ocean perch and producer of frozen branded seafood products. O'Donnell-Usen operated fishing and processing facilities in Nova Scotia, Prince Edward Island and the United States.

In August of 1986, ConAgra Europe bought Avipronto, a poultry processor based in Portugal. The following year ConAgra acquired Longmont Foods, a Colorado turkey processor with annual sales of over $80 million. In 1988 ConAgra bought poultry processor Motts, Inc.

Mike Harper, who pressed turkey chili upon his houseguests with the zeal of the newly converted, was particularly keen on purchasing Longmont. He had John Phillips, by this time assistant to the chairman, lead the acquisition negotiations.

Longmont Foods was started in the early 1930s by Morris Strear, whose son Leonard delivered poultry orders by bicycle. In those days the elder Strear purchased poultry from the neighboring housewives who fed table scraps and corn to their flocks.

Today a fleet of trucks has replaced Leonard's bicycle to deliver 100 million pounds of turkey annually. Longmont Foods, located in Longmont, Colorado, employs 850 people who turn out turkey hams, turkey pastrami, turkey sausage and, of course, full-breasted birds for Thanksgiving and Christmas dinner, and for every-day evening meals.

Turkey chili isn't Mike Harper's only response to the demand by today's diet-conscious consumers for meals that are non-fattening and good for them. With that and his own heart attack in mind, Harper gave his food scientists the assignment of developing a healthier frozen food dinner that was also tasty. Two and a half years later they came up with Healthy Choice, a selection of 10 frozen dinners featuring center-of-the-plate proteins.

Harper introduced Healthy Choice dinners to industry and media representatives at New York City's Plaza Hotel in January 1989. Not only low in calories (310 or less per serving), the new product goes beyond its low-cal competitors in its control of salt, fat and cholesterol, Harper explains.

According to the ConAgra CEO, Healthy Choice is consistent with the dietary recommendations of the National Institute of Health's national cholesterol education program and the National Academy of

Sciences. Its packages carry guidelines for daily sodium, cholesterol and fat intake and show how the portion compares with the guidelines.

Ken Monfort sees no harm in the competition that ConAgra's frozen foods, fish and poultry companies generate for ConAgra red meat companies.

"With the customers we have, particularly the restaurant chains, we can help each other sell to a number of people," he says. "Most restaurant chains and retailers use beef, pork, lamb and poultry. We can help each other in the sales efforts."

And the former chief of ConAgra's red meat operations concedes that there is room for more than steak, pork loin and lamb chops on a menu.

Chickens that "got away" — the Holly Farms/Tyson Foods drama. Holly rejects Tyson Foods' first offer — ConAgra enters the contest.

"I realize people eat chicken," Monfort confesses. "I even eat it once in a while myself."

Then there are the chickens that got away: chickens that will never grace the center of the plate under a ConAgra label. Mike Harper's fondness for the poultry business is well documented, and in the autumn of 1988 ConAgra sought ways to improve both its volume and its bottom line by going shopping for more chickens.

The focus of interest was Holly Farms Corp. of Memphis, Tennessee. Holly Farms was a diversified food company, in the mold of ConAgra although smaller, but its major item was the chicken. It sold fryers by the millions. It ranked fourth among poultry processors; Tyson Foods of Springdale, Arkansas, was first and ConAgra second. And Holly Foods was up for grabs. The target of an unfriendly takeover attempt by Tyson, Holly sought other bidders, including ConAgra.

Tyson resented ConAgra's intrusion and in November 1988 a three-way corporate struggle began, involving Holly Farms, Tyson and ConAgra. It didn't end until the following summer. Some analysts say it was one of the most complex takeover battles in this era of complicated deals.

The struggle began when Tyson offered to buy Holly for $45 a share. Holly directors rejected the offer, and on November 16, 1988, ConAgra entered the contest. Directors of ConAgra and Holly agreed to a merger proposal under which 1.875 to 2.0 shares of ConAgra common stock would be swapped for each Holly share. A separate agreement also gave ConAgra the right to purchase certain Holly assets for $425 million if the deal fell through.

Tyson raises ante several times — ConAgra holds to original bid which Holly's shareholders turn down.

Tyson raised its ante several times — to $52, to $54, to $57, to $60 and finally to $63.50 in January 1989, meanwhile filing suits in a Delaware court to prevent the ConAgra-Holly merger. In mid-January Holly's board called for a new round of bidding. That was when Tyson raised its bid to $63.50, but ConAgra stuck to its November merger agreement.

Holly directors invited Tyson executives to meet with them in New York City and, although the agreement issues were far from resolved at the meeting, Tyson "leaked a statement to the press indicating that Tyson had acquired Holly," charged ConAgra in a court affidavit. Those statements to the press resulted in a dramatic increase in trading activity in Holly stock, ConAgra contended.

Historically, Holly Farms stock had been held by conservative middle class investors interested in results over the long pull. But as negotiations stretched out, arbitrageurs got into the act, and Harper believes they led the vote against the ConAgra merger offer at a special meeting of Holly stockholders in Memphis April 14. ConAgra shareholders in Omaha approved the deal the same day.

Tyson filed a lawsuit to block the Holly Farms special stockholders meeting and was turned down, but the judge did volunteer the statement, "It seems reasonably probable that the ConAgra merger will be rejected by shareholders." *The Wall Street Journal* repeated the judge's comment. So did Tyson — in a full-page *Wall Street Journal* advertisement. That too may have had its impact at the Memphis meeting.

The Tennessee chicken company was left with Tyson as its only suitor. Holly asked Tyson to increase its bid, and invited ConAgra to re-enter the bidding. But Harper had cooled on the idea of acquiring Holly. He decided ConAgra's best course of action was to negotiate with Tyson and accept a fee for dropping out of the race.

On May 15, 1989, ConAgra attorney Bruce Rohde and Tyson's attorney, James Blair, reached a tentative agreement for Tyson to pursue Holly unimpeded by ConAgra and for Holly to pay ConAgra $50 million. ConAgra and Tyson would drop all litigation against one another, and ConAgra would give up its "assets option," the agreement that would have allowed ConAgra to purchase three of Holly's most valuable assets in case ConAgra did not acquire the company.

During the negotiations between Rohde and Blair, Harper had become convinced that ConAgra should complete the agreement with

Tyson and give up the thought of acquiring Holly.

"ConAgra was completely disillusioned with the bidding process," says Harper. He felt that the actions of Holly and Tyson were counter-productive, and had thus far ended in litigation instituted by the two firms when their respective schemes were frustrated. According to Harper, his company had been drawn into the crossfire and was called upon to defend itself, at enormous expense, against charges leveled by both Tyson and Holly.

ConAgra, disillusioned with bidding — decides to negotiate withdrawal with Tyson.

On May 18 the Delaware court denied a request by Holly to prevent ConAgra and Tyson from negotiating a settlement. It also rejected a request from Tyson to stop Holly's auction.

Then the Tyson-ConAgra arrangement began to unravel. As Harper recalls, ConAgra asked for $25 million up front and $25 million later, but Tyson said it wanted to defer payment of any money until it acquired Holly. ConAgra offered to reduce the up-front amount, but Tyson was adamant. Meanwhile, Holly wanted everything settled by 5 p.m. Eastern Daylight Time on May 19, the deadline its directors set for new bids from Tyson and ConAgra.

To settle the Tyson-ConAgra agreement before Holly's deadline, Mike Harper called Don Tyson. The two competitors discussed the $50 million settlement, with Don Tyson unwilling to pay any money up front until he was positive his company would gain control of Holly. But he wanted to check with his lawyers. He promised Harper he'd ring him back in 15 minutes.

Over an hour passed. When Don Tyson did call back, Harper recounts, he told Harper that his lawyers claimed the previous day's ruling by the Delaware court was highly favorable to Tyson, and that Tyson was now willing only to pay ConAgra's expense of $5.5 million. ConAgra could file suit to try to collect more. In other words, see you in court — again.

"I told him that was unsatisfactory, and I terminated the conversation," says Harper. "I was shocked, as I believed the only sticking point was the up-front money, not the $50 million."

Although Harper was certain that negotiations were over, Rohde immediately got a call from Tyson's New York City attorneys. After a lengthy conversation, Rohde was informed that Tyson would "consider" a $30 million payment, but later that afternoon the figure was raised to $37 million.

It was becoming apparent to Harper that ConAgra had better look

Negotiations with Tyson are on again, off again. Finally, deal with ConAgra is struck.

to its back-up position. When $37 million was billed as Tyson's final figure, Harper, unwilling to accept any less than $50 million, decided to submit a new bid to Holly. Reluctant as he was to re-enter the bidding, he saw this as the only course of action left to ConAgra.

Not long before the 5 p.m. deadline, ConAgra's newest proposal for acquiring Holly Farms was fed into the facsimile machine. It called for swapping 2.1 shares of ConAgra stock for each Holly share, for a total value of $1.3 billion. The new bid represented an increase of 5 percent over the 2 shares ConAgra expected to issue under the earlier merger agreement. As Harper recalls, the fax machine was transmitting this information to Holly's Memphis office when the phone rang in Omaha. It was Don Tyson. He asked Harper where their negotiations stood. Harper told Tyson he wanted $50 million, with $7 million to $10 million up front.

Tyson told Harper to write it up. When he hung up the phone, Harper learned only eight pages of the 30-page bid had been sent to Holly. Harper stopped the fax transmission to Holly, and directed that the settlement with Tyson be concluded.

The last phone call? Not at all. Within minutes, Harper recounts, Don Tyson dialed Harper again. His lawyers advised him to cancel the deal because of problems caused by the partial transmission. ConAgra turned the fax machine back on and submitted its full proposal to Holly. It was 5:15 Omaha time, 6:15 Eastern Daylight Time.

Letters flowed back and forth between Tyson and Holly, with Tyson trying to forestall Holly from taking any action on the latest ConAgra bid. Tyson's last message arrived at 11 p.m., Saturday, May 20. It was 30 minutes too late. At 10:30 p.m. the Holly board had voted to accept the ConAgra bid. At 11:30 that night Harper signed an agreement to consummate the transaction. The deal was conditioned on approval by the stockholders of both companies, with a vote scheduled in July.

A Minneapolis securities analyst predicted the obvious: ConAgra's offer wouldn't necessarily end the bidding war for Holly. "ConAgra has begun Round 3," he told the *Omaha World-Herald*. "Tyson will probably come back with a revised bid." A Holly spokesman acknowledged that although his company intended to go forward with ConAgra, Holly could end that agreement if "someone else" submitted a better proposal.

That "someone else" was Tyson, of course. The offer came on June 20, raising Tyson's bid from the $63.50 a share first offered in January — to which Tyson had stubbornly held — to $70 a share, totaling $1.4 billion.

Harper left a meeting when he heard of the Tyson bid and called Don Tyson to offer congratulations, but hinted ConAgra might try to top Tyson one more time. Harper reminded Tyson the two had earlier agreed to deal directly, without intermediaries, if they had another opportunity to negotiate. Less than half an hour later Tyson called back to invite Harper to lunch in Fayetteville, Arkansas, and Harper flew down there immediately. Within 10 minutes, during the drive from the airport to the restaurant, Don Tyson and Mike Harper agreed to end their war, shook hands on it and left the details to their lawyers.

Harper believes final settlement is in best interests of ConAgra shareholders.

When the accord was reached, the three parties — Tyson, Holly and ConAgra — went before the Delaware Chancery Court to get its blessing, which was granted June 23. All previous agreements were terminated. Tyson would acquire Holly for $70 a share, or $1.4 billion, and Holly would pay ConAgra $50 million for pulling out. ConAgra would forego its claim, under the November 1988 agreement, to purchase three key Holly assets for $425 million.

"We are pleased with the outcome," says Harper. "We were not willing to raise our bid because a higher bid would have taken us past the point where we were confident a merger would meet ConAgra's demanding financial standards. The settlement will provide a substantial amount of cash to invest elsewhere in ConAgra's growth."

As for winning or losing Holly Farms, Harper commented: "We can't ever go into a potential acquisition with a win-lose mentality. People do dumb things when they think about deals that way. You'll never read about all the private deals we've walked away from because the price was too high to meet our financial standards.

"Sure, ConAgra could have acquired Holly Farms by raising our bid. But our job is to look after our shareholders' interests, not to 'win' in the acquisition arena. Moreover, we're patient. We've learned that what goes around often comes around."

The sum of $20 million was paid immediately to ConAgra, and the final check for $30 million was banked July 20, 1989. After expenses and taxes, ConAgra realized $27 million, or 33 cents a share. A decent payday.

Harper congratulated Tyson and Holly president R. Lee Taylor: "We wish them well together — at least until the next time we meet as competitors in the marketplace."

CHAPTER 15

NEBRASKA – IT'S
GOOD FOR BUSINESS

IN full military regalia — medals, pearl-handled pistols and riding boots — Mike Harper stood at attention against the backdrop of a huge American flag, just like George C. Scott in the movie "Patton". Hand on heart, Harper surveyed his housed audience. He took a deep breath and, to the tune of "America the Beautiful", belted out the inspiring words:

"Oh beautiful for wrecking balls
In our new neighborhood;
We're going to build a Taj Mahal
Where Jobbers' Canyon stood.
In Omaha, in Omaha,
That's where we want to be;
You paid the price to keep us here
Instead of Tennessee."

Two other similarly satirical stanzas had Harper's viewers calling for an encore. The occasion was the 1988 Omaha Press Club Gridiron Show, an annual gala at which public and press personalities take a cockeyed look at the past year's events. Harper had been coaxed into the Army uniform because of his unexpectedly prominent role in the 1987 Nebraska political scene.

In the years since he had assumed the top spot at ConAgra, Harper had grown used to being in the public eye. He accepted the fact that, as the CEO of an important corporate citizen, he had the personal obligation to participate in community activities. And he encouraged ConAgra's corporate involvement in charitable causes and public affairs.

"The corporate philosophy is that we should actively pursue being good citizens of the community where we are located," explains vice president of public affairs Marty Colladay.

Thus ConAgra supports a wide range of community charities, funding projects in health and welfare, education, civic affairs, and the arts. The combined annual plans for ConAgra IOC's and the ConAgra Charitable Foundation allocate 1% of profit before taxes for charitable causes.

One of ConAgra's top charitable priorities is to support projects that improve the educational system. The ConAgra Charitable Foundation helped fund the University of Nebraska-Lincoln's "Agri-business" program, the first of its kind in the nation. By offering the new undergraduate major, the university can better prepare young men and women for careers in agri-business.

"Our vice president of public affairs, Marty Colladay, led this effort. We have close to $350,000 invested in a reciprocal program between the

ConAgra believes in corporate involvement in charitable causes, public affairs, education, and Harper has practiced personal involvement in civic affairs and local politics.

University of Nebraska Colleges of Agriculture and Business, to promote cooperation between them and to promote agri-business and agri-economics," Harper explains. "Where most departments in the College of Agriculture are going down in enrollment, this one is going up."

In addition to directing corporate charitable activities, Colladay's small but busy public affairs department monitors federal legislative and administrative decisions in Washington, D.C., and state decisions in Nebraska. Because ConAgra operates across the food chain, it is governed by a broad array of laws and regulations pertaining to agriculture, trade and taxes.

Mike Harper also takes an active role in writing to and meeting with Congressmen involved in agricultural policy. As a member of the National Commission on Agricultural Trade and Export Policy, he was able to express ConAgra's views on how the 1985 farm bill could improve U.S. agricultural exports.

"Mike's name carries a lot of weight in agricultural circles," notes ConAgra economist Dick Gady. "Mike was the head of the Commission's 'objectives committee,' which put together a set of issues affecting trade and agricultural policy. He was very instrumental in laying out the kinds of issues that the Commission should look at, and in many cases he tried to nudge the Commission toward some specific point of view. I think that, particularly in the trade areas, the Commission had a great deal of input into what finally was written into the 1985 farm bill.

"You know, Mike's kind of funny. We'll sit around at a table and talk about what good agricultural policy ought to be, and Mike will have some ideas. And pretty soon those are your ideas. So Mike's good at planting the seed, and then letting other people nurture it."

"I've been involved in civic affairs my whole career," says Harper. "I've been active in the Republican Party for a long time. I was a councilman in Excelsior, Minnesota, for five years and mayor for one. I think those are important things.

"We all owe loyalty to our community, our state, and our country. We all have to pay our citizenship dues. By that I mean get involved in politics, get involved in your Chamber of Commerce or your church. Each of us has to pay back a little bit."

But Harper's previous forays into local politics and community affairs didn't prepare him for the experience of becoming Nebraska's most prominent business spokesman.

"We got involved in something called 'economic development'," he explains. "It came up because of the success of Banquet, whose headquarters is outside of St. Louis. Banquet employees developed a number of new products, and came to us and said 'We have to have a new laboratory.'"

ConAgra companies operated product labs here and there across the country. The St. Louis lab developed new frozen foods for Banquet and Armour, as well as for the recently acquired Morton's, Chun King and Patio frozen food lines; an Omaha laboratory handled flour quality control; a lab in Scottsdale, Arizona, experimented with new Armour processed meat products. Harper knew, however, that many of ConAgra's competitors located their headquarters and their major food development plants in the same city. Perhaps ConAgra would operate even more efficiently by doing the same.

Characteristically, Harper approached the question by looking at the long view. If ConAgra were to build a new office complex encompassing corporate headquarters, selected independent operating company facilities and a product development laboratory, would Omaha, Nebraska, be the best place for it?

According to the Greater Omaha Chamber of Commerce, in 1985 Nebraska ranked 46th in the country in new business incorporations. Statistics compiled by the Nebraska Labor Department showed that between 1980 and 1986, manufacturing jobs in the state decreased by 11%, from 96,400 to 85,800. Between 1986 and 1988, as state residents abandoned their plains homes for greener pastures elsewhere, Nebraska's population declined by 11,000.

"We started out trying to determine whether Nebraska wanted an economic climate that was conducive to the growth of businesses here, and particularly big businesses," Harper explains.

In November of 1986, Harper commissioned a study on the issue. ConAgra retained the University of Nebraska Bureau of Business Research, headed by Donald Pursell, because it had a reputation for objectivity.

"Besides, if there was a bias it would be in the right direction," notes Harper. "The study brought some bad news."

According to Pursell's research, Omaha compared unfavorably with 18 other U.S. cities as a location for ConAgra's corporate headquarters, headquarters for various IOC's and a central lab. The Bureau's study examined two general types of costs: ConAgra's taxes and business operating

A study of possible locations for a new headquarters location begins with University of Nebraska research, commissioned by ConAgra. Says 18 U.S. cities would offer better financial climate for the company and employees than present location in Omaha.

costs, and ConAgra employees' taxes and living costs. Specifically, Pursell computed ConAgra's probable costs for unemployment compensation tax, corporate income tax, corporate property tax, and building operation and leasing. He also calculated ConAgra employees' likely expenditures for individual income tax, personal property tax, sales tax, mortgage payments, and residential utility payments. ConAgra wanted employees' costs examined because the company must pay workers more in areas where their cost of living is higher.

The study hailed Knoxville, Tennessee, as the financially most attractive city for ConAgra. Depending on its choice of certain alternative building plans, ConAgra could save from $3.6 to $10.5 million a year by locating its new facilities in that southeastern city. In declining order of desirability, the other contenders besting Omaha were Houston; Nashville; Memphis; Seattle; Orlando; Louisville; Sioux Falls, South Dakota; Jacksonville, Florida; Kansas City; El Dorado, Arkansas; Tampa; Dallas; Little Rock, Arkansas; Salt Lake City; Ballwin, Missouri; Austin; and Indianapolis.

The Bureau of Business Research estimated that if ConAgra undertook its most likely expansion plan in Omaha, the company's Omaha payroll would increase from 670 to 1108 employees. The annual positive economic impact upon the city: $143 million. Conversely, a ConAgra exodus could cost the community $97 million a year.

ConAgra published the results of its study. Knoxville wasted little time. Its Chamber of Commerce sent Harper a videotape called "Knoxville: Take a Look."

Many Nebraskans, on the other hand, disputed Pursell's results. As Harper observes, "A lot of people don't like to hear bad news." Critics complained that the study failed to consider non-economic factors, like Nebraska's quality of life, its public education system, or its residents' strong work ethic. Harper replied that in any business decision the bottom line is based upon economic factors.

"Money is the language of business," he asserts. "During this time I had calls from more governors than there are states in the union.

NEBRASKA: GOOD FOR BUSINESS

Everyone talked about how great their state was, and not one of them said 'We have a lousy work ethic' or 'We have a real poor quality of life.'

"ConAgra had a basic decision to make in January of 1987. One alternative was to lay a long-range plan and quietly, over the next three or four years, to move our headquarters to a more desirable location."

Enron, a major Omaha employer and the parent company of Northern Chemical, ConAgra's co-tenant in the downtown Omaha Twin Towers building, had moved to Houston in 1986. Community leaders confronted the possibility that ConAgra, too, could depart for the Sun Belt. Shortly after the January, 1987 publication of Pursell's study results, Nebraska Governor Kay Orr called on Mike Harper. The previous November, Republican Orr had defeated Democrat Helen Boosalis in the nation's first gubernatorial race between two female major party candidates. Now, Governor Orr was interested in demonstrating Nebraska's hospitality to business development.

State and local politicians become concerned about damage to the economy and to civic morale; ConAgra's lawyers help Harper draft a tax revision proposal.

"I told her of the several things that concerned us, economic factors, that we really wanted to stay but that those were problems," recalls Harper. "She said she didn't want to get into specifics. I told her that she had to get into the specifics. We couldn't deal in generalities. Her staff said shortly thereafter that you can't write something complicated so quickly.

"So our general counsel Bruce Rohde and his colleague Nick Niemann came out to my house one Saturday morning. We sat around our kitchen table, eating turkey chili. Over that weekend we wrote the principles of what became Legislative Bill 775."

By this time Rohde was general counsel, replacing the retired Jack North, and Niemann was the tax law specialist.

Brainstorming, Harper and the two attorneys developed the outline of a specific proposal that included business tax incentives and a limited capital gains exclusion.

Nebraska State Senator Vard Johnson, chairman of the Revenue Committee, had also contacted Harper after hearing of ConAgra's study. Perhaps an unlikely ally, Senator Johnson was a Democrat, an Omaha attorney who represented a largely blue-collar district. (In Nebraska's unique unicameral, or one-house, Legislature, all 49 legislators are called "senators" and, while a senator might belong to a given political party, he

Nebraska Governor Kay Orr presents legislative proposals to the state legislature designed to carry out ConAgra's suggestions; the debate begins.

or she runs for office as a non-partisan candidate.) Johnson had taken a hard look at Nebraska's economy and was disturbed at what he saw.

"Nineteen-eighty-six was an election year for me," he explains. "During the process of getting re-elected I had heard from a lot of people in my legislative district about their fears for our economic vitality. Many of their fears were not entirely well-articulated, but one could sense the genuine worry and concern they had for the well-being of their children as well as themselves, in terms of what would happen economically.

"I thought to myself, in the event that ConAgra does decide that they will leave Omaha, we probably will suffer a psychological cloud for a long time."

Senator Johnson urged Harper to draft a tax revision proposal. In a series of discussions as contentious as any corporate merger negotations, Johnson helped Harper, Rohde and Niemann fine-tune their proposal.

"We were all trying to solve the problem," says Harper. "I give Vard a hell of a lot of credit because we were all able to find a compromise."

Finally, Harper presented ConAgra's brief proposal to Governor Orr, her chief of staff Hans Brisch, and Nebraska Tax Commissioner Don Leuenberger. In Harper's opinion, these legislative changes would prove that Nebraska offered an environment friendly to business.

Working from ConAgra's suggestions, Governor Orr formulated a legislative package combining tax reductions and economic incentives for Nebraska employers and employees. She unveiled most of her proposals in February of 1987.

Nebraska Legislative Bill 270 raised the state's corporate income tax credit for a small business that increased employment and investment. LB 772 permitted a corporation to base its state income tax only upon its Nebraska sales, rather than upon its Nebraska sales, property and payroll. LB 773 revised Nebraska's individual income tax laws, reducing the tax rates of some upper-income residents.

Legislative Bill 775 was the fourth, and clearly the most controversial, economic development measure. LB 775 contained the tax credits and the limited capital gains exclusion proposed by ConAgra.

The bill provided that a corporation making new investments of at least $3 million and creating at least 30 new jobs became eligible for a 10% investment tax credit on property related to the project, and a 5% income tax credit for the newly created jobs.

A corporation making new investments of at least $20 million without creating any new jobs could receive a sales tax refund on depreciable property related to the project. This provision was added by Senator Johnson to help the Goodyear Company of Lincoln.

A corporation making new investments of at least $10 million and creating at least 100 new jobs became eligible for 15-year personal property tax exemptions on corporate airplanes, mainframe computers and agriculture processing equipment, at the discretion of the various county boards. If a business failed to create the requisite jobs or investment within seven years, or failed to maintain the added jobs for seven years, it lost its credits.

Finally, the bill permitted an employee who held stock in a Nebraska corporation that employed him to exclude from state individual income tax any capital gain resulting from a one-time sale of that stock.

The state attorney general reviewed the measure. He questioned the provision allowing counties to grant personal property exemptions, so Senator Johnson, Bruce Rohde and Mike Harper devised substitute language. One of ConAgra's concerns was the personal property tax bill it would owe on aircraft and mainframe computers housed in Omaha for corporate business use. The substitute language exempted all corporate aircraft and mainframe computers bought or leased in connection with an expansion program.

"This was the real test of whether Nebraska wanted big business," says Mike Harper. "Jets and giant computers are the hallmarks of larger corporations."

In late March, the Revenue Committee voted unanimously to send its new version of Governor Orr's economic development bill to the floor of the Legislature. In the Nebraska unicameral, bills are debated three times before passage. The legislature advanced LB 775 to the second stage of debate in April, 1987 and on May 11 the second round of discussion began. Nearly 70 amendments — some serious attempts to clarify technical language, some frivolous attempts to stall a vote — had been submitted for consideration.

Proponents of the bill included the business community, the various Chambers of Commerce, the Nebraska Association of Commerce and Industry, the real estate and construction industries, the University of Nebraska, the AFL-CIO, Douglas County and Omaha's mayor and City Council.

Opponents cited sundry reasons to defeat LB 775. Some critics charged that the bill would boost the economies of Omaha and Lincoln without helping smaller businesses in the state's ailing rural communities. Others objected to the limited capital gains exclusion. And the tax exemptions for corporate airplanes and mainframe computers rankled detractors unaware that aircraft and information systems were characteristic features of the headquarters companies Nebraska sought.

ConAgra assembled its team of persuaders to work the Capitol rotunda and halls. Marty Colladay, vice president for public affairs, and attorneys Bruce Rohde and Nick Niemann drove to Lincoln and back countless times, to meet with Governor Orr and her staff and with senatorial friends and foes.

"The legislation had very high visibility," says Colladay. "There was a lot of media interest, and we were being bashed almost daily by some senators who were not very friendly."

Colladay led ConAgra's efforts in the legislature, but Lynn Phares, vice president for public relations, and Walt Casey, vice president for corporate communications, were the designated spokespersons. Colladay's role did not include briefing the press, and therein lay one of his most embarrassing moments during LB 775's tumultuous journey through the legislature.

One newspaper reporter was particularly diligent in tracking Colladay's whereabouts; he was just as diligent in avoiding her. Colladay and Niemann often traveled in tandem. When they exited a senator's office, Niemann invariably led to signal that the coast was clear.

As they entered Governor Orr's office one day, at the last moment Niemann spotted the reporter already inside conversing with the governor. He quickly gave Colladay the high sign, and the public affairs v.p. ducked into an anteroom to cool his heels until the journalist left.

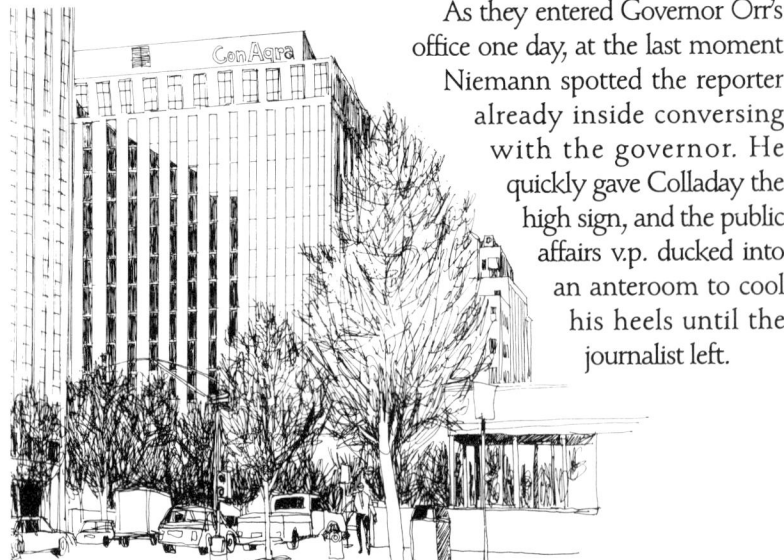

Present ConAgra headquarters building at Omaha, Nebraska.

Harper found Colladay's evasive action highly amusing.

"Here is Marty, a former Air Force three star general, hiding out from a young reporter," he observes.

Despite vocal opposition, on May 12 Nebraska legislators voted 35 to 13 to advance the bill to the third stage of debate. In the process, the senators had adopted two seemingly innocuous amendments. One amendment, designed to encourage a Washington-based potato processor to relocate to Nebraska, provided a personal property tax exemption for purchases of new agricultural equipment.

This would help a rural community in western Nebraska. So far, so good.

The other amendment had been introduced by a senator who was a professor at a state college. Senator Johnson recognized it as a potential troublemaker but, wearied by the battle, didn't protest. The other senators took their cues from him.

Within 48 hours after both amendments were adopted, ConAgra officials realized that, in the words of the second amendment's sponsor, the company "got snookered". The language of the amendment made it impossible to take full advantage of the airplane and computer tax exemption as well as the job-creation tax credit. For each $1 credit claimed for airplanes and computers, a company had to relinquish $1.25 in other tax credits. The amendment succeeded where the direct approach — rounding up the support to remove the airplane and computer exemption — had failed.

ConAgra announced that the amendment could cost the company up to $800,000 a year. Harper viewed the Legislature's action as proof that Nebraska was not truly interested in making the state a good place for business — particularly big business. Having arrived at this conclusion, Harper and his fellow executives believed that it made little sense to maintain the company's headquarters facilities in Nebraska.

Harper called a meeting of the corporate office's 500-plus employees. Never one to mince words, he reported that he was now soliciting proposals from other states for the location of ConAgra's new laboratory, corporate headquarters and Omaha-based IOC headquarters.

Some senators insisted that ConAgra was bluffing. "Blackmail," they called it.

Any number of corporate executives could have told the Nebraska Legislature that bluffing wasn't Mike Harper's style.

"Governor Orr thought I was bargaining with her," Harper recalls. "I told the governor that if the amendment passed, that was a clear signal to us that Nebraska wasn't that concerned about being competitive. She thought I was bluffing and told me so. I told her I never bluff. If you get a reputation for bluffing, than you can't bluff. So I never bluff. Not knowingly, anyway."

Walt Casey, vice president of corporate communications, explains that Harper was just doing business in his customary candid, forthright — and blunt — manner.

"With just about anything we do, we come at it in a straightforward way," says Casey. "That's the way we operate, you know, just 'Bam!', confrontation, take it head on, tell it like it is.

"Nobody likes to be called names. Nobody likes to have their way of doing things criticized thoughtlessly. It was a baffling experience."

Several legislators thought that many of their colleagues would have rejected the amendment had they fully understood its effect. Even so, to remove the new language would be an unwieldy task. A majority of the Legislature would have to send the bill back to the second stage of debate, even as the body's May 29th adjournment date approached. Over the weekend, Governor Orr and her staff lobbied as many senators as they could nab.

On Tuesday, May 19, after sending LB 775 back to the second stage of debate, the Nebraska Legislature voted 29 to 11 to remove the troublesome amendment. At the same time, ConAgra disclosed that Missouri's governor had commenced an aggressive campaign to lure the company to Banquet's home state.

At 6:10 p.m. on May 26 — three days before adjournment — Nebraska senators cast a 35-to-11 vote in favor of Legislative Bill 775.

The next morning, ConAgra's Omaha employees sat on folding chairs, under a string of portable lights, in the makeshift auditorium where Harper had spoken to them just days earlier. The room was an unfinished wing of the Twin Tower building, with a cement floor, unpaneled walls, and exposed heating and air conditioning pipes.

As public relations vice president Lynn Phares joked, "It's in keeping with our image."

Harper rose to address the group.

"You've read about this bill," he said. "At one time there was an amendment to give a tax rebate for hair pieces. I didn't ask that that amendment be introduced, but I was unhappy when the damn thing lost.

"What has happened in the Legislature in the last six months is almost unbelievable. Nebraska has now sent a signal to businesses that the state does want them here. We join 23 other states with favorable tax laws. All these things make Nebraska more competitive and should bring jobs — good jobs. We are very pleased with what Governor Kay Orr and Vard Johnson have accomplished. We accept them on good faith, both the Legislature and the administration, and as of this morning we are no longer sending out solicitations for possible locations outside Nebraska.

"The one big question on your minds: We will build our laboratory here and in due time build our new headquarters here."

Those words were greeted with enthusiastic applause. So were the comments of an employee who rose to thank Harper for keeping workers informed, on the good news and the bad news.

"I have never felt better about the quality of our employees than after our previous meeting," Harper responded. "It wasn't entirely pleasant, but you kept your poise and your sense of humor. Now let's go make some money."

ConAgra publicly announced its plan to build a $60 million headquarters and laboratory complex in Nebraska. The state had extended its hand to headquarters companies. It had unequivocally declared, "Business, we want you here."

Business responded immediately. On Thursday, May 28, Peoples Natural Gas announced that it would move its headquarters across the Missouri River from Omaha's neighbor, Council Bluffs, Iowa.

By July 1, 1989, the economic development package would attract nearly $2.3 billion in proposed investment by 195 companies, to create more than 19,855 new jobs in Nebraska.

Although he laughs at Marty Colladay's close escape from the persistent reporter covering the Legislature's deliberations, Harper gives the former Air Force general and attorney Bruce Rohde the lion's share of the credit for LB 775's successful passage.

"Marty carried the day," says Harper. "And Bruce worked his tail off."

As for Harper himself, if he thought that he could now retreat to his office's computer-laden round table, he was mistaken. There remained the issue of precisely where in Nebraska to construct ConAgra's multimillion dollar facility.

Harper believed that ConAgra's new headquarters and laboratory complex should reflect the firm's commitment to the independent operating company concept. He wanted to avoid housing corporate headquarters, IOC headquarters and laboratory in a single skyscraper, where company presidents "go downstairs to visit somebody and upstairs to

ConAgra employees in the Omaha headquarters finally get the good news — Nebraska has passed the favorable tax laws needed to keep the company in Omaha.

Now begins the job of planning the company's new multi-million dollar headquarters and laboratory complex; Omaha city officials urge location on the city's riverfront.

visit the boss." Harper wanted a campus environment in which various low-set, attractively landscaped — and above all, independent — buildings were scattered along a grassy parkway and joined by glass-enclosed walks.

Shortly after Harper announced ConAgra's intent to remain in Nebraska he was approached by City of Omaha and Douglas County officials, as well as by a group of businessmen active in the Chamber of Commerce's Omaha Development Foundation. Their goal was to entice the company to locate its new complex on Central Park East, 30 acres of cleared land on the Missouri River just east of downtown Omaha's Central Park Mall.

For two decades, downtown Omaha had suffered the steady decampment of office, retail and residential occupants to suburban sites miles away. The Central Park East site was originally called Marina City; ten years earlier developers had abandoned an ambitious plan to erect apartments there, alongside a harbor connected to the river. City planners and business leaders yearned for another major development project to help bring to fruition their dreams for a revitalized downtown Omaha.

But several much larger sites in suburban Omaha lent themselves more easily to the spacious campus environment Harper envisioned. And to make Harper's decision tougher still, Lincoln, Nebraska, offered ConAgra 240 acres of free land if it chose to build in the capital city.

Nonetheless, ConAgra was willing to oblige the proponents of a downtown Omaha site. Harper felt that locating ConAgra's new complex on the riverfront would have a far more significant effect upon the city than would locating it in a suburban area. Furthermore, he shied from uprooting the company's hundreds of Omaha employees just to take advantage of Lincoln's land offer.

There were, however, certain notable drawbacks. Central Park East was criss-crossed by high-transmission power lines in the air and by railroad tracks on the ground. And there was the problem of what Harper called "some big, ugly red brick buildings."

Several square blocks of turn-of-the-century brick warehouses, nicknamed "Jobbers' Canyon," encroached upon the acreage ConAgra needed for its campus-like complex. When Harper broached the subject of razing the buildings, it became clear that they weren't just any old warehouses.

Some preservationists considered Jobbers' Canyon historically significant, and wanted the area designated a local historic district, protected from destruction.

"Once we decided on the riverfront, it aroused a very small group of people who would like to have kept those old warehouses," explains Harper. "I don't think most people in Omaha cared. Most had never been down there. A goodly number have driven there now to see what the fuss is all about. Most people felt like 'Let's get downtown going again.'"

In September, members of the Omaha Development Foundation, anxious to see Omaha's long-delayed riverfront dreams materialize, entered into purchase negotiations with the owners of the Jobbers' Canyon warehouses. The bargaining progressed slowly; the warehouse owners wanted to ensure that they got their money's worth for their contribution to downtown development. Exasperated by the continuing controversy, Harper finally set a deadline. On January 5, 1988, he would announce the location of ConAgra's new headquarters complex. If the Jobbers' Canyon blocks weren't available, Harper would cheerfully choose a more congenial site.

Preservationists oppose the necessary clearing of "Jobber's Canyon" warehouse buildings; warehouse owners protract negotiations; but finally the way is clear. ConAgra begins construction of the new complex.

On December 31, 1987, the owners of seven buildings rejected the Omaha Development Foundation's final offer. On January 4, 1988, Foundation members reluctantly informed Mike Harper that they couldn't seem to strike a deal with the warehouse owners.

Harper pointed out that this day didn't end until 11:59 p.m.

Negotiations resumed. At 11 p.m. — 59 minutes early — the bargainers reached an agreement. Together, business and government leaders have paved the way for Omaha's downtown redevelopment.

On January 5, 1988, ConAgra announced its decision to build on the riverfront. And on August 30, 1988, a crowd of over 500 employees and well-wishers watched Mike Harper and assorted dignitaries sink their shovels into the riverfront soil. At the official groundbreaking, Harper saluted all who had contributed to the project's success.

"The location of this campus on the Missouri riverfront — the gateway to Omaha, the state of Nebraska and the Great Plains — is a dream becoming a reality," state the ConAgra CEO. "People from all across the

Kiewit Plaza building in Omaha was the headquarters before present location.

state of Nebraska, including state and city government, county officials and private citizens, worked together to create innovative legislation, like the Nebraska 1987 Employment Investment Growth Act, that encourages businesses to create jobs and invest in Nebraska."

A year later, in August 1989, 360 employees — about 200 of them transferred from St. Louis — went to work in the headquarters of ConAgra Frozen Foods Company, the first of five buildings to be completed on the ConAgra campus.

The second building, a food development facility and pilot plant, was completed and occupied before the end of 1989, and construction was under way on the facility due to house Armour Food Company, Armour Dairy & Food Oils Company and ConAgra Deli Company. The building for the corporate headquarters will be occupied in October 1990 and the one for ConAgra Grain Processing Companies will be finished by 1992.

Public officials anticipated that the riverfront area, anchored by ConAgra's office complex, would draw $250 million in additional development, hotel and office facilities. By 1993, as many as 2,100 employees could be working in Central Park East. Downtown Omaha would flourish again.

Public and private sectors had joined forces to accomplish this goal.

Sketch of the ConAgra office complex now in construction.

The City of Omaha contributed $11.3 million for site preparation and acquisition, streets and sewers. Douglas County provided $6.3 million to develop an adjacent 24-acre public park and lake. The Peter Kiewit Foundation donated $2 million and loaned $10.5 million to the city to help finance the project. Additional corporate and foundation contributors pledged over $10 million.

Less than 30 days after ConAgra announced it would build on the riverfront, its first neighbor materialized. Chairman and CEO Michael H. Walsh of the Union Pacific Railroad, whose headquarters are in Omaha, said the railroad would renovate and convert its 110-year-old freight warehouse into a $50 million dispatching control center for the 23,000-mile rail line.

The warehouse, which sits at the edge of Jobbers' Canyon and adjacent to the southwest corner of ConAgra's first building, was remodeled into a highly sophisticated computer center. U. P. could have established the center in any of its 21 states, but remained in Omaha because of LB 775. "It provided an absolutely key role in the decision on Union Pacific's part to house this center here," said Walsh at the center's dedication in July 1989. "We own the building, and this gives us a chance to do something nice for Omaha."

Another nearby project spurred by ConAgra's decision is the $90 million in new construction undertaken by BetaWest, the real estate arm of U. S. West Communications, formerly Northwestern Bell Telephone Company. BetaWest began constructing a 15-story office building and five-story computer center on two square blocks facing the Central Park

Mall. Again, LB 775 and its computer tax concessions were an important factor in the decision to build in Omaha.

"The completion of this project will be another significant step in the city's plan for redevelopment of the Central Park Mall and the riverfront areas," says Ken Power, CEO of U. S. West Communications for Nebraska.

As for the seven major businesses that vacated Jobbers' Canyon: one became the cornerstone of a new industrial park in west-central Omaha and two moved to a new industrial site a mile upstream from ConAgra's riverfront buildings. All told, the seven businesses made plans for $28 million in new construction. Each has expanded its Jobbers' Canyon operations.

Harper now stumps the state and the nation singing Nebraska's praises. He has addressed the Federal Reserve Bank directors, Chambers of Commerce, service clubs, educators and food processors' organizations, and press and public relations associations. The 1987 economic development package proves to be a powerful selling tool when Harper invites out-of-state companies to Nebraska.

"The whole subject of economic development is important to ConAgra," says Harper. "Every person and every job that comes here or stays here, or every job coming from a company that expands here rather than someplace else, means less pressure on corporate taxes and less tax pressure on ConAgra employees in the state of Nebraska. That is true. It really is true. It is a part of our consistent story that more jobs mean more taxpayers, and more taxpayers mean less taxes for us all to pay.

"But it takes time to convince companies to move. Our best chance is in convincing companies already in Nebraska to expand rather than going someplace else to build a plant. The test of reversing the trend of losing jobs in Nebraska will probably come in two to four years."

Harper counters critics who contend that business development would have occurred in Nebraska regardless of the new legislation.

"Some will say, 'Why, half or one-quarter or three-quarters of those jobs would have occurred anyway,'" Harper acknowledges. "Fine. Flip that around. Half of those, 25% of those, 75% of those would not have happened. I know of 400 in ConAgra that would not have happened.

"When businessmen want to invest millions of dollars, they don't just look at the governor. They look at what the Legislature does. Governors can be replaced in one election, just like that. It takes 49 individual elections to change the character of the Legislature. The Nebraska Legislature passed each economic development initiative by an overwhelming majority. Our Legislature made a clear, long-term commitment to improving the environment for business in Nebraska. Our Legislature has said, 'Come here. Put your bucks here. We want your jobs. We want you here and we want to have a good environment for business.'"

"Mike wanted to change Nebraska's tax structure so it would be attractive to business," observes ConAgra board member Walter Scott, Jr. "Not just attractive to ConAgra, but attractive to business. He was very sincere in wanting to do that, and obviously he spent a lot of time and effort at it. And he was successful.

"I don't think he wanted to leave Nebraska, but he was in a position where if it made good sense for his company to leave he would, unless there was a change in the tax structure. A lot of us wouldn't be willing to stick our necks out. Mike's unusual in that he was willing to do it. He was not only willing to do it, but he did a tremendous job."

"I have had business people and other citizens come up to me specifically to say that they appreciated ConAgra's taking the lead — and taking the heat," says Marty Colladay.

Harper acknowledges that involvement in community issues can wreak havoc with one's popularity. He accepts his debut on the Press Club stage as a small price to pay for having received the opportunity to energize Nebraska's economy.

"We have had bad things said about the company and about me," he says. "I think that is the price of being in the game. There is one good way to avoid criticism, at least for a while. Don't do anything. Then later on you get criticized for not doing anything.

"I think the greatest lesson of all is that each of us can change our

Scoreboard at Nebraska U. football stadium carries ConAgra message.

own economy here in Nebraska. There is no need to put our heads down. There is a better tone out in the country; there is a better tone in the cities. People have optimism and feel they can change their own fate. The state is healthy. Compare that with 1986, when we were down in the dumps."

ConAgra runs an advertisement on the 40-odd radio stations that carry play-by-play coverage of the University of Nebraska Cornhusker football games. The spot touts Nebraska as a good place for businesses to locate. It includes a toll-free number to call for further information.

On a sunny Saturday afternoon in Lincoln's Memorial Stadium, few spectators are cogitating about Nebraska's economic climate. They're too intent upon watching the Huskers chalk up another victory. On any such autumn afternoon the stadium becomes the third largest city in the state. That city's population never drops below 76,000: for the last 26 years every home game has been sold out.

ConAgra sponsors one of the computerized electronic scoreboards overlooking the playing field. The scoreboard doesn't advertise ConAgra products. It sells Nebraska. In large red letters it reads: NEBRASKA IS GOOD FOR BUSINESS.

CHAPTER 16

CONAGRA: BUILDING ON BASICS

CONAGRA: BUILDING ON BASICS

IT has been 15 years since newcomer Mike Harper came to Omaha to help rescue a beleaguered ConAgra. During that time, Harper has more than fulfilled his pledge in the elderly ladies who relied on their ConAgra dividends for their livelihoods.

"Our dividends have been going up, averaging about a 15% increase every year over the last 10 years," says Harper. "There aren't very many places you can go and be fairly certain of a 15% increase each year. I feel good about that, and I think that helps take care of those elderly ladies I met at my first annual meeting. Fifteen percent a year means four times the dividend today that they had 10 years ago."

The value of the stock has done even better. In 1974, an investor willing to stake a bet on Harper's leadership could have purchased 10,000 shares of ConAgra stock for $30,000. On March 1, 1989, after stock splits, that investor would have owned 90,000 shares, worth more than $2.7 million.

The company's sales growth has been equally impressive. In the 70 years from its modest beginning, ConAgra has grown to become one of the country's elite corporate giants. As it entered the decade of the 1990s, the company had reached a level of over $15 billion in annual sales. And management confidently expected such growth to continue.

ConAgra's dividend increases have taken care of the elderly stockholders which Harper met at his first annual meeting. ConAgra keeps meeting the financial goals set in the Vail meeting over 10 years ago. "Building on Basics" continues to be the philosophy.

Over a decade after Harper and his top executives and board members met on the Vail mountaintop, ConAgra still announces its financial goals on Pages 4 and 5 of its annual report. And it keeps meeting them: an average after-tax return on equity exceeding 20%, an annual increase exceeding 14% on trend line earnings per share; a ratio of long-term debt to equity of 35% or less and the elimination of most short-term debt at the end of each fiscal year; and a steady increase in dividends that is consistent with growth in trend line earnings, and averages 30% to 35% of earnings.

The unique management philosophy ConAgra's managers set forth, based on Harper's "white paper" — encouraging personal initiative and responsibility, fostering cooperation through openness and conflict — continues to cultivate and reward the most energetic, creative and hardworking managers in the food industry. ConAgra's strategic planning processes help its top executives seize unanticipated opportunities,

> By "Building on Basics," ConAgra intends to reach Harper's goal: "Best damn food company in the world."

bringing about constant growth and change in the company.

In 1884, Henry Glade printed his name across the Glade Roller Mill in Grand Island, Nebraska. Following in his footsteps, industrious and innovative leaders like A. R. Kinney, R. S. Dickinson, J. Allan Mactier and Claude Carter led Nebraska Consolidated Mills from its frontier origins to a position as a well-respected food business, the low cost producer in an industry of small margins.

Mike Harper built upon the strengths of that modest company rooted in the prairie towns of the Nineteenth Century. Harper's abiding commitment to the independent operating company concept has fostered leaders — like current office of the president members Phil Fletcher, George Haefner, Floyd McKinnerney, Dick Monfort and Truck Morrison — with the vision as well as the management savvy to advance the company into the international markets of the Twenty-first Century.

ConAgra continues to pursue virtually infinite opportunities across the food chain. Even as the company's sales approached the $15 billion mark, they still represent only a little over 1% of the food opportunities in the United States — and .1% of those world-wide.

By doing things just a little bit better, by increasing profits just a freckle — by building on basics — ConAgra intends to reach Mike Harper's goal of being "the best damn food company in the United States." On second thought, make that "the best damn food company in the world."

Meanwhile, Harper monitors the steady progress of ConAgra's new riverfront office complex.

"The steel for the fourth and fifth buildings is going up now," Harper reports. "I drive by there almost every week, mostly on Sundays. I'll get out of the car and walk around, see what they're doing, kick a few clods of dirt.

"The security guards all know me."

Not only have riverfront security guards come to know Mike Harper, so have many others. The food industry knows him well. Any food executive who happens to be the best at his job knows he may receive a call from Omaha whenever ConAgra has a high level vacancy to fill.

The analysts on Wall Street know Harper and ConAgra. No longer does Harper hop, skip and jump his way across the Great Plains in a tiny airplane to attend brown bag lunches with area stockbrokers. Now the doors of New York City's financial markets are open wide to him.

Area civic leaders know Mike Harper will good-naturedly participate in community affairs, whether they be spoofs of himself or serious events. Politicians, luncheon club members, food processors — just about any group seeking a speaker — are fair game to hear his talk about Nebraska's advantages for business and about American agriculture's future in the world food market.

Business writers are familiar with Harper, ConAgra and the independent operating company philosophy. *Fortune, Barron's, Business Week,* the *Wall Street Journal, Forbes, Time, Newsweek* — all have featured the balding executive and his booming company.

University campuses know him. University of Nebraska-Lincoln journalism students and Harvard University MBA candidates have studied ConAgra's successes and have learned the corporate theme: "Building on Basics."

It's the essence of the ConAgra story.

CONAGRA DIRECTORS
From Company Records
Dating back to 1952

Claude I. Carter	1964 to Present
Robert B. Daugherty	1968 to Present
Philip B. Fletcher	1989 to Present
Charles M. Harper	1975 to Present
Robert A. Krane	1983 to Present
L. D. McGehee	1974 to Present
Kenneth W. Monfort	1989 to Present
Gerald Rauenhorst	1983 to Present
Walter Scott, Jr.	1987 to Present
William G. Stocks	1983 to Present
Frederick B. Wells	1983 to Present
Thomas R. Williams	1979 to Present
John W. Teets	1984 to 1986
Dr. Clayton K. Yeutter	1980 to 1984
Gen. Alexander M. Haig, Jr.	1979
Dr. Earl L. Butz	1977 to 1980
Terrance Hanold	1976 to 1983
Ralph T. Birdsey	1974 to 1976
D. L. Barber	1972 to 1974
Jim B. Cooper	1967 to 1983
Lewis H. Durland	1967 to 1978
Alger W. Lonabaugh	1964 to 1970
John A. Nixon, Sr.	1964
Gilbert C. Swanson	1958 to 1967
L. E. Ray	1958 to 1970
Edward M. Curtis, Sr.	1958 to 1970
Robert K. Andersen	1956 to 1974
Roy H. Park	1956 to 1981
J. Allan Mactier	1954 to 1974
E. W. Augustine	Pre-1952 to 1961
J. V. Bass	Pre-1952 to 1958
A. W. Glade	Pre-1952 to 1964 (honorary)

CONAGRA DIRECTORS *(Cont'd.)*

Harold A. Prince	Pre-1952 to 1954
J. H. Weaver, Jr.	Pre-1952 to 1954
Louise Kinney Platt	1947 to 1975
Earnest G. Kroger	1943 to 1970
R. S. Dickinson	1936 to 1971

A YEAR-TO-YEAR CHRONOLOGY OF CONAGRA

1919   Four Nebraska flour mills consolidated to be incorporated as Nebraska Consolidated Mills Company.

1922   Company's milling capacity was doubled by acquisition of the Updike Mill in Omaha.

1926   The Brown Mill in Fremont, Nebraska was acquired to add needed capacity.

1931   The Omaha mill was destroyed by fire, but rebuilt and modernized with larger capacity.

1936   A new mill was built at Grand Island, Nebraska doubling the original capacity at that location.

1941   In first expansion outside of Nebraska, a new flour mill was built at Decatur, Alabama, to take advantage of river transportation of Midwestern grain to Southeastern markets.

1942   The company made its first entry into the feed business — Red Hat Feed's sales began at the Decatur plant.

1947   New Red Hat Feed mill was added at Decatur. Following WW II, flour sales and production began to shift from family flour to bakery flour.

1951   First major move into the grocery products field with development of Duncan Hines cake mixes.

1956   New Red Hat feed mill was built at Tunnel Hill, Georgia. Cake mix business was sold to Proctor & Gamble netting nearly $1 million to provide important growth capital.

1957   First expansion outside the Continental U.S. Molinos de Puerto Rico — a feed, flour and corn milling complex — was built in 1957–58.

1961   First broiler growing operations were begun by the company to stay in the Southeastern feed picture.

1963   Sheridan Flouring Mills Company at Sheridan, Wyoming was acquired. Produced flour, feed and some regional grocery products — a key location for West Coast bakery flour sales. (Mill was closed in 1972.)

1964	Poultry processing plants at Dalton, Georgia and at Athens, Alabama were purchased.
	Five feed manufacturing plants in Nebraska and Iowa were acquired with purchase of Nixon and Company. (Nixon operations were sold in 1976.)
1965	Fant Milling Company of Sherman, Texas was acquired — with two flour mills and a product line of Gladiola brand family flour, corn meal and baking mixes. (Branded grocery products business was sold in 1974. Gainsville, Texas flour mill had been closed in 1967.)
	A new Saprogal feed mill was begun at LaCoruna, Spain, in a joint venture.
	Maplecrest Turkey Farms growing operations and processing plant in Iowa were acquired. (Maplecrest operations were closed in 1969.)
1966	Harris Milling Company was acquired giving the company flour mills in Michigan and North Carolina and a feed mill in Michigan. (Feed mill sold in 1976, Michigan flour mill sold in 1972 and North Carolina mill was sold in 1967.)
	Mauser mill in Treichlers, Pennsylvania was acquired for soft wheat flour milling.
1968	Colorado Milling and Elevator's flour mill and elevator in Omaha were purchased for added grain storage and baking mix production.
	Birdsey Milling Company, Macon, Georgia was acquired to expand Red Hat Feed sales and also to provide soft wheat bakery flour production.
	Martel mix plant, Cincinnati, Ohio, was acquired to provide production of private label cake mixes and other baking mixes. (This plant was sold in 1974).
	Grain storage at Molinos de Puerto Rico was nearly doubled to supply expanding island sales.
	Red Lion (PA) flour mill was acquired.
1969	Montana Flour Mills Company was purchased, adding flour mills in Montana, Minnesota and California, also feed mills in Montana. (Also, country elevators that were sold in 1974. The Great Falls, Montana flour mill was sold as part of Peavey acquisition agreement in 1984.)

Dixie Lily Milling Company and affiliated companies in Florida and Georgia were acquired providing grocery products and direct store-door delivery distribution systems. (These operations were sold in 1974.)

The Stral Company with processing facilities in Greensboro, Alabama was acquired to launch ConAgra into catfish aquaculture. (Stral facility was closed in 1975 and operations transferred to Tippo, Mississippi.)

Milling plant of Flour Mills of America, Inc., in North Kansas City, Missouri, was purchased and converted to dry corn milling. (This facility sold in 1974.)

1970   Acquisition of McGehee Poultry Company of Ruston, Louisiana added a hatchery, feed mill and poultry processing plant to increase broiler production by 25%.

1971   Fruen Milling Company, miller of specialty oat products and horse feeds at Minneapolis, was purchased.

Harrell Poultry Company with processing facilities in Enterprise, Alabama was acquired.

On February 25th, the company name was officially changed from Nebraska Consolidated Mills Company to ConAgra, Inc.

1972   H.C. Cole Milling Company's soft wheat mill at Chester, Illinois was purchased.

Feedright Milling Company of Augusta, Georgia was acquired.

The four feed mills of Security Milling Company headquartered in Knoxville, Tennessee were purchased.

1973   Kasco dog food plant at National City, Illinois was purchased.

Geisler Pet Products Company at Omaha, Nebraska was acquired, completing the company's first entry into the pet food and pet care markets.

1976   Norso Distributors, an Oakland, California pet accessories distributor, was acquired.

McMillan Company grain merchandising operations in Minneapolis were acquired.

	ConAgra acquired Biota International, Inc. (pet accessories) and Sapropor (formula feed, hog breeding, trout aquaculture) in Portugal.
1977	J.P. King and Sons, table egg production facilities in Blountsville, Alabama was acquired.
	Pet Dealers Supply Company of Los Angeles, California, distributor of pet supplies was acquired.
	Bow Wow Dog Food Company, Rolla, Missouri was acquired.
	Taco Plaza Corp., a Texas chain of Mexican fastfood outlets headquartered in Fort Worth, gave company an entry into the restaurant business.
1978	ConAgra acquires three agri-business companies in Venezuela (49%).
	ConAgra acquires United Agri Products, Inc. (UAP) (49%).
1979	ConAgra acquired Atwood-Larson Company (grain merchandising company).
	ConAgra acquires United Agri Products, Inc. (remaining 51%).
1980	ConAgra acquires Oklahoma-Kansas Grain Corp.
	ConAgra acquires Interstate Terminals, Inc. (river grain facility).
	ConAgra acquires Hess and Clark, Inc. (agricultural chemicals).
	ConAgra acquires Banquet Foods Corp., a major frozen food processing company.
1981	ConAgra acquires Singleton Packing Corp., (shrimp processing, packing).
	ConAgra acquires Bioter-Biona, S.A. (50%). (Food company in Spain.)
	ConAgra acquires Westfeeds, Inc. (livestock feeds).
	ConAgra acquires Grower Services, Inc. (agricultural chemicals).
	ConAgra acquires Sea-Alaska Products, Inc. (seafood processing).

1982	ConAgra acquires Peavey Company (flour miller, grain merchandiser, food processor, operator of specialty retail stores).
	ConAgra and Imperial Foods Limited form Country Poultry, Inc. (each 50% interest) with ConAgra's Country Skillet Poultry Co. and Imperial's Country Pride Foods.
	ConAgra acquires Southern Micro Blenders of Tennessee, Inc. (vitamin premixes for livestock, poultry feeds).
1983	ConAgra acquires Occidental Chemical Company (Hawaii — agricultural chemical distributorship).
	ConAgra acquires Seeco, Inc. (feed vitamin premixes, animal health care products).
	ConAgra acquires Armour Food Company (certain operating assets).
1984	ConAgra acquires Geldermann and Company, Inc. (commodity futures brokerage).
	ConAgra acquires Florida Feed Mills, Inc.
	ConAgra acquires Pacifex, Inc. (fertilizer marketing).
	UAP acquires Ag-Chem, Inc. (agricultural chemical distributor).
	ConAgra acquires Glendon Corporation (49% Woodward & Dickerson, Inc. — international trading company).
	ConAgra acquires remaining 50% of Country Poultry, Inc. from Imperial Foods Ltd.
	UAP acquires Omaha Vaccine Company and Stockyards Veterinary Supply.
	ConAgra acquires Northern States Beef, Inc.
	UAF acquires Security Chemical Co.
	ConAgra acquires Saprogal, S.A. (animal feeds, hog breeding, poultry production in Spain) — remaining 50%.
1985	ConAgra Feed Ingredient Merchandising Company acquires Mid-America Milling (animal protein blending plant).
	ConAgra acquires Glendon Corporation (Woodward & Dickerson, Inc. — remaining 51%).
	Home Brands Company acquires Velvet peanut butter branded business.

ConAgra acquires Berger and Company (worldwide trader of commodities).

ConAgra and Scoular Company form AgriBasics Fertilizer Company, Inc. (50-50 joint venture).

ConAgra acquires Sandvig's farm stores.

ConAgra acquires U.S. Tire, Inc.

ConAgra acquires The Cropmate Company (fertilizer supplier).

ConAgra acquires Scoular's 50% in AgriBasics Fertilizer Company.

Berger and Company acquires Edible Protein Division of the Pillsbury Company.

ConAgra International acquires Biotersa Portuguesa (commodity trading — renamed ConAgra International S.A.).

1986 ConAgra and Kurt A. Becher GmbH & Co.KG, complete agreement for 50% partnership (grain and feed ingredient merchandiser).

Saprogal acquires INTRA (meat processing).

ConAgra acquires Webber Farms, Inc. (producer, marketer and distributor of fresh sausage, processed meats).

Geldermann, Inc. acquires Heinold Commodity Futures Brokerage subsidiaries.

ConAgra acquires Camerican International (international food marketing company).

ConAgra acquires Del Monte frozen food business from RJR/Nabisco (principal brands are Morton, Patio, Chun King and Award).

ConAgra acquires Canadian Harvest Process Ltd. (dietary fiber business).

ConAgra acquires Squillante & Zimmerman, Inc. (international food marketing company).

Sapropor acquires Avipronto (poultry processing).

ConAgra Poultry Company acquires Institutional Foods Company assets.

The Cropmate Company acquires Howe, Inc. assets (fertilizer, ag chemical business).

ConAgra acquires Acfin S.A. (three Swiss companies with Canada and U.S. grain and feed trading operations).

1987   ConAgra acquires The Mearns Company (50%) — cotton merchandising business.

ConAgra acquires Dyno-Singer Merchandise Corp. (sewing notions) and Unique Packing (notions packaging).

ConAgra acquires E. J. Miller Enterprises, Inc. (processor and regional marketer of boxed beef).

Geldermann acquires Clayton Brokerage assets.

ConAgra purchases two feed mills from Union Alimentaria Sanders. The mills are located in Lugo and Valencia, Spain.

ConAgra's Sea-Alaska Products Company merged with Trident Seafoods Corporation. The new company is called Trident Seafoods Corporation. (ConAgra's interest is 45%.)

Monfort of Colorado, Inc. merged with ConAgra (beef and lamb processing and distributing).

ConAgra acquires O'Donnell-Usen Fisheries Corp. (fishing and fillet-processing operations, processor and marketer of seafood).

ConAgra acquires the Becher family's remaining 50% interest in Kurt A. Becher GmbH & Co.KG.

ConAgra acquires a 50% interest in Swift Independent Holding Corporation, the parent of Swift Independent Packing Company (SIPCO) and Val-Agri, Inc., a meat processor and food distributor.

ConAgra acquires assets of Natural Food Commodities (distributor and merchandiser of a wide variety of dried fruits, nuts and specialty agricultural commodities).

ConAgra acquires Longmont Foods (a turkey processing business).

ConAgra's NutriBasics Company and The Du Pont Company form 50-50 joint venture called DuCon (industrial chemicals and chemical applications to serve selected feed, food and electronics markets).

1988   ConAgra acquires assets of International Multifoods' U.S. flour milling business.

ConAgra and Golden Valley Microwave Foods, Inc. each own 50% of a new company formed to acquire Lamb-Weston (a leading U.S. frozen potato processor).

ConAgra acquires Blue Star Foods (a manufacturer of private label and branded frozen foods, canned products).

ConAgra Poultry Company acquires Mott's Inc. (poultry processing business).

Armour Dairy & Food Oils Company acquires assets of SpiceTec, Ltd. (spice import and marketing business).

ConAgra and The Du Pont Company formed a partnership, Canadian Harvest U.S.A., to develop and market dietary fiber products. (ConAgra subsidiary Canadian Harvest of Ontario has been incorporated into the partnership.)

United Agri Products Company acquires Pfizer Inc's Canadian crop protection chemical business (a leading formulator and distributor of crop protection chemicals in Canada).

Cook Family Foods, Ltd., Lincoln, Nebraska, (a producer of branded smoked ham products) merges with ConAgra.

ConAgra and D.L. Berger Associates form Berdex International, Inc., an International trading firm based in San Francisco. (ConAgra will not be involved in operation or management — passive investor only.)

Home Brands Company acquires Holsum Foods peanut butter processing plant in Albany, Georgia and its related business (producer and marketer of peanut butter for retail, industrial and foodservice markets).

1989	ConAgra completes acquisition of Pillsbury grain merchandising division.

ConAgra and W. Jordan Millers Ltd. form 50-50 joint venture to process/distribute oat products for human consumption in U.K. and Europe. The joint venture is called Cereal Millers Europe Ltd.

ConAgra Pet Products Company acquires the Sergeant's Pet Care Division of A. H. Robins Company.

Pfaelzer Brothers Company acquires the mail order catalog division of Ace Pecan Company.

ConAgra Fertilizer Company acquires assets of Agricultural Fertilizers and Suppliers Ltd., a wholesale fertilizer distributor based in Exmouth, United Kingdom.

ConAgra purchases the remaining 50-percent interest in SIPCO, Inc. and Val-Agri, Inc., a smaller unit associated with SIPCO. SIPCO, formerly known as Swift Independent Packing Co., and Val-Agri process and distribute fresh beef, pork and lamb products. (ConAgra purchased the initial 50-percent interest in Sept. 1987.)

ConAgra acquires 50-percent of Gelazur, S.A., headquartered in Nice, France. Gelazur is a leading European seafood distributor, marketing a wide variety of frozen seafood products to retail markets in France and throughout the rest of Europe.

CONAGRA (NCM Co)
Sales and Earnings History
1920-1989

Note: NCM Co was incorporated in September, 1919. However, combined operations apparently did not begin until March 15, 1920.

Fiscal Year	Sales	Earnings
3/15/20–6/30/21	$6,500,000	($115,000)
FY 1922	9,000,000	140,000
1923	11,850,000	162,000
1924	12,540,000	158,000
1925	13,500,000	170,000
1926	13,100,000	166,000
1927	12,800,000	98,000
1928	13,500,000	147,100
1929	12,400,000	131,040
1930	11,200,000	119,000
1931	12,000,000	151,200
1932	14,300,000	170,000
1933	11,800,000	(102,000)
1934	12,200,000	89,000
1935	13,100,000	165,060
1936	14,200,000	178,900
1937	13,800,000	173,880
1938	14,900,000	164,000
1939	15,700,000	197,800
1940	16,200,000	204,280
1941	17,500,000	140,750
1942	21,000,000	264,600
1943	22,800,000	287,280
1944	20,400,000	257,040
1945	22,100,000	278,460
1946	23,150,000	291,690
1947	24,500,000	388,000
1948	25,147,524	408,720
1949	20,332,095	161,777
1950	19,753,157	306,404
1951	24,612,483	379,060
1952	29,217,160	323,084
1953	35,688,115	642,835

Sales and Earnings History *(Cont'd)*

Fiscal Year	Sales	Earnings
1954	41,658,411	346,724
1955	48,881,668	601,224
1956	49,046,480	697,188
1957	34,333,606	393,252
1958	36,625,931	500,005
1959	41,434,876	477,875
1960	50,450,682	450,450
1961	57,165,020	959,332
1962	66,339,122	917,884
1963	76,718,676	1,957,960
1964	99,658,743	2,684,370
1965	102,050,000	3,044,578
1966	126,653,951	3,151,421
1967	148,316,234	532,093
1968	159,411,357	4,002,925
1969	191,937,157	5,096,090
1970	245,137,920	5,003,431
1971	272,625,316	3,001,600
1972	301,705,587	3,060,115
1973	422,125,471	6,062,928
1974	633,643,845	(11,853,118)
1975	573,543,906	4,071,317
1976	504,114,000	19,126,000
1977	532,218,000	12,831,000
1978	543,852,000	15,144,000
1979	644,830,000	21,034,000
1980	842,905,000	18,515,000
1981	1,376,808,000	27,071,000
1982	1,705,169,000	32,873,000
1983	2,319,973,000	47,770,000
1984	3,301,524,000	62,648,000
1985	5,498,157,000	91,728,000
1986	5,911,046,000	105,285,000
1987	9,001,553,000	148,726,000
1988	9,474,951,000	154,698,000
1989	11,340,414,000	197,878,000

NOTE: Results are as reported at end of each fiscal year. In some cases, these have been restated in later years.

INDEX

A
Adcox, Willard, 12, 13, 85
Albers, Rita, 212
Allen, Newton, 11
Amsden, Don, 139
Andre, Arlee, 42, 51
Annaplains Land and Cattle Co., 92
Armour Food Company, 189
Atwood-Larsen Company, 164
Avipronto, 252

B
"Bag of Money" concept, 12
Balcom Group, 129
Banquet brand, 144
Barber, Del, 11, 43, 56
Barnard, Bob, 11
Bates, William, 8, 74, 75
Becher, Kurt A., 225
Berger and Company, 225, 231
Beta West, 275
Bioter, 89
Birdsey Flour Mills, 93
Blackburn, Earl H., 29
Blair, James, 254
Board of Trade, 7, 8
Bow Wow Company, 125
Brady, Tom, 9, 13, 105, 115, 133
Brisch, Hans, 266
Brown Mill (Fremont), 35
Bundrant, Charles H., 252
Burdick Grain Company, 164
Butz, Earl, 248

C
Camerican International, 226, 231
Cargill, Inc., 9, 187
Carter, C. I., 9, 76, 88, 105, 108
Casey, Walter, 210, 270
"Classic Lite" brand, 202
Clean Crop brand, 135
Clemons, Jane, 62, 64, 76
Clemons, Rex, 3, 43, 76
Cole, H. C., 97
Colladay, Marty, 217, 261, 268
Colorado Mill and Elevator Company, 163
ConAgra Fertilizer Company, 227
ConAgra Trading Company, 224
ConAgra, asset sales, 15
ConAgra, new name, 98
ConAgra, NYSE listing, 100
ConAgra, philosophy, 109
Cook Family Foods Company, 251
Cookin' Bag brand, 146
Cotton, Owen, 71, 88

"Country Pride" brand, 181
"Country Skillet" brand, 181

D
Dalton Poultry Company, 86
Daugherty, Robert, 4, 109, 111, 115
Decker Meat Company, 197
Dickinson, R. S., 29, 72, 84, 96, 120
Dickinson, Carrie, 34, 48
"Dinner Classics" brand, 194
Dixianna brand, 52
Dixie Lily brand, 9, 105
Doering, George, 129, 136, 156, 223
Dominican Republic, 91

E
Enron Company, 265
Etting, Catherine, 22
Etting, Albert, 22
Etting, Lee, 24, 38

F
Fant Milling Company, 93
Farmer, Jack, 227
Feedright Milling Company, 97
Flagg, Gould, 58
Fletcher, Phil, 156, 244
Formax brand, 97, 123
Fruen Milling Company, 97

G
Gady, Richard, 138, 249, 262
Garland Mills, 93
Geisler Pet Accessories, 97, 123
Geldermann, Inc., 226
Glade Roller Mill, 22, 38
Glade, Henry, 20
Glade, August, 22
Glade, Arthur, 23, 38
Glade, Phil, 23, 38
Glade, Fred Sr., 23
Glade, Fred Jr., 24, 39
Gleacher, Eric, 14, 129, 145, 166, 191
Gonzalez, Jesse, 184, 231
Gosko, George, 168
Grand Island Mill, 106, 161
Granneman, Don, 144
Graves, Didi, 209
Grower Service Company, 134

H
Haefner, George, 182, 244
Hall, Ron, 11, 89
Haney, Roger, 217
Hanold, Terry, 109, 114, 115
Hansen, Chris, 3, 11

Harper, C. M.
- first annual meeting, 3
- boyhood and early career, 5
- first employment by ConAgra, 105
- meetings with analysts, 107
- appointed Director, President and CEO, 108
- Vail, CO meeting, 114
- UAP acquisition, 132
- corporate planning process, 136
- Banquet negotiations, 145
- Peavey acquisition, 165
- building poultry operations, 181
- seafood expansion, 184
- MBPXL merger agreement, 187
- Armour acquisition, 191
- personal, home and piloting, 205–219
- forming international operations, 223
- Monfort and other red meat acquisitions, 244
- negotiations with Holly Farms, 253
- corporate headquarters relocation, 263

Harper, Carolyn, 10, 207
Harper, Josie, 205
Harper, Charles Michael, Jr. 207
Harper, Kathy, 207
Harrell Poultry, 96
Harris Milling Company, 93
Hartley, Abbott, 24
Hasson, Merle, 37
Hastings Mills, 24
Healthy Choice brand, 252
Heffelfinger, Frank, 162
Hess and Clark Company, 134
Hill, Roy, 11
Hines, Duncan, 53, 61
Holland, "Tuffy", 130
Hollenbeck, Jim, 215
Holly Farms Inc., 253
Holmes, Robert, 124

I

Imbs, J. F. Milling, 105
Irvine, Elsie, 191

J

James, Phil, 130
Jobber's Canyon, 272
Johnson, Vard, 265, 267

K

Kansas City Corn Mill, 9
Kasco brand, 97, 123
Kennedy, Jim, 109, 110, 115, 123, 132, 145, 147, 148

Kinney, Alva R., 24
Kinney, Louise (Platte), 27, 108

L

Legislative Bills 270, 772, 773 and 775, 266
Leuenberger, Don, 266
Levy, "Sy", 4, 109, 112, 115
Linkletter, Art, 91
Longmont Foods Company, 252

M

Mactier, Allan, 4, 51, 71, 83, 105
Mactier, Ann, 51
Mactier, Jean, 71
Malin, Maurice, 99
Maplecrest Farms, 87
Martha White, Inc., 9
Mary Ann brand, 36
Mathias, Frank, 73, 78
Mauser Mill, 93
McCoy, Warren, 106, 110
McGehee Poultry Company, 96
McGill, Jack, 91
McKinnerney, Floyd, 133, 135, 139, 244
McMillan Company, 164
Miller, E. A. Inc., 239
Miller, John, 239
Miller, Ted A., 251
Monfort of Colorado, 241
Monfort, Kenneth, 241, 244, 250
Monfort, Richard L., 251
Monfort, Myra, 243
Montana Flour Mills, 7, 93, 227
Morrison, "Bud", 7, 95, 114, 137, 156, 177
Morrison, "Truck", 161, 167, 224, 228, 244
Mothers Best brand, 36
Motts Inc., 252

N

Nebraska Consolidated Mills Company, 24
Niemann, Nick, 265, 268
Nigro, Joe, 64, 72
Nino, El, 7
Nixon Feed Company, 88, 106
Norso Distributors, Inc., 124
North, John, 124
Northern States Beef Inc., 202, 240
Northwest Fabrics, 163

O

O'Donnell-Usen Fisheries Corporation, 184, 252

INDEX

Oklahoma-Kansas Grain Corporation, 164
Olson, Earle, 212
Omaha Flour Mill, 24
Omaha Press Club, 261
Orr, Kay, 265

P

Pannier, Boise, 36, 101
Park, Roy, 9, 53
Peanuts characters, 125
Peavey Company, 106, 161
Peavey Retail Stores, 175
Peavey, Frank, 161
Pet Dealers Supply Company, 125
Peters, Tom, 129
Petty, Joe, 212
Peyton, Robert, 173, 224, 228
Pfaelzer Brothers Company, 202
Phares, Lynn, 270
Phillips, John, 151, 156, 242
Port ConAgra Inc., 164
Power, Ken, 276
Prince, Harold, 58
Prince, Mary, 58, 64
Pueblo Chemical Company, 130
Puerto Rico — subsidy, 6
Puerto Rico — price controls, 6
Puerto Rico — "crown jewel", 15
Puerto Rico — operation bootstrap, 71
Puerto Rico — Molinos de, 72
Pursell, Donald, 263

R

Racciatti, Thomas, 173, 177
Rasche, Donald, 148, 152, 158
Ravenna Mills, 24
Red Hat brand, 46
Red Hat poultry division, 87
Red Lion Milling Company, 93
Remele, Lewis, 171
Robbins, Mary, 205, 208
Rohde, Bruce, 188, 254
Rude, Jim, 165, 208, 214

S

S & S Farm Stores, 163
Sanem, Michael L., 251
Saprogal, 89
Sapropor, 97
Sasser, Clyde, 182
Satterwhite, Jack, 227
Schuler, Harold, 5, 128, 135, 148, 206, 208
Schulz, Charles, 125
Schuster, Frances, 64

Scott, Walter Jr., 277
Sea-Alaska Company, 185
Security Mills, Inc., 97
Sheridan Flour Mills, 88, 93
Singleton Seafood Company, 184
SIPCO, 246
"Snoopy" Dog Food, 125
Squillante and Zimmerman, Inc., 226
St. Edward Mill, 24
Stamper, F. M. Company, 143
Stamper, Howard, 144
Stephens, Rod, 196
Stocks, William, 165
Stone, Don, 172, 175
Stral Catfish Company, 97, 183
Sweet Sue Poultry Company, 86

T

Taco Plaza Restaurants, 127
Tamsen, Don, 198
Teets, John, 189
Thomas, L. B., 13, 78, 105
Thomas, Harry, 76
Three Star Special Cake Mix, 55
To-Ricos brand, 96
Trident Seafood Corporation, 251
Tyson Foods, 253
Tyson, Don, 255

U

United Agri Products, 132
Updike Mill, 33
USDA, 7, 8

V

Valmont Industries, 4
Victoria Feed Company, 125
Vin Fiz flight, 199

W

Wallen, Don, 195, 198
Walsh, Michael H., 275
Weaver, Joe, 38
Weaver, Joe Jr., 62
Wells, Frederick, 163
Wheelers Farm Stores, 163
White Elephant brand, 36
White, Bob, 115, 136, 138, 246
Wilkening, Marv, 212
Wittnam, Don, 134
"Woodstock" Bird Feed, 125
Woodward & Dickerson, 225, 231
Wurster, Bill, 226

Y

Yeutter, Clayton, 224, 233